W0036893

FLASH VIDEO CREATIVITY

KRISTIAN BESLEY
ERWAN BEZIE
MURAT BODUR
NEAL BOYD
HOSS GIFFORD
TIM HAWKINS
BRUCE HERBERT
DIANA JOHNSON
KEN JOKOL
LEONHARD LASS
LIFAROS
DOUG MCDERMOTT
ANTHONY ONUMONU
JEROME TURNER

FLASH VIDEO CREATIVITY

© 2003 Apress
Originally published by friends of ED in 2003

First Published February 2003

Trademark Acknowledgments

friends of ED has endeavoured to provide trademark information about all the companies and products mentioned in this book by the appropriate use of capitals. However, friends of ED cannot guarantee the accuracy of this information.

ISBN 978-1-59059-159-8   ISBN 978-1-4302-5129-3 (eBook)
DOI 10.1007/978-1-4302-5129-3

CREDITS

AUTHORS
KRISTIAN BESLEY
ERWAN BEZIE
MURAT BODUR
NEAL BOYD
HOSS GIFFORD
TIM HAWKINS
BRUCE HERBERT
DIANA JOHNSON
KEN JOKOL
LEONHARD LASS
LIFAROS
DOUG MCDERMOTT
ANTHONY ONUMONU
JEROME TURNER

COMMISSIONING EDITOR
BEN RENOW-CLARKE

EDITORS
DAN SQUIER
JULIE CLOSS

TECHNICAL REVIEWERS
KRISTIAN BESLEY
LIFAROS
JON STEER
JEREMY THOMAS
MICHAEL WALSTON

GRAPHIC EDITORS
AVTAR BHOGAL
MATTHEW CLARK
PAUL GROVE

COVER AND TEMPLATE DESIGN
KATY FREER

INDEXER
SIMON COLLINS

PROJECT MANAGERS
RICHARD HARRISON
SIMON BRAND

PROOFREADERS
SIMON COLLINS
JOANNE CRICHTON
HELENA SHARMAN

MANAGING EDITOR
CHRIS HINDLEY

CONTENTS

Foreword

by Bruce Herbert and Diana Johnson of Sorenson Media

Creative boundaries are being blown apart as Macromedia Flash MX ushers in a new era of moving images on the Internet. At its launch, analysts predicted that the Flash Player would transform itself from being a "lightweight animation tool" to "the de facto technology for simple web interactivity" (Randy Souza, Forrester). Since then though, Flash developers combining vector animation and video have proven that it's capable of much, much more than "simple web interactivity".

We're still just beginning to scratch the surface of the possibilities it opens up to us, but already it looks like Flash MX is becoming the key technology for pushing video creativity on the Web to a new whole level.

Understandably, many people look at Flash as just another way to deliver video on the Web, one more program for showing movies on your desktop. Well, it can certainly do that – but there's a whole lot more it can do besides!

You can use ActionScript to add custom controls, determine a video playback sequence, or mask your video with a custom shape. You can use layering to create special effects, design custom templates for e-learning applications, and use lightweight video streams along with Flash animation in rich media e-mail campaigns.

With Flash MX's unique set of tools to hand, the Flash Player can deliver a brand new range of video applications with a creative scope the like of which has never been seen before!

The impact of video

You only have to look at the massive social impact of film and television to appreciate that moving pictures are a fantastically – perhaps uniquely – powerful medium. Offline video is often used to complement interactive media such as games and CD-ROMs, because it can be dynamic, entertaining, and can leave a lasting impression on the viewer.

Video on the Web isn't a new concept: despite all the technical hurdles involved in sending watchable images across connections with miniscule bandwidth, pioneering designers have struggled for years to find ways of working within (and working around) the limitations of the day. Let's take a quick look at its history, and see why online video content in Flash offers up a whole new frontier for web designers and video producers alike.

Web video production

Video production often falls into two broad categories: **disk-based** and **web-based** media. Disk-based production took off in the early 1990s, as desktop video editing (non-linear editing) and storage solutions began to mature and become widely available. Just a few years later, the Internet began to take off, and the Web started to look like it could be a viable platform for delivering video content. Even though it was early days, the obvious potential of online video sparked off a great demand for reliable encoding tools and delivery services.

To many producers, the Internet represented an untapped medium: a new way to distribute video files for a variety of uses in the entertainment, business, and educational markets. Video players such as QuickTime, MS Windows Media, and Real Media became standard fixtures on millions of desktops. They played a critical role in pushing forward the market acceptance of online video.

Compressing video

There's a fundamental problem with delivering quality video content via the Web: the sheer quantity of data. Raw video files tend to be massive, and they're typically very difficult to compress. Each frame typically contains an enormous amount of information, so just a few seconds of video can easily take up several megabytes. On a hard disk or CD-ROM that may not be a problem, but on the Web (where bandwidth is precious) it's a killer!

A **video codec** (codec = **co**mpression and **dec**ompression) is a decision-making algorithm that video authoring software uses to crunch massive amounts of video data into smaller, more manageable files. The codec does this by looking for redundant data – information that doesn't significantly affect the image quality – and throwing it out. There's just enough data left for a video player (using the same codec) to recreate the original movie from a downloaded file, and play it back.

Deciding exactly what image data is redundant is a tricky call in itself, and even now, it's not something that can be totally automated if you want the best possible results. There's always some trade-off between bandwidth (the amount of data needed per second) and movie quality (the detail and number of frames needed for each second of video).

So, video compression wasn't just a critical step in the preparation of video files – it's the technology that made mainstream delivery of web video possible.

Sorenson and the evolution of codecs

Even once codecs had begun to make online video technically viable, moderately large files, limited bandwidth, and high technology costs still prevented most people from getting much out of it. If a producer wanted to make their video available online, they'd need to figure out how much storage space was required and how many separate hits the server could handle at any one time. Hosting could be expensive, and only users with bandwidth (or patience) to spare would see the finished product in its full glory.

As time went on though, more and more powerful algorithms were developed, each finding new ways to squeeze more quality into less bandwidth. By 1997, the standard Sorenson Video codec (then sold as a product in its own right) was promising to reduce video files to as little as one percent of their original size. Delivering high-quality video to ordinary users over the Internet was really looking like a viable option.

Apple noticed the strengths of this codec, and in the spring of 1998, formally licensed it for exclusive inclusion in QuickTime. Major motion picture studios such as Lucas Film, Disney, MGM and Paramount began to use it to prepare high-profile movie trailers for release on the Internet.

The codec quickly became famous for its powerful compression and high-quality results. Sorenson Media continued to refine it, and began work on an easy-to-use compression application called Sorenson Squeeze, for producers new to video encoding.

Sorenson and Flash

It was during this time that Macromedia began to take notice of Sorenson Media's unique strengths in the video compression industry. Flash developers had repeatedly asked for the ability to import video files into Flash movies for playback through the Flash Player.

Previously, video content had to be included in a standalone video player, or faked by creating bitmap sequences from the video and transforming these into vector-based images. Adding integrated video presented a challenge. The encoded video files created in the Flash application would need to be small enough to be managed by this lightweight player.

Recognizing the strong demand of their customer base for rich video integration into Flash, Macromedia approached Sorenson Media late in 2001 to create a video codec that could be included in the next version of Flash: Flash MX. Macromedia needed something that would be extremely small (less than 70Kb), and easy for the new Flash audience to use, but still offering high-end video encoding capabilities. Sorenson Media created a new codec, **Sorenson Spark,** loosely based on some video conferencing technology that had been previously developed by Sorenson Technology.

On March 4, 2002, Macromedia announced that a standard edition of the Sorenson Spark codec would be included in Flash MX. This would enable developers to import video into Flash and place it in the timeline. Later that month, Flash MX was released to the public and has since been very well received by the Flash community. Reviewers predicted that its impact would change the very nature of the creative presentation of websites.

> "Flash MX offers what Macromedia calls a rich client: a highly experiential, integrated thin-client environment for content, communications, and applications. Until now, Flash has provided only the ability to integrate multimedia elements into existing web pages, but the new version radically extends Flash – from content display, to database connectivity, to video, to debugging. The result is unprecedented: Flash's integrated multimedia authoring power comes close to making standard websites obsolete."
>
> – Ian Bogost, DevX

Creative Uses of Flash MX Video

Since its inception, Flash has raised the bar on the way people are informed and entertained on the Web. Many websites offer a variety of eye-catching Flash animations that compel people to keep watching, or to come back regularly.

The recent addition of video into the mix has raised the bar yet again. It may have been mere months since the release of Flash MX, but there are already plenty of sites out there showcasing the effective and creative use of Flash video on the Web.

Hillman Curtis

Hillman Curtis, who has designed a variety of web-based projects for Intel, MTV, Rolling Stone, Hewlett Packard, 3Com, Sun, and Capitol Records, recently published a book on media design based on his industry experience. He selected Flash MX video to communicate his own inspiration for the book, because the technology best illustrated his message.

"I used ActionScript to create a non-linear player that reinvents the viewer's experience each time the video is selected," explained Hillman. While the Flash MX video allowed him to share his own inspiration, the ActionScript gave him the ability to generate different selections of the video interview in a random order – resulting in a unique interview every time.

The promotional video supported Hillman's own design goals and business approach of looking at something in a new way while adhering to the core message and brand. "All my years of designing for some of the top brands has pointed to one thing - provide an experience rich enough to warrant a return visit and even better, word of mouth traffic. With Flash MX video and Sorenson Squeeze I can do just that."

http://www.hillmancurtis.com/mtiv_mx

EXPN

EXPN (an affiliate of ESPN) hosts the X Games and video segments of action sports such as snowboarding, motorcycle racing, and skateboarding. Its site uses Flash MX video to target a very specific demographic for their corporate sponsors. The use of Flash MX video complements their business objective to create a technology solution that defines extreme sports for their viewers.

> "At EXPN, our focus is on creating technology solutions that show top athletes pushing the limits of each sporting event. Our viewers demand engaging content and our sponsors understand that this type of content captivates their target audience."
>
> –Loren Schwartz, EXPN

With thirty-six separate cameras arranged in an arc, video production company Kewazinga shot the "extreme tricks" of snowboarders, skiers, and skateboarders from a range of different angles. The EXPN web team then used Squeeze to compress all this high-motion video, and loaded it into their custom "axis cam" player. This is simply a Flash MX movie that can play back all thirty-six shots at the same time, allowing users to switch angles as they watch the video.

The results are impressive! Within the custom Flash MX player, a viewer can see these tricks from whichever angle they choose – they can even pause the video and swoop round the athletes frozen in the middle of a trick.

http://expn.go.com/xgames/wxg/2002/archive/axis/index.html

Future uses for creative Flash MX video

Whether it's being used by a large corporation, a portal site, or a design firm, the emerging uses of Flash MX video we've been looking at here are just a taster of what's to come. It's perfect for online advertising, but can also be important to the e-learning market. It not only has the potential to change how businesses communicate with their customers and clients, but can also change how they communicate with employees, investors, and partners.

The creative presentation of online video is becoming more and more important as websites and applications compete to educate, entertain, and influence the buying habits of growing numbers of web users. Flash MX designers can now create content that reaches a larger audience, and engage viewers with additional functionality and flair to provide a rich media experience.

Macromedia is already developing a new array of products and services that will push the limits of how video is creatively used to meet real-world market uses of video. Flash Communication Server MX provides the building blocks for developers to build a webcast with navigational elements, slides, animation, and much more. Flash video-enabled PDAs may soon make personal video messaging an everyday reality.

While beta testing of cutting-edge applications with Flash MX video continues behind closed doors, a whole new era of video production has begun.

Kristian Besley is a freelance writer, technical reviewer and web developer, specialising in Flash MX interactivity (including applications and games) and PHP database integration.

He has written in a large number of friends of ED book titles including Foundation Flash MX, Flash MX Video, and Learn to Design with Flash MX.

He was born and raised in Wales and attended a Welsh-language school.

Thanks to Katy, Ben, Pete, Cath, Richard, and Dan.

Special thanks to Jake for the superb fireworks.

Introduction

Kristian Besley

The purpose of this chapter is to provide you with some simple grounding in the practical business of working with video in Flash MX. The rest of the chapters, as you might already have seen, will take the concepts a whole lot further. For now though, we're just going to concentrate on getting up to speed.

If you're fairly new to Flash, I definitely suggest you work through the whole of this chapter before delving into the others. On the other hand, if you're an experienced Flasher you may just want to dip in and out. Either way, it's all meant to serve as a foundation for the later chapters – the concepts we'll be looking at here are echoed and expanded on throughout the rest of the book.

We're not going to go into too much video theory here, so we'll start with the most basic video task in Flash MX – importing your pre-edited video file.

> *All the footage in this chapter was captured and edited using Apple's iMovie2. If you're looking for a decent, cheap DV editing application for importing and editing your footage, it's well worth a look. It's only supported on Macs though, so if you're a PC user, you might want to try Microsoft's MovieMaker instead.*

Importing video

Importing video into Flash is a painless operation. However, to make sure you end up with the best possible results while keeping your finished files reasonably small, there are several factors you should take into consideration before you even start up Flash MX.

Firstly, when you export an edited video file from your video editing application, you should aim to use the best possible quality and avoid compression. Why? Well, the simple answer is that Flash has its own codec (called Sorenson Spark) for compressing video. Codecs like Spark will produce the best possible results (smaller file size, more detail) when they're dealing with high quality, uncompressed video.

> *The Sorenson Spark Pro codec is a more powerful (and versatile) version of Spark, provided as part of a standalone application called "Sorenson Squeeze for Macromedia Flash". This can offer better results than the built-in Flash codec, but it'll cost you a little extra – Squeeze is currently priced at $119.*

Another consideration is framerate. Many web video enthusiasts hold to the opinion that web-based video should never aim to run at more than twelve frames per second – mainly due to considerations of bandwidth. If you're working on a project that's destined for a mass audience accessing it online, then it's usually best to go with this rule. Even if your video isn't as smooth as you'd like it be, your audience will thank you for saving them the download time.

Finally, if you want small files, it's best to try and keep motion to a minimum during filming. What? Surely this goes completely against the idea of using video in the first place! Well it does, but it's just one of those facts of life: codecs like Spark work by comparing consecutive frames and duplicating any sections that don't change much from one to the next. If nothing changes, it can say "same again"; but if everything changes, it has to describe a whole new image from scratch.

Lots of movement means lots of data, so a few seconds of shaky Grand Prix in-car camera footage will probably make for a larger file than several minutes' footage of a botoxed newscaster up against a dull blue background. It's a good idea to use a tripod whenever possible, and ration yourself when it comes to showing big movements. Of course, there's nothing saying that you *can't* have lots of motion; it's just important to remember that file size will suffer if you do.

> *Not all of this book's experiments are necessarily intended for use on the Web, so you may find these file size considerations going out of the window in later chapters! It's always good to keep them in mind though – at least that way you can avoid some nasty shocks when you get to the end of a project.*

Okay, that's way too much theory! Let's do what we set out to do: import that video!

The video footage I used for this first project was exported from iMovie at 25fps with no compression. The source file is called jumping.mov, and you can find it on the CD if you'd like to work along.

Create a new Flash document and use Modify > Document to set the frame rate to 25fps. We do this to make sure that our movie runs at the same rate as the video we're about to import (which just happens to be 25fps).

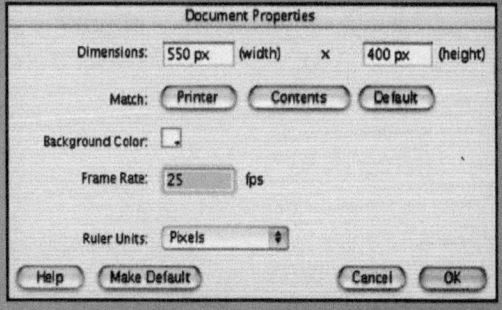

Now select File > Import and track down the jumping.mov video from the CD.

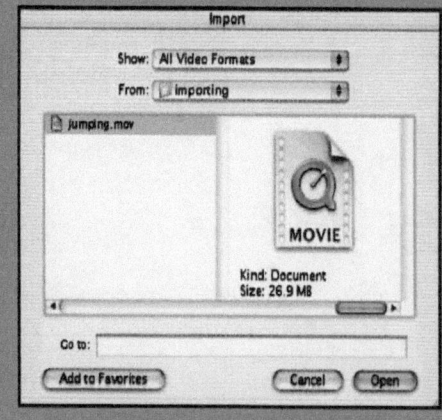

As you can see, this file is over 26MB in size – rather hefty for a clip that's only four seconds long! The reason for this extortionate size is because there's no image or sound compression on it: it's all raw data.

Click Open or OK to proceed, and the following dialog will appear. Make sure that the Embed video in Macromedia... option is selected and click OK.

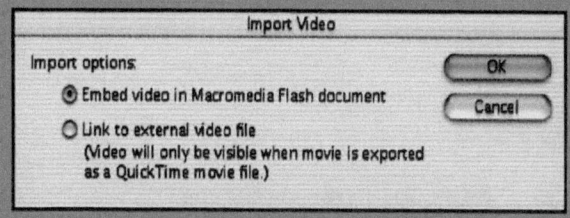

If you want to export video to the SWF format for playback through the Flash Player, you should always use this option. The other option is for exporting to the QuickTime MOV format.

Now you'll be greeted with a slightly more complex dialog, with many sliders and options. This allows us to change the import settings for the file.

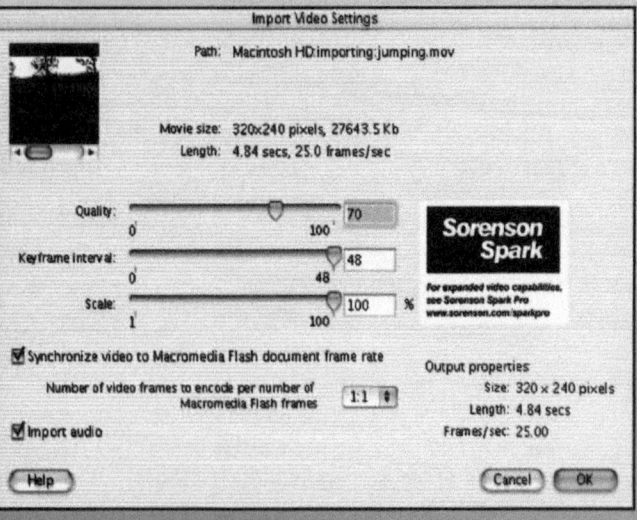

These settings aren't especially complex, but some are worth a brief explanation.

- **Quality** specifies how much compression should be applied to the video. The greater the value, the better the overall quality. To squeeze MBs out of your imported video, reduce the value of the quality setting – this tells Spark that it can throw away more picture information, and therefore gives you a smaller (more highly compressed) file.

- **Keyframe Interval** tells the codec how often to store a complete frame (known as a keyframe). If you set it to 0, Spark will store every frame in the video as a keyframe (like a series of JPEGs) resulting in a fairly large file. Alternatively, if you set it to the other extreme (48), Spark will store a keyframe once every 48 frames, and figure out all the in-between frames by tracking differences from one to the next. This will generally result in a smaller video file, but there'll usually be some loss of quality, and more demand on the processor when seeking changed parts of the video during playback.

- **Scale** just sets the imported scale of the video.

- **Synchronize video** is used to synchronize sound with the video track. On slower machines (which may tend to skip video frames when they can't keep up) Flash will make sure that the sound doesn't jump ahead or lag behind.

- **Number of Frames to encode** tells Flash how many frames it should import from the source file – for example, a setting of 1:2 means that every other frame should be used. To account for the lost frames, Flash lengthens the remaining ones, so the video will be the same length after import. This can be very useful for keeping file sizes down.

These two screenshots show the same output length for the clip:

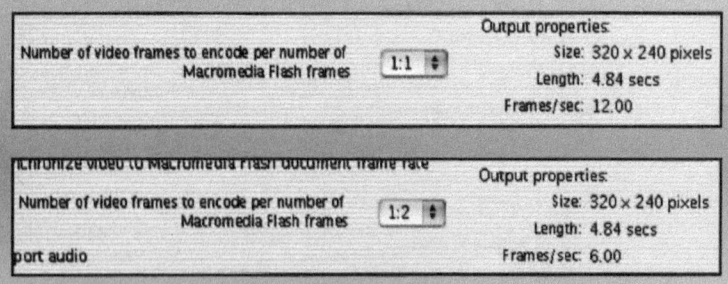

- **Import Audio** lets you to specify whether to import audio data along with the video. Audio data can also use codecs to keep down file sizes, but Flash can't always import compressed audio. As with video, it's best to import audio at the highest possible quality, and without compression data.

Once you've selected all the necessary settings (my clip was imported using the ones shown previously) click OK. After a little while, the clip is imported and you're greeted with the following dialog:

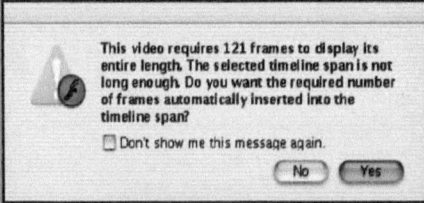

As the lengthy text suggests, Flash is offering to increase the timeline to show all of the frames of the video. In most cases, you should click Yes at this point – a video timeline must be fully extended to show all of its frames. So, click Yes for now to extend the clip on the main timeline. The movie will then be shown on the main stage.

Okay, now test the movie: the video should run in a loop. My published movie here weighs in at 424KB. Compared to the original 26MB, I'm sure you'll agree that's not a bad saving!

That said, 424KB for just four seconds still isn't really good enough for use in a website. It'll still take over a minute to download via a 56K modem. This is where experimentation with the import settings pays off.

Ways of working with video

There are two ways to manage video in Flash.

If you intend to simply play a video in Flash and don't really want to manipulate or mess with it, then the best option might be to have the video **streaming**; this way the video will run progressively – through from beginning to end. Video streaming in Flash works in the same way as traditional Flash animations stream in. To allow your movie to stream, place the video on the main timeline – then that's it. Each frame will then play once it's loaded, so it's usually best to provide some other content before you reach the video, to allow some of it to load in and prevent staggered playing.

Alternatively, you can place the video clip **within a movie clip timeline**. This is a totally different affair, since it eradicates any streaming (a movie clip must be fully loaded before it plays at all). However, it does let you manipulate the clip in many, many ways, so this option is far more suitable for creative video work.

Right now, we'll look at some basic manipulations available for videos embedded in movie clips, before looking at scripting in detail in the next section.

Manually changing video properties

A video movie clip can be manipulated just like any other movie clip in Flash: you can change its size, position, color, rotation, and so on. This gives Flashers many more creative options than users of other applications that handle video content on the fly. Let's take a quick look at these options before we get stuck into some scripting.

Coloring

The first set of options available to manipulate your video are found on the Color drop-down menu on the Property Inspector:

The Brightness option here is very useful because it will allow you to brighten up dark or dull footage if you are unable to clean it up from the source video. The other notable is the Advanced option – you can use this to selectively increase or decrease the contrast of your video footage, or create some very dramatic color effects:

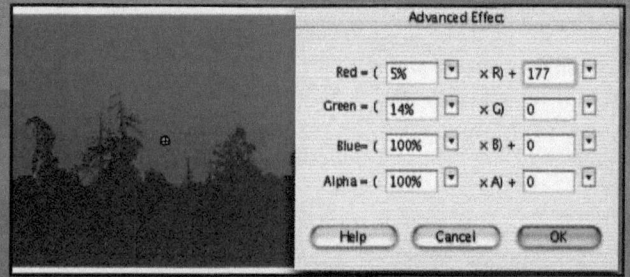

Transforming

The Free Transform tool (or Transform panel) allows you to manipulate your videos in all sorts of ways– from rotating to skewing and scaling.

You can also flip your video in either horizontal or vertical directions (Modify > Transform > Flip Horizontal / Vertical).

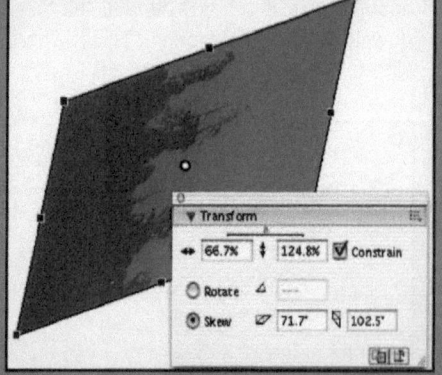

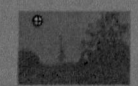

Masking

Videos can be masked just like any other movie clip using a masked layer.

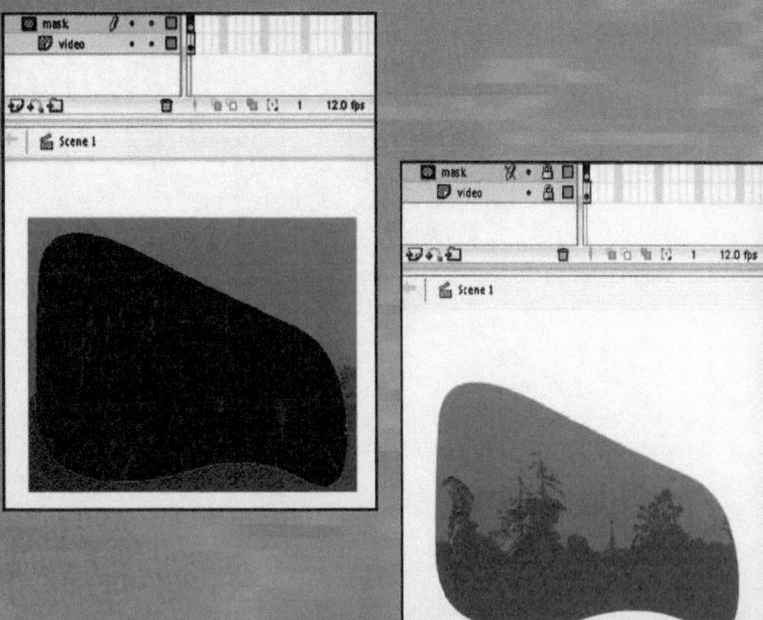

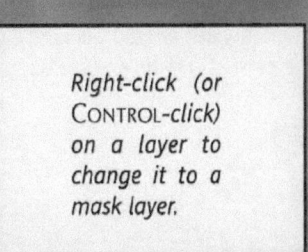

> *Right-click (or* CONTROL-*click) on a layer to change it to a mask layer.*

Now that we've seen what it's possible to do manually, let's take a look at how to change video dynamically with ActionScript.

Scripting with video movie clips

In this section, we'll run through several FLAs that show some of the ways in which we can manipulate our video movie clips using ActionScript. We'll see how to modify the video's appearance, position, and scale.

Video appearance

All the properties we'll look at in this section are generic to all movie clip instances, but we'll work with them creatively to see how they can be used with video in mind.

The basic properties available to video and other movie clips are as follows:

■ _x and _y control the position of any object, as measured in pixels down and to the right of the origin (0,0). For movie clips in the main timeline, the origin is at the top left corner of the stage; on other timelines, it's marked with a crosshair. We can use these properties (often with setInterval or onEnterFrame) to create motion. For example, to position a movie clip myClip at 300 pixels to the right of, and 100 pixels below, the origin:

```
myClip._x = 300;
myClip._y = 100;
```

■ _rotation controls the orientation of any object -- which way it's pointing. It's measured in degrees, with a default value of 0. Increase it and the clip will turn clockwise, doing a complete turn when you hit 360. For example, you can make a North-pointing clip point in various different directions:

```
myClip._rotation = 45;    // clip points North-East
myClip._rotation = 90;    // clip points East
myClip._rotation = 180;   // clip points South
```

- _width and _height control the width and height (in pixels) of any object instance. For example, to make a clip 150 pixels wide and 200 pixels high:

```
myClip._width = 150;
myClip._height = 200;
```

- _xscale and _yscale also control the size of the object instance, but they're different to _width and _height because they're measured (in percent) relative to the library original. Using the default value of 100 for each will give you an exact copy of the object as defined in the library. Other values will scale each of the dimensions up and down accordingly:

```
myClip._xscale = 200;    // twice original width
myClip._yscale = 10;     // one tenth original height
myClip._xscale = -100;   // mirror image of original
```

- _visible controls the visibility of an object using true or false settings. If you want to hide an object from view, you can make it invisible like so:

```
myClip._visible = false;
```

There's one other property to mention – although you'll probably detect a note of caution in the description.

- _alpha controls the opacity of any object instance, and is measured in percent. The default value is 100, giving full opacity. Lowering the value makes the instance less opaque (more transparent) until it's completely transparent (invisible) at 0. Alpha transparency puts a big load on the processor, so it's best to avoid using this property along with video movie clips (which also need a lot of processor attention), or at the very least use it extremely sparingly. A combination of the two can quickly bring your movie screeching to a halt!

Now let's cut to the chase and see how these properties can be used with ActionScript.

Scaling the video (_xscale and _yscale)

In this movie, running.fla, a video appears from nowhere and runs out of the screen.

Open a new Flash movie and set the framerate to 25fps. Create a new movie clip symbol called runningvid and import the video running.mov into it at mid-quality with a mid-keyframe interval. Let Flash extend the frames to cover the whole length of the video.

This footage (along with several of the other videos in this chapter) was filmed in portrait, with the camera filming sideways. This meant I could get the girl's full body length in shot without wasting huge areas of the frame.

Of course, we actually want the girl standing upright, so use the Transform panel to rotate the video 90 degrees clockwise. Now move the video so that the registration point is in the middle of her face.

Whenever an object is scaled up or down, its registration point is the one point that stays in the same place. We center the face on this spot so that it will act as a focal point during the growth of the movie clip.

Return to the main timeline and drag a copy of runningvid onto the stage. Give it the instance name vid and use the Align panel to center it on the stage.

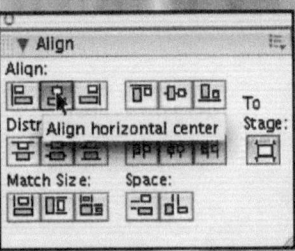
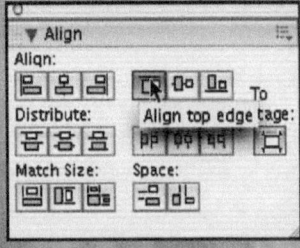

Rename the existing layer video and add a new layer called actions. Now attach the following code to frame 1 of the actions layer:

```
size = 0;
speed = 0;
```

We'll use these variables to control the growth of the movie clip. The first will track how large the clip needs to be, while the second will control how fast size changes as the clip appears to zoom towards us. Now add the following:

```
vid.onEnterFrame = function() {
  speed += vid._xscale/200;
  size += speed;
  vid._xscale = size;
  vid._yscale = size;
  if (vid._xscale>4000) {
    vid.onEnterFrame = undefined;
    vid._visible = false;
  }
};
```

This defines the onEnterFrame function for vid – code to be run every time that instance jumps to a new frame. The first two lines inside the function increase the value of speed according to the current scale of the video, and increase size by the value of speed (which increases the video's _xscale and _yscale properties). The upshot of this is that speed will keep increasing as the movie clip gets bigger, and size will grow, faster and faster, as speed gets larger and larger. This gives the illusion of a video object appearing out of the distance, and moving steadily towards us.

If we incremented speed by the same value every time, the approaching object would seem to get slower as the movie went on. This keeps the apparent rate of approach good and steady.

The last line checks to see if vid has grown larger than 4000% (that's forty times) its original size. If so, it's hidden from view by setting the _visible property to false.

Run the movie and notice how quickly it's all over! That girl is in a hurry...

Let's have some fun with this clip, and get her dodging around a bit – I think a game of British Bulldog is in order! Add this line of code inside the onEnterFrame function:

```
vid.onEnterFrame = function() {
    speed += vid._xscale/200;
    size += speed;
    vid._xscale = size;
    vid._yscale = size;
    if (vid._xscale>4000) {
        vid.onEnterFrame = undefined;
        vid._visible = false;
    }
    vid._x += Math.Random()*40 - 20;
};
```

Now, as she approaches the camera she jolts all over the place!

Although this is a dead simple movie, it starts to show some of the dynamic possibilities of using ActionScript to control your video clips. This opens up a number of possibilities from moving video on the fly to using masked video clips as game sprites (see Ken Jokol's chapter later in the book for more indulgence on this subject).

Moving the video (_x, _y and rotation)

As we've just seen, a video movie clip can be dynamically positioned using ActionScript to manipulate the clip's _x and _y properties. Now let's add in some rotational movement.

circle_walking.fla is a very raw Flash movie that uses one of the basic movie clip properties and an old favorite: _rotation. The girl in the red jacket (not to be confused with the character in "Don't Look Now") just walks and walks around in a circle, defying gravity and boredom.

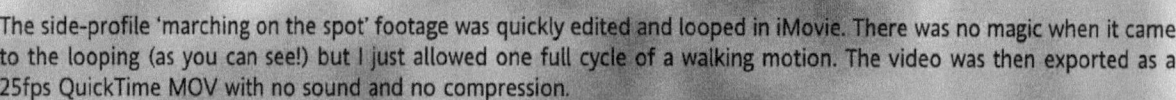

The side-profile 'marching on the spot' footage was quickly edited and looped in iMovie. There was no magic when it came to the looping (as you can see!) but I just allowed one full cycle of a walking motion. The video was then exported as a 25fps QuickTime MOV with no sound and no compression.

Now that we know what we have to work with, let's move on to Flash.

Open a new Flash movie and set the framerate to 25fps and the stage size to 550 x 550 pixels. Create a new movie clip symbol called walkvid and import walkloop.mov into it at mid-quality with a mid-keyframe interval. Let Flash extend the frames to cover the whole length of the video.

Now rotate the video 90 degrees (so that the girl's standing upright) and align the video so that the registration point is halfway along its top edge. This is the point around which we want to rotate the video. You should now have something like this:

Return to the main stage, rename the existing layer actions and add a new layer called circle. On the new layer, draw a circle using a khaki green color (I've used #848C4A). Resize the circle to 440 x 440 pixels and center it on the stage.

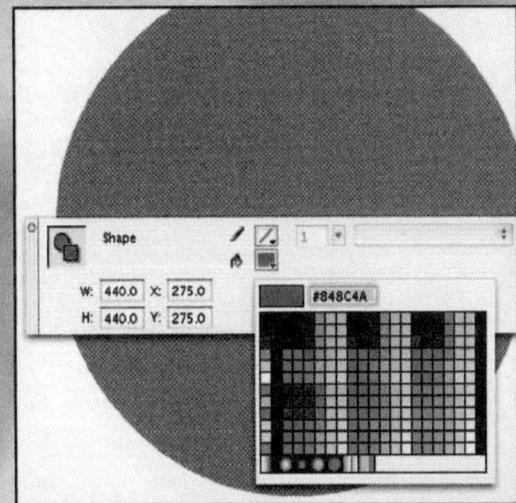

Create a new layer called video and drag a copy of the walkvid movie clip onto it. Give it the instance name vid and place it at the position shown in the screenshot:

Copy the circle from the circle layer and create a new layer called circleMask. Paste a copy onto the circleMask layer (using Edit > Paste In Place). Recolor the circle to a color that stands out (and one that you'd never use).

Now change the order of the layers to match what's shown here on the right, change the circleMask layer to be a mask layer, and make sure it only masks the video layer.

Once you've done this, the graphic elements are fully assembled. Now we need to add a tiny bit of script. Select frame 1 of the actions layer and type the following:

```
vid.onEnterFrame = function() {
    vid._rotation +=2;
}
```

Now run the movie and watch the hamster in overdrive. There isn't much to it as you can see – and it has the minimum script possible.

Iteration: wall_walking01.fla

The next iteration from this is a little different, and has SpiderMan style wall stickiness. We'll carry forward the basic concept from the last example, but now the marching girl will be walking around the boundary of the screen.

Open a new Flash document, change the background color to #848C4A, and set the framerate to 25fps. Import the video into a movie clip as before, but give it a central registration point. Drag a copy of the movie clip onto the existing layer and rename the layer video. Give the clip the instance name vid. That's it for graphic elements in this movie.

Now insert a new layer called actions and add the following code:

```
// initialization
speed = 5;
stagewidth = 550;
stageheight = 400;
hwidth = vid._width/2;
hheight = vid._height/2;
```

Let's look at the variables here: speed is the set speed for the motion, stagewidth and stageheight are used to check the boundaries, and hwidth and hheight store half the height and width of the video movie clip, and are used to add to the boundaries when they're checked.

Now add this chunk of code:

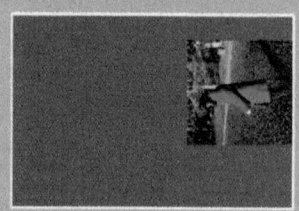

```
vid._x = (stagewidth-hwidth)/2;
vid._y = stageheight-hheight;
xspeed = -speed;
yspeed = 0;
```

This tells the movie clip where to start and what speed to start moving at. It'll start at the bottom center and begin moving to the left.

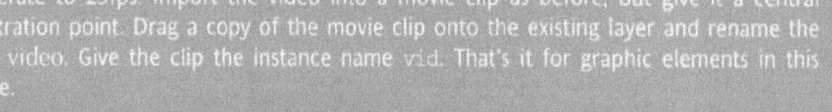

Now for the most important bit of code. This does it all: the boundary checking and the speed, rotation and position changing.

```
vid.onEnterFrame = function() {
    if (vid._x<=hwidth) {
        yspeed = -speed;
        xspeed = 0;
        vid._x = hheight;
        rot = 90;
    }
    if (vid._x>=stagewidth-hwidth) {
        xspeed = 0;
        yspeed = speed;
        vid._x = stagewidth-hheight;
        rot = -90;
    }
    if (vid._y>=stageheight-hwidth) {
        xspeed = -speed;
        yspeed = 0;
        vid._y = stageheight-hheight;
        rot = 0;
    }
    if (vid._y<=hwidth) {
        xspeed = speed;
        yspeed = 0;
        vid._y = hheight;
        rot = 180;
    }
    vid._x += xspeed;
    vid._y += yspeed;
    vid._rotation = rot;
};
```

Firstly, we set the onEnterFrame declaration, and then we get into the crux of it. There are four checks, one for each screen boundary (the video clip moves around the boundaries). Let's look at a couple of them and see what happens:

```
if (vid._x<=hwidth) {
    yspeed = -speed;
    xspeed = 0;
    vid._x = hheight;
    rot = 90;
}
```

OK – this one checks if the video has reached the left edge of the stage. Normally, we would use 0 as the side of the stage, but we need to take into consideration the dimensions of the video movie clip. If we use zero, the movie clip will run up to the registration point and half of the video will go off-screen. By using half the width (the hwidth variable), we're stopping when the left side of the movie clip reaches the left side of the stage.

Once the condition is true, yspeed is set to -speed (-5 by default), and xspeed set to 0. The movie clip will now move up the side of the screen. yspeed and xspeed are used after the if conditions to increment the movie clip's position.

The next thing to do is to update the x position of the movie clip. Since we're just about to rotate the clip by 90 degrees, we use hheight (rather than hwid th) to tell us how far from the boundary to place it.

Finally, we set the rot variable, which stores the correct rotation for the movie clip. Along with xspeed and yspeed, we'll use this to update the movie clip's properties after the if checks are complete.

As long as hheight is larger than hwidth (that is, the movie clip is taller than it is wide) this is all we need to do for our left boundary test. If not, things would be quite a bit more complicated.

The next if check looks like this:

```
if (vid._x>=stagewidth-hwidth) {
    xspeed = 0;
    yspeed = speed;
    vid._x = stagewidth-hheight;
    rot = -90;
}
```

This performs exactly the same function as the previous check, making sure that all the clip is still on the screen. The only difference is that we now use stagewidth to define our right boundary, and *subtract* half the movie clip's width to account for its dimensions. Likewise, when we set the clip's x position, we subtract its height from stagewidth (since it'll shortly be on its side again). The rest of the code follows the same pattern as before, so there's no need to go into it.

The last section of code...

```
vid._x += xspeed;
vid._y += yspeed;
vid._rotation = rot;
```

...simply increments the _x and _y values as appropriate, and uses the value of rot to set the movie clip's _rotation – straightforward enough. Now run the movie and watch the amazing, spectacular SpiderLady stick to those walls.

Iteration: wall_walking02.fla

Hardly anyone is decisive enough to run in one direction, and watching the last SWF for a little while bothered me because of its regularity. Even though it's coded, it could easily have been done with a motion tween. For this reason, I decided to add some indecision, allowing her to randomly change direction on her travels.

Add the following code inside the onEnterFrame code:

```
if (vid._y<=hwidth) {
    xspeed = speed;
    yspeed = 0;
    vid._y = hheight;
    rot = 180;
}
// ITERATION **
if (Math.Random()*50 < 1) {
    xspeed *= -1;
    yspeed *= -1;
    speed *= -1;
    vid._xscale *= -1;
```

```
        }
        vid._x += xspeed;
        vid._y += yspeed;
        vid._rotation = rot;
    };
```

This new code just runs a check on a random value between 0 and 50 – in the event that it's less than 1, it runs a little script to reverse the speed values and flip the video horizontally. `*= -1` here is used to reverse the value from negative to positive, and vice versa. It saves us calculating the current value and working from that.

Leave all the rest of the code as it is and run the movie. This time you'll notice that she runs around and has now acquired an element of confusion, turning every now and again. Elle est folle!

I'm going to leave this movie here so you can take it somewhere else. As you can already see though, the possibilities are pretty huge and the video game idea might be pretty cool. Right now, we'll move on to another set of properties: frames and movie clip timelines.

Video timeline properties and methods

In this section, we'll look at some of the basic timeline-based properties and methods which can be used by video or any other movie clips. The basic timeline methods are as follows:

- `gotoAndStop` is used to send the playhead of any given movie clip to the given value and stall it there. For example, to jump to frame 20 of `myClip` and stop there:

        myClip.gotoAndStop(20);

- `gotoAndPlay` does the same as `gotoAndStop()`, but leaves the playhead moving when it arrives at its destination. So, to jump to frame 20 of `myClip` and carry on playing:

        myClip.gotoAndPlay(30);

- `stop` tells the playhead to stop or pause wherever it currently is. For example:

        myClip.stop();

- `play` tells the playhead to play from the current playhead position. For example:

        myClip.play();

- `prevFrame` sends the playhead to the previous frame. For example:

        myClip.prevFrame();

- `nextFrame` sends the playhead to the next frame. For example:

        myClip.nextFrame();

The basic timeline properties are as follows:

- `_totalframes` is a read-only property containing the number of frames in any given movie clip's timeline.

```
framesTotal = myClip._totalframes;
```

- `_currentframe` is a read-only property containing the number of the playhead's current frame position within the specified movie clip. For example:

```
current = myClip._currentframe;
```

Let's take a look at a few more FLAs to see how these can be put to use.

Using the timeline properties and methods

After many of my feeble attempts to scale the table in one jump, I settled for the step-step-jump combination. Why did I want to jump the table in the first place? Well, to show timeline manipulations, airborne motion is the way to go.

This creation – you can find it on the CD in a file called `tableJumper.fla` – shows some basic timeline manipulations, controlling the table jumping motion. This is a result of a few different iterations, combined into one interface for your clicking pleasure.

The controls I installed here are quite simple, with buttons to play the video in the following modes:

- Slow motion (forward and back)
- Fast motion (forward and back)
- Remix! (a random motion selection from the above)

There are also two input text fields, which allow the user to change the speed. The first sets the frames per second for slow motion, while the second sets the relative speed of fast playback (so 2 will give double speed, 3 triple speed, and so on). The remix button will randomly mix fast and slow motion in either direction, switching between them at frantic speed. Let's make the table jumper...

Open a new Flash movie and create a new movie clip. Import the looped video `tablejumping.mov` – it's only just over three seconds long. Let Flash extend the timeline as before and return to the main timeline. Rename the current layer video layer and drag a copy of the video movie clip symbol onto it. Give it the instance name `vid`. That's all for our video.

Add a new layer and name it actions. All of the code in the movie will be placed on frame 1 of this layer, so you might like to pin it in the Actions Panel so that it's always on show.

Now we need to add some code to the movie. We'll start with the ActionScript to play the video slowly:

```
//functions and methods
MovieClip.prototype.playSlow = function(frameToPlay, direction) {
  this.onEnterFrame = function() {
    this.count++;
    if ((this.count%frameToPlay) == 0) {
      if (direction == "rwd") {
        this.prevFrame();
      } else if (direction == "fwd") {
        this.nextFrame();
      }
    }
  };
};
```

Basically, this code gives movie clips the ability to run slowly in either direction. We'll see in a moment how to use it – first let's see how it works.

The first line might look scary but it's actually dead easy:

```
MovieClip.prototype.playSlow = function(frameToPlay, direction) {
```

MovieClip.prototype tells Flash that we want to define a method that can be applied to all MovieClip objects. Following this is the name of the method: playSlow. We then point the method definition at a function – more on this in a moment.

The next line sets up an onEnterFrame for this (which refers to the MovieClip object that called this method):

```
this.onEnterFrame = function() {
```

Then we increment the object's count variable:

```
this.count++;
```

Our playSlow method accepts two arguments: frameToPlay and direction. We use the first one to find out when to proceed to the next frame:

```
if ((this.count%frameToPlay) == 0) {
```

We use the count variable (which is incremented every time this enters a frame) and feed it into the **modulo operator** (%), along with frameToPlay.

Modulo works by dividing one value (in this case this.count) by another (frameToPlay) and returning the remainder. For example, 7%2 gives 1 (since 2 goes into 7 three times with a remainder of 1), but 8%2 is 0 (since 2 goes into 8 exactly). If the first is exactly divisible by the second, the remainder is zero and the if condition is satisfied, so we run the next few lines of code:

```
if (direction == "rwd") {
  this.prevFrame();
} else if (direction == "fwd") {
  this.nextFrame();
}
}
```

The result of all this is that Flash will play one in every frameToPlay frames in the video. For example, with frameToPlay set to 3, we'll see one frame in every three: frame 3, frame 6, frame 9, frame 12, and so on. With frameToPlay set to 10, we'll just see every tenth frame, putting the table jumper on overdrive...

The direction argument is just the direction the movie is to play in. This is passed in as a string – either "rwd" (rewind) or "fwd" (forward) – and checked out by an if...else if block. Depending on the value, Flash either jumps to the next frame or the previous frame. This check, of course, is only run when the result of the modulo calculation equals 0.

After that exhausting breakdown, add this piece of code to the end of the function:

```
// initialization
vid.playSlow (5, "fwd");
```

> The comment here isn't crucial, but we'll be adding various different variables and things in here later, so you might find it handy to keep as a reminder of where to put them.

Run the movie and the video will play through once, slowly, in a forward direction. The rewind playing won't work yet – not without some changes to the code. Replace the line you just put in with the following:

```
// initialization
vid.gotoAndStop (vid._totalframes);
vid.playSlow (7, "rwd");
```

It won't play because the video is, from a reverse point-of-view, already at the end. Unless we tell it explicitly to loop either or both ways, it won't. In a moment, we'll add a new method to check if the video has ended in either direction. For now though, it's bootlegging I'm afraid. Onto the next method – let's see some speed in the opposite direction.

Enter the following code before the initialization section:

```
MovieClip.prototype.playFast = function(framesToSkip, direction) {
   this.onEnterFrame = function() {
      if (direction == "rwd") {
         this.frame -= framesToSkip;
      } else if (direction == "fwd") {
         this.frame += framesToSkip;
      }
      this.gotoAndStop(this.frame);
   };
};
```

This method accepts two parameters: framesToSkip and direction. The first is used every frame to increment or decrement the frame number (stored as the frame variable). So, if framesToSkip were set to 5 in the forward direction, the frames played would be 5, 10, 15, 20, 25, and so on.

The last line of code here just tells the video to go to the frame stored in the frame variable.

The next function fills in the faults of our previous two methods, providing them with the ability to loop. Enter the following code:

```
MovieClip.prototype.checkIfEnded = function(direction, framesNum) {
    if (direction == "rwd") {
        if (this._currentframe <= framesNum) {
            this.gotoAndStop(this._totalframes);
            this.frame = this._totalframes;
        }
    } else if (direction == "fwd") {
        if (this._currentframe >= this._totalframes) {
            this.gotoAndPlay(1);
            this.frame = 0;
        }
    }
};
```

The basic purpose of this code is to check whether the video has come to the end in either direction of playing. The forward check is simple: if _currentframe is equal or greater than _totalframes, the video is rewound and the frame variable is reset to zero.

The backwards check is a little more complicated. Flash doesn't have a problem going past the last frame, but it tends to choke if it's sent back before frame 0. To counter this, we send a frameCheck argument to the function, which checks against the number of frames being skipped. So, if the video is playing fast in reverse and framesToSkip is set to 10, Flash will check like this:

```
if (this._currentframe <= 10) {
```

This will prevent Flash from trying to jump back past the first frame and choking up. When this is true, the frame variable is set to _totalframes, so that it can play in reverse from there.

Now we've created a loop check, it needs to be applied to the previous two methods. Add the highlighted code to the methods:

```
MovieClip.prototype.playSlow = function(frameToPlay, direction) {
    this.onEnterFrame = function() {
        this.count++;
        if ((this.count%frameToPlay) == 0) {
            if (direction == "rwd") {
                this.prevFrame();
            } else if (direction == "fwd") {
                this.nextFrame();
            }
            this.checkIfEnded(direction, 1);
        }
    };
};

MovieClip.prototype.playFast = function(framesToSkip, direction) {
    this.onEnterFrame = function() {
        if (direction == "rwd") {
            this.frame -= framesToSkip;
        } else if (direction == "fwd") {
```

```
        this.frame += framesToSkip;
    }
    this.checkIfEnded(direction, framesToSkip);
    this.gotoAndStop(this.frame);
    };
};
```

Try out the following lines in the initialization section – but only one at a time – and run the movie. You should see the video play and loop in each direction, at various different speeds. Put in some of your own speed values to see what effect they have:

```
vid.playFast(6, "fwd");

vid.playFast(8, "rwd");

vid.playSlow(3, "fwd");

vid.playSlow(6, "rwd");
```

As you can see, we've now built the basic functionality, and it's almost flawless. However, we still need some vital interface elements – some input boxes for the speeds and buttons to change modes.

Create two input text boxes on a new textbox layer, and give them instance names of slowText and fastText. These will control the speed of each of the two play modes. For each one, activate the Show Border Around Text option, and set the maximum characters to 2. This should prevent absolute craziness on the user's behalf!

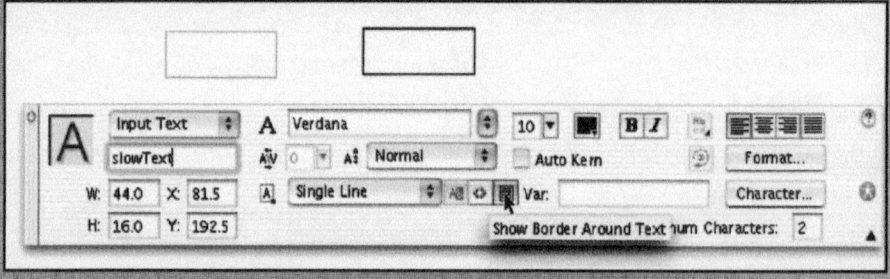

Now for some more censorship! Get rid of any code you've left in the initialization section, and add the following lines:

```
slowText.restrict = "0-9";
fastText.restrict = "0-9";
```

This prevents the user from entering anything other than numbers into the text boxes. Label the left input text box as "fps", and the other as "fast speed".

Since we're expecting users to put an fps value into the slowText text field, we need some way to translate that into the frameToPlay value that's fed into playSlow. The Flash movie's frame rate (which we can store in a variable called framerate) is fixed at 25fps. To make the video run forwards at 5fps, we therefore need to jump forward one video frame for every five timeline frames (25/5 = 5).

So, we use a fairly simple equation to convert slowText values into a frame delay:

```
frameDelay = function() {
    return (Math.round (framerate / _root.slowText.text));
};
```

We use Math.round to round our delay to the nearest whole number (Flash doesn't work in half frames!) and return this value so that a function call to frameDelay will simply give the calculated value. Just to make sure we don't get pesky users trying to exceed the movie's framerate (which just ain't gonna work!), we add an extra couple of lines:

```
frameDelay = function() {
    if (_root.slowText.text > framerate) {
        _root.slowText.text = framerate;
    }
    return (Math.round (framerate / _root.slowText.text));
};
```

This code checks if the value entered in the slowText box is greater than framerate (25 in this case). If it is, the slowText value will be reset to that max value. Simple, huh?

Just before we test the movie, we need to finish things off and give ourselves a working interface. Create a new layer called buttons and create four buttons with the following instance names fastBut, slowBut, slowrwdBut, fastrwdBut. Label and position them as shown:

These will let users change the playing mode of the movie. Now we need to wire them up, so type in the following code:

```
fastBut.onRelease = function() {
    vid.playFast(Math.round(_root.fastText.text), "fwd");
};
slowBut.onRelease = function() {
    vid.playSlow(frameDelay(), "fwd");
};
fastrwdBut.onRelease = function() {
    vid.playFast(Math.round(_root.fastText.text), "rwd");
};
slowrwdBut.onRelease = function() {
    vid.playSlow(frameDelay(), "rwd");
};
```

Add the following to the initialization section:

```
//initialization
slowText.restrict = "0-9";
fastText.restrict = "0-9";
vid.stop();
slowText.text = 5;
fastText.text = 5;
framerate = 25;
```

This simply stops the video on startup, sets a default value for each of the input text boxes and sets the aforementioned `framerate`. Now test the movie and play around with the speeds and modes. It should all function correctly at this point, but if not, check your code and button instance names.

So far we have a functioning interface, and the ability to change the speed and direction at will. However, quickly pressing the buttons sparked an idea that the mouse button cannot replicate: true frantic speed and direction changes – or **video remixing**. If you've ever seen the video for Brown Paper Bag by Reprazent then you'll already know what I mean. If not, you'll soon get the idea when you see the finished SWF in action.

Create a new button with a remix label, and give it an instance name of `remixBut`.

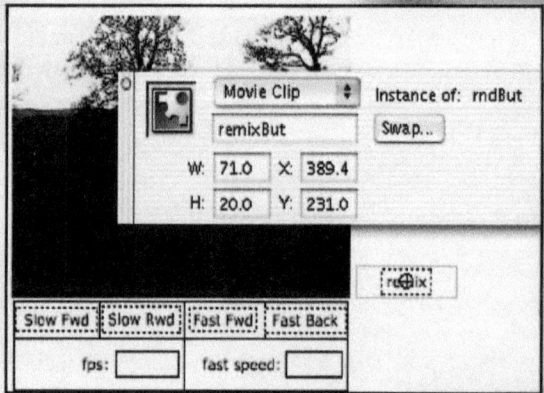

Add the following code to the usual place:

```
remixBut.onRelease = function() {
  _root.onEnterFrame = function() {
    rnd = 100/remixPercentChance;
    rnd = Math.Random(rnd*4);
    rnd = Math.round(rnd);
    if (rnd == 1) {
      vid.playFast(random(10), "fwd");
    } else if (rnd == 2) {
      vid.playFast(random(10), "rwd");
    } else if (rnd == 3) {
      vid.playSlow(random(10), "fwd");
    } else if (rnd == 4) {
      vid.playSlow(random(10), "rwd");
    }
  };
};
```

This code runs every frame, checking a random number for values 1, 2, 3 or 4. The possibility of the mode changing is set as the variable remixPercentChance, which represents a percentage chance – set as 40% in a moment. The multiplication by 4 accounts for there being four chances of mode changing.

If the random number matches up to any of the conditions, the mode is changed to any of the four possibilities. A random speed value is also passed for further insanity.

Add this to the initialization section:

```
remixPercentChance = 40;
```

This variable determines the chance (in percent) of a motion change. This setting gives us a four in ten chance of change – feel free to tweak this value if you want more or less of a headache!

Now run the movie, and press the remix button. Hopefully, you'll get some interesting results. The only problem now is that once you've pressed remix, none of the other buttons will work. We need to provide correction for the other buttons, and let them get rid of the remix effect – add the same line for each of the button handler functions:

```
fastBut.onRelease = function() {
  vid.playFast(Math.round(_root.fastText.text), "fwd");
  _root.onEnterFrame = undefined;
};
slowBut.onRelease = function() {
  vid.playSlow(frameDelay(), "fwd");
  _root.onEnterFrame = undefined;
};
fastrwdBut.onRelease = function() {
  vid.playFast(Math.round(_root.fastText.text), "rwd");
  _root.onEnterFrame = undefined;
};
slowrwdBut.onRelease = function() {
  vid.playSlow(frameDelay (), "rwd");
  _root.onEnterFrame = undefined;
};
```

This will clear the onEnterFrame code, as set by the remix button. If we don't add these lines of code, the remix will continue, even when you're at the controls.

That's it for this movie. It shows you a little of what you can do with movie clip properties like _currentframe, _totalframes and basic methods like gotoAndStop, gotoAndPlay and stop. The only one missing is the play method, but I'm sure you've used this one before anyhow.

The obvious beauty of this is that you can add your own video at will and Flash will pick up the number of frames in the video movie clip; you won't have to change anything. The only variable you need to change is framerate – depending on the speed of your movie.

Advanced Scripting

In this section, we'll look at masking, the drawing API and recoloring movie footage. All of this will be performed using ActionScript for expansion and ease of change.

Dynamic kaleidoscope

Kaleidoscopes aren't new to Flash. The general concept behind their creation is quite simple: just a little flipping and triangular masking. That principle is used here, but this movie is written with a view to allowing ease of changing the number of segments via a variable alteration.

 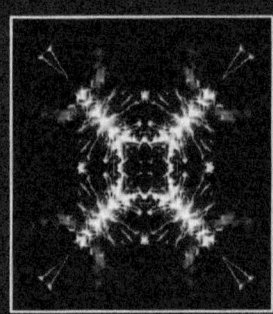 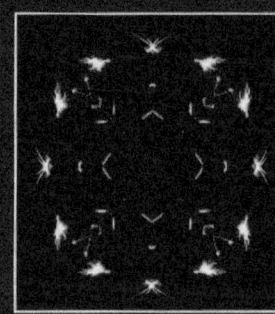 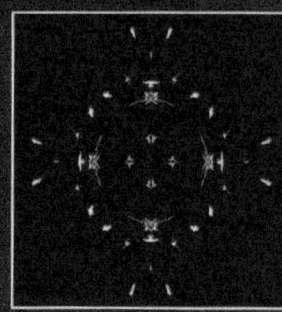

The dynamic element here is provided by the fact that it is very simple to make a change, due to the fact that a triangular mask is created with the drawing API, and it can be made bigger or smaller depending on the number of segments required.

The kaleidoscope will also be user-controlled according to the mouse position on screen.

kaleido01.fla

This first movie does all of the above, using a video of someone having fun with a sparkler (sparkle.mov). Let's see how it's made.

Open a new movie with a black (#000000) background and a framerate of 25fps. Import the sparkle.mov video into a movie clip as normal, with a central registration point. Call the movie clip fireworks.

Create a new movie clip called video and add an instance of the fireworks movie clip. Give it the instance name fworks and center it on the stage.

Name: sparkle.mov
Kind: QuickTime Movie
Size: 6.9 MB
Created: 27/11/02
Modified: 27/11/02
Dimensions: 200 × 150
Duration: 00'04

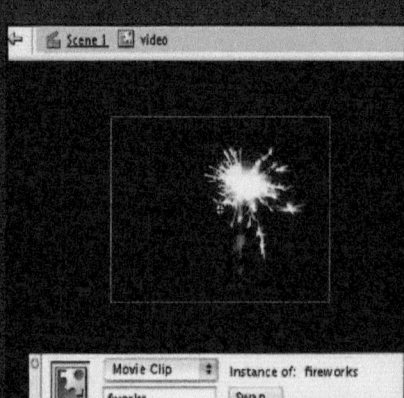

Now right-click (CONTROL-click on a Mac) on the fireworks symbol in the Library and choose Linkage from the drop-down menu.

Click on the Export for ActionScript box and enter vid in the Identifier box. You should have something that looks like this:

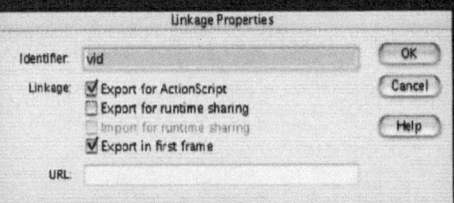

We do this so that the video can be attached dynamically by the code that's coming in a moment. Giving the library symbol a linkage identifier lets us use ActionScript (more specifically the attachMovie method) to pull it out of the library and onto the stage. We'll see how in a moment.

That's it for graphic elements. Easy, huh? We've got a little bit of code to run through, but there's nothing too hard here – just quite a lot of it.

Rename the existing layer on the main timeline actions and pin the Actions panel to frame 1. Enter the following:

```
fscommand("fullscreen", "true");
fscommand("allowscale", "false");

//initialization
slices = 8;
angles = 360/slices;
stageWidth = 550;
stageHeight = 400;
stageMidX = stageWidth/2;
stageMidY = stageHeight/2;
vidHeight = 150;
// depth vars
tCount = 0;
vCount = 100;
```

The first section here just forces the SWF to run full-screen, and prevents it from scaling out of proportion. This few lines initialize a number of key variables. Let's run through some unknowns:

- slices represents the number of segments in the kaleidoscope. As mentioned, this can be changed (within reason) to change the display. We'll see how in a moment.

- angles calculates the amount of rotation required for each segment using the slices value.

- vidHeight stores the actual height of the video. This is used when it comes to drawing the mask so we know its limits.

- tCount is an incremental value for the duplication of triangular masking portions and is used for naming and depth.

- vCount is a depth and name store for instances of the video.

Now let's add the code we need to draw a single mask segment:

```
tri = _root.createEmptyMovieClip("triangle", 10000);

tri.beginFill(0x00FF00, 100);
tri.lineStyle(1, 0x00FF00, 100);
tri.moveTo(0, 0);
tri.lineTo(0, vidHeight);
split = slices/8;
tri.lineTo(vidHeight/split, vidHeight);
tri.endFill();

tri._x = stageMidX;
tri._y = stageMidY;
```

The above code should give us something like this:

This might look like a lot of code, but it's really not that much to take in. First, we create an empty movie clip to house the drawing and reference it with `tri`, so from now on we can refer to it via the new shorthand name.

Next, the drawing API code begins with the `beginFill` method – this tells Flash that we want a filled shape to be drawn using green at 100% alpha. The `lineStyle` code tells Flash what thickness, color and alpha to use for the strokes to come.

The pen is then moved to 0,0 – simple enough. The `lineTo` code draws a line from the current pen position (which we just set to 0,0) to an x position of 0 and y position of `vidHeight`. This draws a line straight down the screen.

The next couple of lines need a little attention:

```
split = slices/8;
tri.lineTo(vidHeight/split, vidHeight);
```

These are basically just deciding where to draw the next line to, and this will depend on the required size of each segment.

We use `vidHeight` to set the height of each triangle, and some fraction of `vidHeight` to get the width. Assuming we have a minimum of eight slices, the largest segment we'll be dealing with is a 45 degree triangle (a little math gives 360/8 = 45). This should be as wide as it is tall, so we divide `vidHeight` by 1 (8/8) to get the width.

If we have sixteen slices, we need a narrower triangle. 16/8 gives us `split` equal to 2 and we use this to draw a triangle that's half as wide as it is tall. Likewise, a 32-slice kaleidoscope will give us a quarter-width (8/32 = 1/4) triangle.

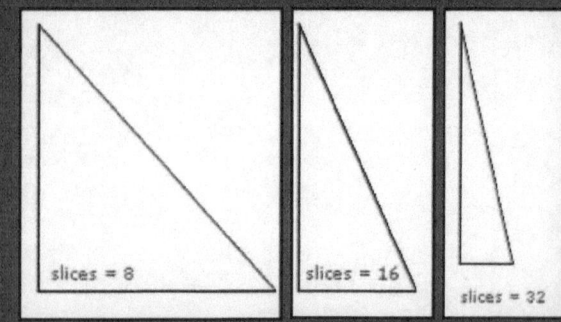

slices = 8   slices = 16   slices = 32

The endFill method closes the shape. Even though we've only drawn two lines, Flash will fill the shape for us. The next two lines position the triangle at the center of the screen.

The next chunk of code takes care of duplicating and attaching the triangle masks and videos – this is the heart of our code.

You may find it useful to know that each of the video instances is given its own triangular mask, so all can work independently of one another. The number of videos and duplicate masks made will obviously come down to the number of slices required.

The next bit of code marries together the masks and videos, moving, rotating and flipping them in the same way as before, using setMask to actually do the magic.

If you've ever made a kaleidoscope in Flash or studied one closely, you'll know that it works by mirroring, so rotating the videos and masks is just not enough. It's the difference between right and wrong – though both look pretty splendid!

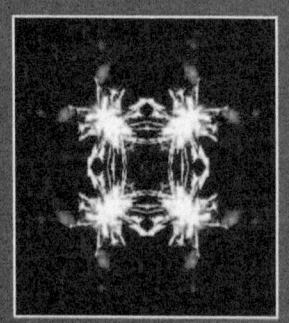

To get around this, I need to use a couple of for loops to position the segments correctly, and to flip certain pieces where necessary.

Add the following code:

```
// attach masked vid segments
for (i=0; i<slices/2; i++) {
  for (j=0; j<2; j++) {
    _root.attachMovie("vid", "vid"+vCount, vCount);
    vid = _root["vid"+vCount];
    vid._x = stageMidX;
    vid._y = stageMidY;
    _root.triangle.duplicateMovieClip("tri"+tCount,tCount);
    nutri = _root["tri"+tCount];
    vid._rotation = (i*2)*angles;
    nutri._rotation = (i*2)*angles;

    if (j == 1) {
      vid._yscale = -100;
      nutri._yscale = -100;
    }

    vid.setMask(nutri);
    tCount++;
    vCount++;
  }
}

//hide triangle
triangle._visible = false;
```

Two loops are set up here to make sure that we draw all the required segments, but more importantly to make sure that we flip some of the segments. The current value of the inner loop is used here:

```
if (j == 1) {
    vid._yscale = -100;
    nutri._yscale = -100;
}
```

This checks whether the piece needs to be flipped. If j is 1, we know the piece is due for flippage.

The only other major departure here is following lines, which rotate the assets at intervals of 2. The assets are essentially overlapped before they are flipped.

```
vid._rotation = (i*2)*angles;
nutri._rotation = (i*2)*angles;
```

Without the flipping code for example, here's how it would look:

This is actually eight segments occupying the space of four.

The last thing we do here is to use setMask to mask the video with the triangular masks and increment the count variables for the next run of the loop.

Okay, test the movie and watch the effect as it is. Feel free to change the slices value – ideally to some multiple of 8 – I'd suggest 32 as a max too!

kaleido02.fla

You might agree that it needs something that is lacking from a traditional kaleidoscope – more movement. There isn't much to this but it makes a difference to the overall effect.

Add the following code before the for loops:

```
MovieClip.prototype.move = function() {
  this.onEnterFrame = function() {
    this.fworks._x = _root._xmouse/6;
    this.fworks._y = _root._ymouse/6;
  };
};
```

Remember we gave the fireworks movie clip an instance name of fworks? This is why. The aim is to position it according to the cursor position on screen. This is also why I put in the full-screen code to begin with: it gives us a larger region to play with.

Now add the line shown in bold:

```
for (j=0; j<2; j++) {
    _root.attachMovie("vid", "vid"+vCount, vCount);
    vid = _root["vid"+vCount];
    vid.move();
    vid._x = stageMidX;
    vid._y = stageMidY;
```

This applies the `move` method to the current created `vid` clip.

Run the movie and you'll notice that mouse movement now creates different patterns because different areas of the video are being displayed.

That's all fine and dandy, but isn't a black & white kaleidoscope missing the point?

kaleido_03.fla

Okay, if it's color you want...

Add the following code at the end of the initialization variables:

```
rndRed = Math.random()*100;
rndGreen = Math.random()*100;
rndBlue = Math.random()*100;

MovieClip.prototype.setColor = function(r, g, b) {
    col = new Color(this);
    colTransform = new Object();
    colTransform = {ra: r, rb:'0', ga: g, gb:'0',
        ba: b, bb:'0', aa:'100', ab:'255'};
    col.setTransform(colTransform);
};
```

Now add this just after the `move` call in the last iteration:

```
for (j=0; j<2; j++) {
    _root.attachMovie("vid", "vid"+vCount, vCount);
    vid = _root["vid"+vCount];
    vid.move();
    vid.setColor(rndRed, rndGreen, rndBlue);
    vid._x = stageMidX;
    vid._y = stageMidY;
```

I won't try and give a complete explanation of the `Color` object here, but all of this code simply applies a random red, green and blue value to the all the `vid` movie clips. Test the movie and take a look at the uniform color spread. If you want a different color, republish it, and do it again and again.

kaleido_04.fla

For another very simple iteration, make a copy of the `Math.random` lines inside the `for` loops, just before the `setColor` function call:

```
for (j=0; j<2; j++) {
_root.attachMovie("vid", "vid"+vCount, vCount);
    vid = _root["vid"+vCount];
    vid.move();
    rndRed = Math.random()*100;
    rndGreen = Math.random()*100;
    rndBlue = Math.random()*100;
    vid.setColor(rndRed, rndGreen, rndBlue);
    vid._x = stageMidX;
    vid._y = stageMidY;
```

Now run the movie again – all the segments are given a different color, resulting in a pretty garish and unlikable combination...eek!

kaleido_05.fla

This time, we'll get the colors to cycle gradually but randomly. Add the following three variables to the initialization section:

```
rspeed = random (10) - random (10);
bspeed = random (10) - random (10);
gspeed = random (10) - random (10);
```

Butcher the `move` function by adding the lines shown in bold:

```
MovieClip.prototype.move = function() {
    this.onEnterFrame = function() {
        this.fworks._x = _root._xmouse/6;
        this.fworks._y = _root._ymouse/6;

        if ((_root.rndRed >= 100) || (_root.rndRed<=0)){
            _root.rspeed *= -1;
        }
        if ((_root.rndGreen >= 100) || (_root.rndGreen<=0)) {
            _root.gspeed *= -1;
        }
        if ((_root.rndBlue >= 100) || (_root.rndBlue<=0)) {
            _root.bspeed *= -1;
        }
        _root.rndRed += rspeed;
        _root.rndGreen += gspeed;
        _root.rndBlue += bspeed;

        this.setColor(_root.rndRed, _root.rndGreen, _root.rndBlue);
    };
};
```

Finally, comment out all the color-setting code left inside the `for` loops:

```
for (j=0; j<2; j++) {
  _root.attachMovie("vid", "vid"+vcount, vcount);
  vid = _root["vid"+vcount];
  vid.move();
  //rndRed = Math.random()*100;
  //rndGreen = Math.random()*100;
  //rndBlue = Math.random()*100;
  //vid.setColor(rndRed, rndGreen, rndBlue);
  vid._x = stageMidX;
  vid._y = stageMidY;
```

Run the movie, and you'll see all the segments cycle nicely through a range of colors. The change is gradual, so the effect is nice and easy on the eye – quite a contrast to the last iteration at least!

Summary

The stuff that you've seen in this chapter is just an opening into the world of interactivity and creativity with Flash. So far, we've looked at movie clip manipulation through the Flash environment and ActionScript, and have started to look at some basic interactivity. From here it can go anywhere – and believe me, it does! So turn the page and begin the ride.

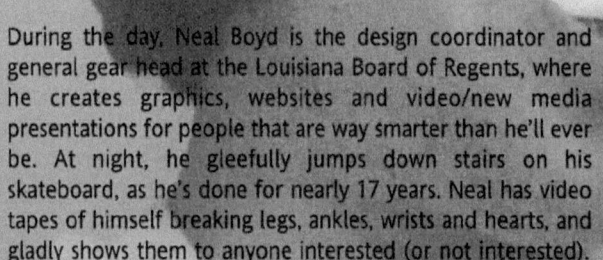

During the day, Neal Boyd is the design coordinator and general gear head at the Louisiana Board of Regents, where he creates graphics, websites and video/new media presentations for people that are way smarter than he'll ever be. At night, he gleefully jumps down stairs on his skateboard, as he's done for nearly 17 years. Neal has video tapes of himself breaking legs, ankles, wrists and hearts, and gladly shows them to anyone interested (or not interested).

He's awful thankful that he has a 'sit-down' job.

You can make fun of Neal at the award-winning website www.loudblue.com, but all he'll do is tell you how pretty your eyes are and crawl away crying like the sad little puppy that he is

Mixing vector animation with video

Neal Boyd

I began drawing at the age of three, inspired and egged on by my immensely talented older brother Raymond. As a child, I tried to emulate his style and technique, while at the same time using what I learned to illustrate the things that interested a kid that age... namely Godzilla, Ultraman and various comic book characters.

As I grew older, my interest in all things science fiction grew into an infatuation. By the time I was twelve years of age, I had created several dozen complete comic books, numerous universes, and had a library of original characters that grew on a daily basis. The comics would get passed around the school, and before I knew it, I was turning fellow classmates into superheroes (as well as transforming kids I didn't like as much into exaggerated, villainous beasties that I would conquer in ways that probably wouldn't be considered healthy by today's standards).

The more I drew, the more my style developed into that of a true cartoonist: I was learning how to simplify my artwork, keeping my use of lines to the minimum necessary to recognize my subject. This style of art allowed me to draw more pictures in one sitting, and also proved to be an asset later on when learning to illustrate in vector-based programs (more on that later).

As I made my way through my school years, my passion for art was fueled by an equal passion for the sport of skateboarding. Much of the artwork that the skateboard companies used was urban in nature, and the act of skateboarding itself gave me a keen insight on how to illustrate the animated human form. I spent many high school lectures drawing flip-book animations of baggy-clothed versions of myself performing fantastic maneuvers in the lower right hand corners of my textbooks (much to the dismay of my teachers). I'd like to offer an apology to any students in the years below whose concentration was ruined by this unwanted addition to their books.

After high school, I started attending classes at Southeastern Louisiana University, majoring in English. My choice surprised a lot of people, but I had my reasons (most of them unfounded). You see, I was under the impression that art classes consisted of beret-wearing pretentious types that sat around all day throwing famous Italian and French names back and forth. For a guy that came from the rural southern United States, English seemed like a safer field of study. So for the next couple of years, I studied Greek and English literature, whilst spending nearly every free moment of my time scratching away with my pen and paper.

Around this time, I developed an interest in learning how to color my work, but my experiments proved frustrating. Oil and acrylic paint tended to cover my line work, and water-based inks and paints always seemed to bleed out over the edges of my shapes. Just as I was ready to return to a black and white world, my good friend and fellow sci-fi and comic geek Fred Goodspeed introduced me to a wonderful program called Adobe Photoshop (it was in version 3 at the time). It was a revelation to be able to get the vivid color I had been looking for, without ruining my time-consuming line drawings.

I found a computer in one of the labs in the University that was equipped with both Photoshop and a scanner, and I spent nearly every day coming in to the lab, scanning images, and terrorizing my work with the abundance of tools I now had at my disposal. That particular semester ended, and as the summer semester started, I chose to not attend class so that I could spend more time in the lab... Oh, the irony.

The particular computer that I worked on at the school became my workstation. I spent an average of four hours on the machine (before going to work in the evening) and up to twelve hours on days I had free from vocational duties. Out of all of this time digitally manipulating my drawings, I had yet to log one hour on the Internet.

Truth is, I didn't exactly know what it was.

When the summer semester was over, the computer lab became too busy. *My* computer was hijacked by essay-writers and other folks that were actually spending time working on subjects they were studying – the nerve! My classes were also getting in the way of my education. As I spent my class periods discussing the different Cantos in Dante's Inferno, I secretly thought about how I could create metal textures for the androids I had been doodling the night before. My academic future in English was walking down a path of doom. My fate was sealed when a 24-hour internet café opened up across the street from the school.

As I mentioned earlier, I'd never surfed the Internet. My only computer knowledge consisted of scanning line art and spending the rest of the day giving it new life. When I found out the new (and now defunct) Star Route Café had Photoshop running on one of its boxes, I was ecstatic. I was disappointed at the fact that using this machine meant I had to pay an hourly rate, but as I frequented the café very regularly, the owner and I were able to come to an arrangement.

Dubois spent much of his day at the café too, building websites on a freelance basis, so he saw my graphics and liked what he saw. We developed an informal deal: he would allow me to work on a computer for free, as long as I made graphics or flyers for him every once in a while.

But even this wasn't quite enough for me. Eventually, I accepted the inevitable and saved up for my own machine.

At this point, I was still learning the ins and outs of the Internet, but I consumed as much information as possible. My English textbooks gathered dust, as I was spending all of my free time wrapped up in HTML guides and Photoshop tutorials. I spent the next couple of months creating my first website on a free hosting site, where I began to learn about file optimization and some of the fundamental rules of usability and navigation.

It was at this time a friend of mine introduced me to www.gabocorp.com. "How is this possible?!? What kind of magic is this?!?" I had never heard of Flash before witnessing the beauty that was gabocorp, but I was hooked.

The creator's imagery was everything I tried so hard to create with the tools I had been using – bold, vivid colors, smooth crisp lines and *motion*! I had been experimenting with daffy little animated GIFs, but this was real animation! Not only did the site interact with me, but it loaded twice as fast as my graphic-intensive site! Needless to say, this discovery truly changed my life. Within a very short space of time I had my very own copy of Flash 3.

I've always had the ability to learn things quickly, but Flash was a different story. The interface was completely alien to me, so I stuck to using the tools that looked familiar at first – mainly the paintbrush and the bucket. For the first part of my relationship with Flash 3, I used it primarily as a drawing tool. I loved the way it smoothed my lines, and I found myself being able to easily emulate different styles of cartoon illustration, from the clean lines of Jim Davis (the creator of *Garfield*) to the bold style of Sam Keith (*The Maxx*).

As I became more familiar with creating characters and objects in this new environment, I started taking my flip-book experience and applying it to my digital work. I happily created cartoons frame by frame for a little while, but creating progressive design pieces eluded me. To be honest, I was making cool artwork, but lacked the discipline of a designer. I needed some more skills. I changed majors.

When I began studying design under the tutelage of Professor Gary Keown, the curriculum was undergoing a drastic change. The semester I signed up, a great deal of the class work was done by hand, but the curriculum was being converted into an all-digital format. I studied art and design for a couple of years, and was able to land a job doing web design for a local web development firm.

After a couple of semesters, I decided to quit school so that I could work in the field full time. I spent my days building websites for mostly local clients, nothing too fancy, so I wound up spending my evenings (and complete nights in many cases) creating new movies. I played around with layouts, navigation interfaces, character animations and 3D experiments, but I lacked focus. Part of my problem was the fact that I wanted to do everything I saw, but didn't know exactly how to put it all together.

I made more cartoons, and began implementing more Flash elements into my site. After a while, I was using Flash for everything – well, everything *except* for video.

From Flash 3 (where I started off) up to Flash 5, the only way I could achieve the effects I wanted was to import sequential images, add my effects, then export. This would only work for very small files. One of the biggest hassles I had was that Flash tended to choke on me when importing a few thousand bitmaps at one time, and importing them a few hundred at a time was not only time consuming, but also a very stressful process as well (doing a large import like this made my system extremely unstable).

Another issue was that audio had to be imported separately, and then matched up later. When scrubbing the timeline, the audio and video almost never matched up correctly, no matter how everything was arranged, so I had to export everything over and over until I got lucky. As you might have guessed, this process got very old very quickly. I basically quit doing these projects because of the frustration.

And this was the way it stayed, until a short time ago, when I learned that the new Flash MX would be able to import video. "Now anything is possible," I realized, with a mixture of excitement and dread that my social life would officially become ruined...

While Flash MX was being beta tested, I was sketching out ideas with the same fervor I used to have when creating comic strips. I didn't (and still don't) have plans for a full-length feature, but I did have some pretty cool ideas for some short clips. When Flash MX came out, I was ready to go.

My first video didn't amount to much more than me standing in a parking garage interacting with various abstract vector shapes all around me. It was a very silly video, but to my knowledge nobody had done it before, and even if they had, it was very fulfilling to actually be in one of my own Flash animations. My next mini-feature, a clip called "Loud Blue Kung Fu", didn't have me interacting with vector elements, but used the elements to help communicate a sense of continuity and style through the piece.

The way I work, and what I create in Flash, is heavily influenced by both my background as a cartoonist, and the vector/bitmap use of some of the current pros that I look up to today. I like sharp, bold, simple images, and prefer to use them to put the focus on the subject in the video.

As far as blending vector images with video goes, the works of Eric Jordan (www.2advanced.com) and Mike Baker (www.highradiation.com) quickly come to mind. Eric has been an influence on lots of us dedicated Flash aficionados, and his ability to blend the borders of vector art and reality into a seamless mix leave me in awe. Mike Baker – one of the most prolific videophiles I know – is constantly topping his previous efforts, and destroys my senses with pure energy every time I watch his work.

Some of the inspiration I get these days comes from movies like 'The Matrix', 'The Cell', and 'Ninja Scroll'. On the screen, I enjoy fast, in-your-face motion; in production though, I like to take a much lighter approach as far as tone goes.

One other source of inspiration for me is the act and art of skateboarding. I'm getting a little older, and although I do skate on a regular basis, I find that I appreciate watching other people ride almost as much as I enjoy riding itself. I currently spend a great deal of time filming other skaters, and use many of the filming techniques I learned while following people on boards on my own projects. Documenting a sport like skateboarding not only helped me to learn how to get the best shot of a particular maneuver, but it also helped me to learn how to incorporate physics into my animations, making them organic and natural to help temper the contrast that most vector images tend to have when placed on top of grainy film footage.

I try to incorporate a sense of humor into everything I do, because, quite frankly, when I try to make important work, it comes off as pretentious and preachy. It's pretty simple really – I'm not out to change people's lives, I really just want to make cool stuff that people like watching. Having a whole lot of fun isn't too bad either.

Well, that's the story of one designer located in the muddy southern region of the United States. I'm currently a web developer at Pixelstix Web Development in Hammond, Louisiana during the day, and by night I run Loud Blue Studios (www.loudblue.com). When I'm not making client sites or adding new experiments to Loud Blue, you can often find me at one of the local coffee shops working on Flash projects and presentations with my pal Eric Gilley. If you come by and I'm not there, I'm probably hiding out with my fiancé Becca (making her watch scary movies with lots of clowns) or I'm trying very hard to break my leg through the media of skateboard and any unlucky set of steps I happen to come across.

The idea

I'm sitting at work, creating a Flash intro for a client site. The client explicitly stated that he wanted his intro to jump off the screen and kick the viewer's ass – now there's an idea! (Imagination starts here.) Imagine this – you're sitting at your computer creating a really sweet animation that will blow everyone's mind. You preview what you've done so far, but there's a problem. The animation stops for no reason. "Did I accidentally put a stop action on the frame?"

All of a sudden, the screen begins to flicker and pulsate wildly. At first, you think your computer is about to blow up for no reason; then you witness something you thought you'd never see: one of your movie clips has crept out of your monitor and is now in the real world!

"Wow, that's pretty cool," you think to yourself. For a second, you stare at the living animation flowing from your screen with amazement and befuddlement, but your fascination quickly turns into horror as the twisting shapes and wingdings start rampaging out of your machine, knocking you out of your chair and onto the floor.

As you look up and around, you see vector graphics flinging themselves wildly around the office like a wild bull. Then the shapes focus on you. You quickly get up and start running as fast as you can with the rabid lines and shapes whipping at your heels...

Yeah, that should make a good start.

Getting started

I needed to document this idea while it was still fresh in my head. Instead of writing it down in text, I opted to jump directly into thumbnail sketches. Drawing thumbnails helps me in several ways – having a visual image helps me decide where I need to film, what my graphics need to look like, how I pace the shots, what camera angles I should use (especially since I'm my own cameraman), and most importantly, whether or not the idea is feasible to go ahead with.

When creating thumbnails, I don't attempt to create a master work of art. I want to be able to sketch out the idea fast enough so that the spontaneity is still present, but make the illustrations decent enough so that I'll be able to use the best initial thought that popped into my head at the beginning.

I only draw key shots that I know must be in the movie – there's no point in wasting time on the filler shots, as I may get a better idea while on location, but I don't deviate from the important shots that I illustrate.

I'm a doodler by nature, so I use this to my advantage. When I'm not trying to compose the layout of a shot, I sketch out patterns and designs that I may or may not use for other vector elements – in this case, the evil vector objects attacking me.

When I'd finished sketching, I was left with this:

Planning the shoot

I now had a pretty decent image of what I wanted this film to look like. My next step was choosing a location. Now, since I'd be sharing the screen with lots of whipping, flickering images, I wanted to make sure that I could get shots in locations that have lots of open spaces. The places I planned to film needed to allow me the ability to film from far away.

Luckily for me, my office is in a converted warehouse, affording me room to get the camera angles I sketched out earlier. I planned to do the rest of the shoot outdoors, primarily at two different parking garages (that would appear to be one single location if everything worked out right), so I hoped that wouldn't pose too many problems.

This particular shoot took three days: about two hours for the office scene, and close to seven for the outdoor parts. The filming took a little longer than I'd like it to, but since I was doing it by myself (and in some instances the camera was several floors above me) I had to do a lot of traveling back and forth from the action to the equipment on every take to make sure the sequences came out correctly.

Preparing the video

Once filming was complete, my main goal was to create any and all pre-Flash assets I'd need. When I'm adding vector work to video in the Flash environment, I like to try to have all video editing and audio work completed beforehand.

I use Adobe Premiere to do 100% of my video editing, but not to worry if you don't have it yourself – the editing can be done on virtually any decent DV editing program. The only manipulation actually done to the video is cutting, rearranging, and (every once in a while) slowing down the footage.

When I export the footage, I remove the audio, since then the file size will be considerably smaller (especially important if the video winds up on the Web). There won't be any talking going on, so I can arrange my soundtrack and sound effects in Flash.

I'm not making this video for broadcast on television, so I opt to export out in MPEG format at a resolution of 352x288. I'm using an older computer and juggling precious drive space, so I choose to compress my video before setting it on my hard drive.

> *Flash can import MPEG, DV (Digital Video), MOV (QuickTime), and AVI files. Importing DV footage would look a lot better, but in my case, saving such a large file might prevent me from doing other things...like saving goulash recipes.*

At this point, I had one file weighing in at about 18 MB. The majority of the rest of the process will be done in Flash (with one exception that I'll focus on later). This is where we finally get to open Flash and start filling up the composition with vectors.

Building the FLA

Before we start looking at the creation of the FLA, I'd like to comfort some of you by letting you know that there's virtually no scripting involved in this project. If you have a handful of Flash intros (or the like) in your portfolio, you should feel right at home.

First of all, I imported the video into Flash and adjusted the settings so that it would play the way I wanted it to. I created a new movie and adjusted the stage to the dimensions of the MPEG I was importing. In this case, the video is 353x288 pixels.

I then changed the movie's frame rate to 25 fps – this matches the frame rate of the MPEG, and should play through the Flash Player almost exactly as the video plays in its native format. If you were to bring the video in at 12 fps, it would appear clunky (as a result of discarding over half of the frames).

Once the stage was set, I selected File > Import > VIDEO.MPEG, and wound up looking at this dialog:

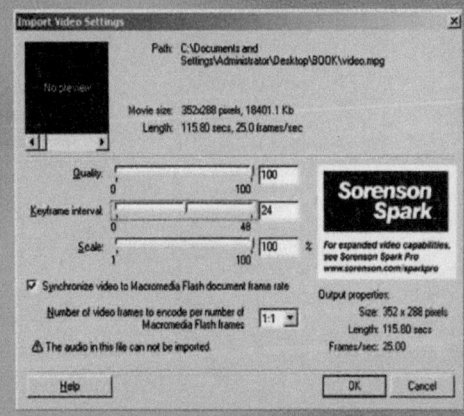

At this point, we get to decide on our Flash compression settings. If you're importing some really high quality footage and hope to upload your finished piece to a web server (without angering the server administrator), this is where the magic happens – you can compress your video to a fraction of its original size.

Alternatively, if you were planning on exporting your final project for further editing in After Effects or Final Cut Pro, you probably wouldn't want to apply any compression settings at all.

Once I'd successfully imported the video, I centered it on the stage using the Align panel:

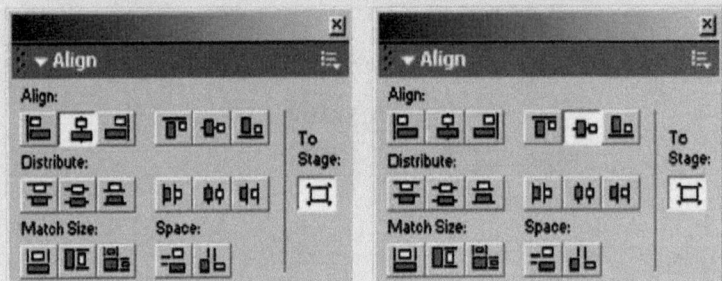

I normally tend to draw directly on top of the video, so I always make sure to lock the layer that it's located on. It's good practice to create every graphic element on a separate layer, as it makes editing a lot easier, and also allows us to utilize shape tweens if we choose to use them (its virtually impossible to use shape tweens on two separate objects resting on the same layer and get usable results).

Since Flash MX now has layer folders, we can add as many layers as we need without worrying about getting lost in a mass of confusion. It also allows us to categorize, then sub-categorize each element on the timeline so that they'll be easier to find if we need to go back and fix anything (always name your layers for easy reference).

Next, I needed to create a few assets for this video: some using Flash, and some using other software. My first concern was creating a border for the movie. Should this video wind up on a website, the border can help complement the site design or separate it if necessary.

I used the Line tool with a weight of 2 to draw around the video. I then selected the frame that the border was on, converted it into a symbol (*F8*), and locked the layer (so that I couldn't accidentally nudge it later on).

From this point on, I worked in between the layer containing the video and the layer containing the border. Anything placed below the video will be hidden, and working under the border gives me a better idea of how the final product will appear, as I can see exactly how it's framed.

We'll start by creating our opening title and credits.

Creating blurred text

For the title and opening credits of this production, I wanted to have some blurred text speed in, come into focus, flicker in and out of focus, then speed away in the same blurred fashion that it came in.

Pseudo blur (Flash only)

Here's one way you can create a pseudo blur inside Flash. First, select some text:

Then, break it apart once (*CTRL+B*), converting it from a word into a series of letters:

Break it apart once again, converting each letter into a fill:

Finally, select Modify > Shape > Soften Fill Edges. In this case, I made the edges expand a distance of 4 pixels, in as many steps:

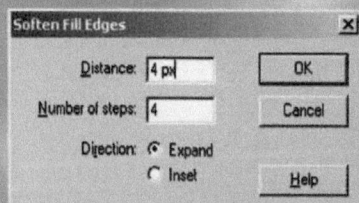

The results look rather like a Gaussian blur:

However, I actually want a motion blur effect for my titling and credits, so this won't do.

Flash allows us to achieve some incredible text effects, but it does have its limitations. Making text blur natively in Flash is a pretty time-consuming affair, and although the final results might work for other projects, they just don't fit here.

Motion blur (Photoshop and Flash)

Getting the result I wanted took a little outside assistance. I needed a program that can (a) apply a motion blur effect to a piece of text, and (b) export the blurred text as a PNG file with alpha transparency. I used Photoshop, but Fireworks can do this task equally well.

Start off by typing the word in Flash, and then convert it into a movie clip symbol (*F8*):

Now double-click on the symbol, so that you're working on the movie clip's timeline. We only want to export the text, so this guards against accidentally exporting the video frame as well.

Select File > Export Image, and save the image in EPS 3.0 format. Now you can launch Photoshop 7 and import the EPS file ready for surgery.

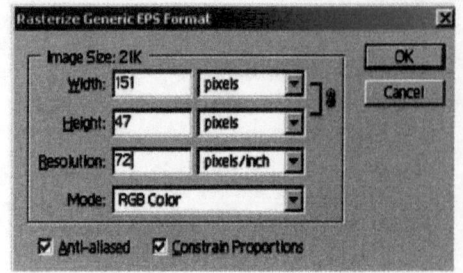

Make sure your resolution is set to 72 pixels/inch, so that you don't wind up with the text being too large or too small – resizing it in Flash later will just make the blurred text look pixelated. Also, make sure to set Mode to RGB Color (especially important if you're using colors other than white).

Once the EPS is imported, you'll see crisp text sitting on a background of gray and white squares (which mark it out as being transparent). I like to add an additional layer below the text, and fill it with a solid color (in this case black) so I can see exactly what I'm doing.

Since we want to blur the text from left to right, you'll need to make room on either side of the text – select Image > Canvas Size and add about 20 pixels to either side of the image.

Now select the layer containing your text, and apply Filter > Blur > Motion Blur:

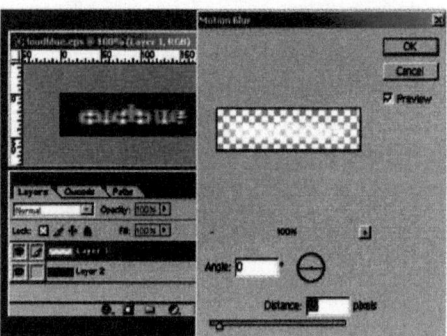

In this case, I blurred the text by 15 pixels. In the screenshot above, you can see what my text looks like with a background, as well as how it looks transparently.

Remove the background layer, so that the blurred text is once again resting on a transparent background. Now we just needed to export it. To export an EPS, go to File > Save for Web, and choose PNG-24 from the settings drop-down, and also make sure that the Transparency checkbox is marked:

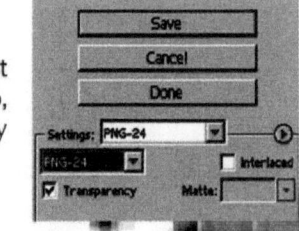

> We use PNGs (rather than GIFs, TIFFs, or some other image format) because they're perfect for our purposes. Not only do they support transparency, but they also export with alpha channels that Flash can recognize. So, instead of getting undesirable blobs of solid pixels, we'll wind up with an image that's true to what we saw in Photoshop.

Hit Save to save the image, and import it back into Flash. It's now possible to animate the text without any tweening or scripting.

Drag the blurred text onto the stage, slightly to the left of the vector text movie clip, and convert it to a symbol. Copy and paste to create another instance of this symbol, and place it just to the right of the vector text. You should end up with something like this:

Hit *CTRL+A* to select all these instances; now right-click (or *CONTROL*-click) and select Distribute to Layers to place each object on its own layer.

All I then had to do was space out the frames in each layer, and (where appropriate) insert blank keyframes at the end of each one so that the images wouldn't overlap. The result is the appearance of very fast movement, despite the fact that there's no motion happening!

I repeated these steps for various other bits of text and graphic elements. Using different types of blurs (such as the flickering caption text at the beginning of my sample video) can help give certain graphic elements rough, film-like qualities.

Special effects

Besides being able to do some really neat text effects, Flash gives us the ability to do lots of other special effects pretty easily: from practical effects that will help move the film along, to tricks that would take forever to do, even using many of today's powerful video editing programs.

On the practical side of things, one of my most faithful companions is the square. By making a large black square (the size of the stage) and converting it into a movie clip, I can fade in and out of shots by tweening its opacity from 100% to 0% (using the Alpha channel tool under the properties panel after selecting the "Big Black Square" movie clip on the stage).

When I'm cutting between shots, I like inserting a white square (for a duration of one frame) to give off a "flicker" effect – these are used on several cuts throughout the movie. For an added touch, I've inserted my logo into each "flicker frame". It's not quite subliminal, but it does add another detail to the movie. In yet another instance, I use two animated squares to create a 'letterbox' look on one particular camera angle (near the beginning of the video, while I'm typing).

Security camera

You can even use squares to add a slight tint to your video – a color filter if you will. Near the beginning of my video, there's an overhead shot of me typing; I wanted it to look like as if it had been filmed by a security camera.

I placed a green, mostly transparent square over this shot to give it the basic look. I also added a fake timecode, along with a couple of hairlines and a blinking red dot. Squares can do anything!

You can find these assets in the layer folder called 1a. Security Camera, from frame 726 onwards.

Evil vectors part 1

Everything I've talked about up to this point has been setting the stage for my favorite part of working with video inside Flash. Now comes the fun part: creating the shots in which the vector animations jump out of my computer and into the real world.

There isn't any scripting going on here; I just whip out my pen pad and start getting crazy. The thumbnails I drew originally served as a basis for the look I wanted to get, but since the shapes needed to move, change and morph, most of my efforts in this movie, as with everything I make using this method, involved making things up as I went along.

The first shot that vectors appear to be coming out of my computer is the close-up profile shot of me at the desk. On the video, I look surprised at something:

Well OK, maybe I don't look that surprised, but I'm here for my Flash skills rather than my acting talent.

Drawing the whipping and flickering shapes wasn't a problem – some of the elements were animated by tweening, some flicker in and out, and some were keyframed – but I was left with a slight predicament. As you can see, the computer I'm using is a laptop, and its side is facing the viewer. I want the make the vectors leak out of the screen, hopefully without giving the appearance that the vector work is drawn *on top* of the video.

There are two ways I can create this effect, having things spill out from an invisible horizontal plane:

- I can take a screenshot of everything, cut the image in half, and add in a bitmap of my computer and the static background. Then I can animate all the vectors on a layer underneath.

- I can draw the animations right on top of the video and use masking to hide the trailing artwork.

Both would produce acceptable results, but for time's sake, I decided that the second option would be more practical.

You can find the assets for this section in the layer folder called 2. Evil Vectors, from frame 1181 onwards.

I created a new layer folder and started to get busy. I used several common techniques to create the animation, such as shape and motion tweening. I drew right on top of the video in the location I'd like it to come out of the computer:

Each layer was converted to a movie clip, so I now had six separate movie clips tweening from right to left. Some of these movie clips have motion tweens inside their own timelines, while others are static movie clips that I move around on the main timeline. I gave them some slight transparencies, helping the vectors to blend in more with the environment.

My next task was to mask out the parts of the movie clips that I didn't want to be visible, making them appear to be coming out of the screen rather than laying on top of everything.

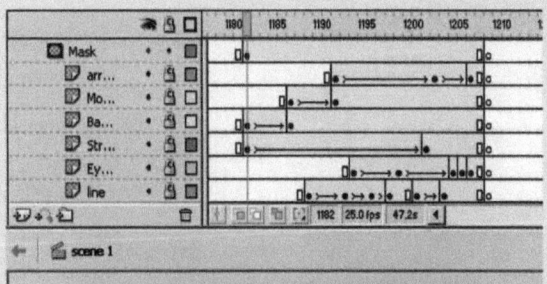

I made all of the movie clips temporarily invisible, and began creating my mask. I added a mask layer above all of the movie clips in the 2. Evil Vectors layer folder, grabbed the Line tool, and started tracing the outline of my computer's screen (the side facing me). The stage looked something like this:

To finish the mask, I made all of the layers under the mask layer visible again, locked all of the layers, and then got back to the mask layer. I traced round all of the vector elements, and filled the mask. Here's what my screen looked like at this point:

Once I'd finished, I locked the mask layer – it then became invisible, so I could see the effect I had created:

When I created this mask, I made it towards the end of this particular shot, to make it easier to cover the vector animations' finishing position. If you're following a similar workflow method, make sure you move the mask layer's frame to the beginning of the shot! The effect is quick and effective.

For the next couple of shots, the technique I used was even more simplistic. I added movie clips directly on top of the video (just as before), but masked it in a slightly different way.

Evil vectors part 2

In the next shot, I'm knocked out of my chair by a flood of vector animations with evil intent. Previously, the graphics were right in front of me and easy to see. Now though, I'm being filmed from behind. To give the appearance of an explosion of vectors, I chose not to add anything to the footage until my monitor's screen was visible:

This shot's assets are in the layer folder 3. Evil Vectors, from frame 1216 onwards.

This part of the process is really fun – I create the final image first (on the last frame of the shot), and then work backwards (with the masks) to animate the vector animations as they manifest themselves.

I created new layers for all my vectors, and moved down the timeline to the last frame of the shot. I then began creating the movie clips that would ultimately look like they're popping from my computer. Some trace the contour of the office, while others reach out haphazardly – all of them are revealed by a mask that uses shape or motion tweens.

As far as my masking techniques go, there's really not much to them. I basically drew some random shapes (each on a different layer), and added a mask layer above each unique shape. That mask itself is (in most cases) a skewed square that I motion tween the heck out of. Be sure to check out the FLA for my deep dark secrets!

When I was done with the masks, I went back and added some more vector elements (some 3D arrows and lines) to fill up some of the empty spaces, and to give the appearance of more chaos.

Computer spew

For the next shot, I simply wanted to show vector animations pouring out of my computer screen. I made some cycles (movie clip animations that loop seamlessly) and added three or four movie clips that are tweened on the main timeline. This helps to disguise the looping, and adds a few more details to the piece.

You can find this in the FLA in the layer folder called **4.**Computer Spew, from around frame 1250 onwards.

I also manually tweened the opacity of three looping animations being used here, as this lets the viewer see that there's a computer on the desk, as well as giving an impression that the vectors are flickering (and emanating power). I then added some bending, looping lines on top of the whole mix.

> *The lines are laid out in a way common to lots of Japanese animations. They help point the focus of interest into the center of the computer's screen, which is in turn spewing out the evil vector shapes.*

For good measure, I added a few large white squares to give another flickering effect.

Running from computer

So far, I've been trying to give the appearance that I'm closer to the camera than the vectors are. For the next shot, I wanted to let the animations get closer to the camera. I figured this would help to give them some dimension, and also make them seem larger than life.

In this shot, I wanted them to fly up into the air, temporarily leave the framing, and then reappear as if they were swooping down at a high rate of speed:

You can find the assets for this shot in the layer folder, 5. Running from Computer, *from frame 1330.*

Running part 2

For the next shot, you'll see me running directly away from the camera. The effect I wanted here was to have random shapes creeping after me on the floor and on the wall, as well as having some things flying at me in midair. For the elements on the floor and wall, I drew directly on top of the footage, turned the objects into symbols, and followed up by animating masks on top of everything. The end result is a rather sinister looking chase scene.

All the vectors and masks used here are in the layer folder 6. Running part2.

Elevator

For this following shot (beginning at frame 1893), I got a chance to take it easy – or cheat, if you will. I grabbed all of the animated vectors I could find from earlier in the movie, and then recycled them, in the folder 7.Elevator, by surrounding the frame of my video.

I wound up with several pointy objects focusing towards the center, with me standing in fear. In the lower center, I inserted a 3D arrow (made in Swift 3d V2) and made it look as if it was tracking me. In this case, having a bold 3D object in front of me adds tension to the shot, and also helps to draw attention away from my poor acting.

For the next shot, I'm running full speed away from the elevator, again being chased by multitudes of villainous vector shapes. I went about this shot just like the one I talked about a little while ago (with the vectors on the floor and wall). I just drew out some random shapes on the concrete, and then later used some shape and motion tweened masks to reveal my potential assailants.

In the next two shots, I used exactly the same masking technique as I'd used to make the vectors come out of my computer. The only difference was that I needed to pay a little more attention to how well the mask fitted the environment I was placing the vectors in.

In the shot from frame 2092 onwards, there are two walls that I had to trace around. Once I'd got those traced, and defined the bottom of the mask, I was good to go. I then started creating and placing all the necessary movie clips where I wanted them, and made sure to pace them to my running speed. I let a few arrows pass by me for two reasons: for one, the effect adds depth; and for another, it looks so darned cool!

Again, I recycled some of the graphics I made earlier. This helps reduce workload and file size, and because the images will be small (supposedly being a long way away), they'll barely be recognizable. If the masking is successful, I should seem to be getting chased by a bunch of resolution-independent graphics coming from behind a wall, out into the open, then behind another wall.

Finishing touches

And that's about all there is to it. I added some sounds in at the beginning – a whooshy noise to go with the motion blurs, and a sound loop to accompany the high-speed vector chase.

I left the export settings pretty much as they were, as I had already compressed the video. If you're doing similar work of your own, you may want to play with your audio settings so that everything sounds as good as you want it – not to mention the fact that you can also shave a bit of size off the finished product.

I know that for anyone reading this that has any professional Flash experience, the techniques used to gain these various effects are nothing new. However, the fact that we can do these things with such ease *is*.

Even for users without high-end digital video editing suites, creating special effects-rich video is incredibly easy. Not only can we crank out titles and credits with ease, we can blend vector animation with the real world, giving ourselves the ability to alter reality (or at least taped reality) however we see fit.

I remember a few months back being incredibly happy that I was able to import a JPEG sequence into Flash, make it loop, then and add some minor touches (like flickering lights and such). Now... now I can make VIDEOS of myself being CHASED BY A FLASH INTRO!

Sorry to scream at you like that, but this is an *amazingly* cool new step on Macromedia's part. To be able to do things with video that we could once only do on a blank stage (I'm talking to the Flash developers here, not video producers) gives us a remarkable resource that I hope to see many other developers embrace.

Not only does the work come out clean, but the file sizes that Flash can export makes this stuff easily accessible to almost everyone with a connection to the Web. Bear in mind that the finished movie (complete with audio) is about the same size as a typical MP3. With these tools at our disposal, we can turn videos into design elements on our websites, and in most cases, we don't even need to worry about our users having the right kind of media player!

I beg of you, fellow Flashers... take any and every old video you have on your hard drive and start tinkering with 'em. Add a talking bunny rabbit to your old family reunion footage; add Star Wars text scrolling to your son's baseball game... anything! A full-on moving video comic strip would be totally possible. Go for it.

The first time I blended vector animation with DV footage, I guessed my social life would be ruined forever. So far, I've been proved right. Who's got time for friends when you can shoot laser beams out of your eyes?

Erwan Bezie's passion for graphic arts started early with illustration and black & white photography. However, he studied music and was a professional bass player for ten years, touring with jazz and pop bands around the south of France. In 1998 he bought a computer to do some proper music editing, but quickly switched back to graphics as a means of expressing himself. He decided to move to London to study web design and start a new career. After three years of working for corporate clients, he moved back to France and now runs his own web design agency, lebonze.com.

Tim Hawkins is a multimedia developer (and occasional designer) based in the UK, where people pay him to make Flash do things it probably shouldn't. He infrequently updates his website (www.cellpattern.com) with content of wildly varying usefulness, although now people like you know about it there's some chance he'll be more diligent in future. At the time of writing, Tim likes Indian food and tiny cameras, and hates French keyboards and people who steal guitars.

Video masking
lebonze with Tim Hawkins

Video on the Web undoubtedly has a nice, bright future ahead of itself, thanks to faster Internet connections every year. However, the majority of users are still on a dial-up connection, and this is where the ability to manipulate video with ActionScript comes in handy. At last, web designers have the opportunity to remain creative without forcing tens of megabytes of raw video data down a poor viewer's modem connection. Adding ActionScript to video also opens up a whole new world of interactivity. By combining code with your own creativity, your video work will become richer and more noticeable.

The French sociologist Pierre Bourdieu talks about a 'collective intellect' when he mentions the necessity of the world's thinkers to collaborate in tackling the numerous drawbacks of neo-liberalism. Why not then a 'collective intellect' for designers and artists? Admittedly, it's not neo-liberalism that's at the forefront of a designer's mind when faced with a creative task, but the point is that collaboration frequently produces better results that doing things on your own. Environment, cultural influences, gender and age difference, and even the straightforward fact of having more than one mind interpreting the subject at hand, all lead to more finely tuned and advanced results.

> *When we were asked to participate in this book, we decided to do a joint chapter. Each of us felt that our own skills would complement the other's, and that a collaboration would produce some interesting results.*
>
> *We met about two years ago through* dreamless.org – *Joshua Davis' now dead-and-gone forum – when several designers from the London area decided to confront the real world. At first we met for drinks, and then collaborations started to emerge. Meeting like-minded designers in person was, for me, the most enriching of all my online experiences. Dreamless' most characteristic forum was probably '04 – battle arena + digital landfill' where, as the name suggests, designers engaged in graphical combat. Being under pressure to compete with others is a very effective way of discovering and affirming your own style. It is also a great way of assessing your weaknesses, and to begin addressing them. Indeed, anyone can do this on their own as an exercise – just choose a random topic and force yourself to complete a piece on an extremely tight deadline.*

Expanding your knowledge is certainly another good source of inspiration in itself. If you haven't done it yet, you might want to learn all about trigonometry and how to use it effectively in your code. Go to your local library. The simple act of browsing through a shelf of books might well trigger a thirst to learn about a whole range of different subjects.

Thinking creatively

When I need to think creatively on a particular quandary, I find that the following exercise helps me to approach the problem from a new angle, and find an innovative solution:

I allow my mind to wander off the creative obstacle completely – in fact, the further the better. I may pick a random word in a dictionary and then find connections to the subject I'm trying to tackle. There's a good chance that the paths along which my mind meanders turn out to be new and surprising directions I'd never have considered otherwise.

Seemingly unrelated disparate material can emerge into a very coherent ensemble. It will also have a certain amount of 'freshness' not found in other creative processes. It's an exercise I would recommend to all designers faced with a creative block – improvisation is an essential source for creativity.

I also find that forcing myself to get out from in front of the computer and seeing the real world renews my innovation, enthusiasm and ideas. If you have a digital camera, get out and start snapping. Take pictures of anything – uniqueness frequently lies in the most obscure images.

I personally find that nature is probably the most inexhaustible of all sources of inspiration. Whether I'm amazed by the colors of the autumn leaves or a weed that's managed to fight its way through a concrete paving slab, whether it's the dappled colors of sunlight through a canopy of trees or the sound of a waterfall, life always offers the most incredible and moving of experiences.

Yet even if you have no shortage of inspiration, a difficult question remains: how do you assess your work's aesthetic value, or, sometimes just as importantly, its market value? What is it that gives your work this value? On the Internet, your name may constantly be competing against millions of others. Does the legitimacy of design and art work only come with popularity?

We often hear people coming out of an art exhibition saying, "I could have easily done exactly the same thing!" This might well be the case, but chances are it wouldn't have actually made it into the gallery without their name or style being previously acknowledged by those critics who define the art world. Though I may have a concept equal to the artists' work hanging in the exhibition hall, getting my piece hung in its place isn't straightforward.

So does this hold true for those of us trying to make a name for ourselves online? The anonymous nature of the Internet can certainly make it equally difficult to get recognition. Furthermore, its vastness makes it hard to know exactly how legitimized you are.

In an ideal world, artwork of any kind should not be quantifiable. The relationship between a visual piece and its viewer should be of a passionate, intense kind, its value derived not from its institutional price, but from how it moves and affects the viewer. The aim of this relationship would not be to satisfy criticism. Rather it would be a relationship where artwork imposes its own and self-sufficient rules onto a game the viewer accepts they are playing. But that's in an ideal world, right?

Well, perhaps not. The nature of the Web – forwarding amongst a peer group, 'word of mouth', linkage, specialized forums open to almost anyone with a passion of the same subject matter – allows an idea to be viewed and appreciated by millions without any kind of institutional patronage. If an idea is *good*, it will be passed on from one person to another in seconds.

Great, you may say, I want to get cracking! But there are still some practical constraints to this. You may have the creative idea of the century, but if a user has to wait ten minutes for your masterpiece to download, chances are they won't hang around to see it, and no one will pass it on. An online user, rather like a television viewer or any other person wishing to be entertained, requires almost instant results. This is where the ActionScript outlined in this chapter can help.

We hope this chapter will give you, as a reader, the **confidence** to pursue your own ideas, however random, the **inspiration** to get out there and collaborate with other designers, and the **tools** to spread your ideas easily and effectively.

The concept

You live in a personal 3D virtual reality invented by your visual cortex. The electrical signals from your two eyes are compared, filtered and processed by this area of your brain, resulting in the world you see around you. This allows you to pick matching furniture, drive fast in traffic, distinguish between your friend and an inflatable doll, and catch a Frisbee (some cortices are evidently better than others).

Compared to real life, video seems pretty easy to process. It's a two-dimensional picture projected onto a screen. So maybe if we make folks' brains work a little harder, we'll attract more viewer attention.

It's possible that by fragmenting an appropriate video clip with a moving mask, we can create the illusion of depth and motion – that the guy in the movie is walking behind the canvas of the screen. In other words, we might be able to encourage a bit of spatial awareness as well as increased object recognition (as the whole image is always partially occluded).

Or maybe not.

Worst-case scenario: we make yet another arty effect to put on a website!

Setting up

Let's start with a new FLA called `lookin.fla`. Make sure the main stage is set to 550 x 400 pixels with a frame rate of 21 fps, rename the first layer as gradient, and add a simple color gradient background. Lock the layer, so that none of our other steps risk interfering with its contents.

Next, create a new movie clip symbol called myMovie, and select the Linkage section. Check Export for ActionScript, and use the default identifier `myMovie`. Import your chosen video (I've used a file called `lookin.flv`, which you can find on the CD) and place it at (0,0) in the movie clip, giving the movie clip a top left-hand registration point.

We'd like to thank our friend Ivan who kindly agreed to have his face chopped up for the sake of the project!

Back in the main timeline, create a new layer called actions to house some ActionScript. Select the first frame of this new layer, call up the Actions panel, and get ready to start typing!

Initializing the code

First, we set two variables for the x and y coordinates of the video clip where they can be used by the rest of the code:

```
this.xPos = 100;
this.yPos = 90;
```

Now make a function we will use to start everything going:

```
this.init = function() {
```

Create an empty movie clip called canvas, which we'll use to draw the mask on later, in level 10, and put it in the right place on the stage, using the coordinates we stored a second ago:

```
this.createEmptyMovieclip("canvas", 10);
var c = this.canvas;
c._x = this.xPos;
c._y = this.yPos;
```

It can be useful to temporarily alias variables that will get used often, like I've done here by declaring that variable c is a reference to this.canvas. It can make code tidier to look at, and therefore a bit easier to understand.

Attach the myMovie movie clip:

```
this.attachMovie("myMovie", "mmov", 9, {_x:this.xPos, _y:this.yPos});
```

We need it to be on level 9 so that it will be under the mask we're going to draw in our canvas movie clip. The placing parameters within the curly brackets make sure that mymovie is attached in the same position as its masking movie clip.

Now we've put the video movie clip on the stage, we can get its dimensions:

```
this.width = this.mmov._width;
this.height = this.mmov._height;
```

These will be useful later, so storing them somewhere memorable is a good plan.

To finish the initialization, we set the canvas as a mask of mmov, make an array to store our block objects in, and set the processFrame function to run every frame:

```
this.mmov.setMask(c);
this.blocks = new Array();
this.onEnterFrame = this.processFrame;
};
```

Now let's look at the functions we need to write.

The processFrame function

The first is the processFrame function we called earlier:

```
this.processFrame = function() {
```

Every time we enter a new frame, we want to do three things:

- possibly add a new block
- move and rescale all the existing blocks
- remove blocks that have moved out of the visible area, as drawing them consumes CPU power, even though they can't be seen

With just a couple of tweaks, this code can utterly swamp slower PCs and Macs. How processor-intensive it gets depends on the number of blocks on screen, the size of blocks, and the movie frame rate.

Of course, we can change the number of blocks on screen by changing how often a new block is generated and how quickly each one disappears – in other words, how fast it moves across the canvas.

First, set an alias b to the blocks array because we'll be using it loads:

```
var b = this.blocks;
```

Next, we need to set up some code to generate new blocks on some frames:

```
if (Math.random() < 0.5) {
   var nB = new Block(0, Math.random()*this.height,
➡         20+(Math.random()*40), 20+(Math.random()*60));
   b.push(nB);
}
```

Math.random spits out a number between 0 and 1, kind of like the 'random' button on a calculator. Since it's random, it will be less than 0.5 half the time. Therefore, our if statement will be true 50% of the time it's called, and on average we will make one new block every two frames.

To add a block, we instantiate an object called nB from the Block class which we will define in a minute. Don't worry too much about that yet – just notice that we're varying the initial y coordinate, the width and the height of it with some randomization.

When it's made, we push it into the blocks array ready for use. Simple!

Next, we loop through the entire blocks array and alter each item:

```
for (var i=0; i<b.length; i++) {
   b[i].w *= 1.03;
   b[i].h *= 1.01;
   b[i].x += b[i].w * 0.3;
```

It might look good if each block grows as it gets older, so width is increased by 3% each frame, and height by 1%.

Then we increase the x coordinate by 30% of the current width. This means that the wider a block is, the faster it goes. So, not only do they get faster as they move across the canvas, but some are quicker to begin with – remember we randomized the initial widths when we make a new block. Why? Well, it might be quite dull if they were all the same!

This loop is a good place to remove the blocks that have gone past the edge of the video clip:

```
   if (b[i].x > this.width) {
      b.splice(i, 1);
      i--;
   }
}
```

When a block's x coordinate is greater than the canvas width, we delete that block from the array by splicing one value at position i. Since the array has just been squashed up, we reduce i by one so the loop still catches everything.

At the end, we fire the drawAll function to paint the blocks onto the canvas:

```
this.drawAll();
};
```

The drawAll function

So far, we've been working only with pure data – an array full of block objects with properties representing the dimensions they should have. The drawAll function will be used to represent our blocks visually, using some methods of the Flash MX drawing API:

```
this.drawAll = function() {
    var c = this.canvas;
    var b = this.blocks;
    c.lineStyle();
    c.clear();
```

First, we set lineStyle to undefined – lines won't mask anything, so it's a waste of time drawing them. Then the canvas is cleared to wipe away the stuff we drew last time.

Next, we use the drawBlock function with the x, y, w, and h attributes of each block:

```
for (var i = 0; i<b.length; i++) {
    this.drawBlock(c, b[i].x, b[i].y, b[i].w, b[i].h);
}
};
```

The drawBlock function

This is the drawBlock function we just used. It takes five arguments: cvs is a reference to the movie clip to draw on, while the others are pretty obvious (x and y coordinates, width and height).

```
this.drawBlock = function(cvs, x, y, w, h) {
```

Our first line moves the virtual 'pen' to our starting coordinate, ready to draw:

```
cvs.moveTo(x,y);
```

Then we say we want to start making a filled shape:

```
cvs.beginFill(0xff0000);
```

Since it's a mask, the color is completely irrelevant – but I made it red anyway.

Then use the lineTo function to draw a rectangle through the specified points, and end the fill:

```
cvs.lineTo(x+w, y);
cvs.lineTo(x+w, y+h);
cvs.lineTo(x, y+h);
cvs.lineTo(x,y);
cvs.endFill();
};
```

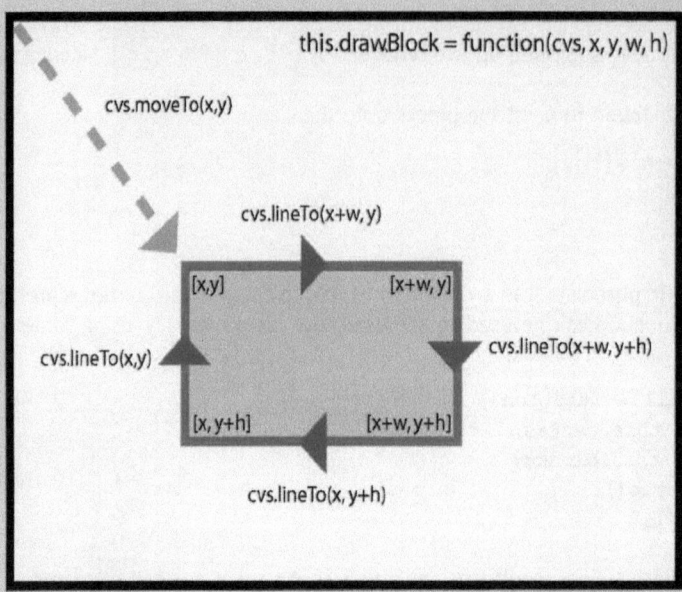

The block class

The user-defined block class we used earlier is very basic. A class is a template for an object that we can make using ActionScript.

Probably the most confusing thing about this is that Flash uses function to define a class, which means it's hard to tell a class from a method at first glance. Personally, I distinguish between them in my own code by writing traditional methods-that-do-things with syntax like this:

```
this.doSomething = function(arg) { trace(arg) }
```

Meanwhile, I define my classes like this:

```
function BeSomething(arg) { this.aProperty = arg }
```

There's a lot more you can do with classes – if you're interested, look for material on OOP in Flash.

So here, the Block class just takes four arguments and stores them as properties in the constructed object.

```
function Block(x, y, w, h) {
  this.x = x;
  this.y = y;
  this.w = w;
  this.h = h;
}
```

Finally, we get everything running by firing the init function:

```
this.init();
```

When you've finished, try commenting out the setMask line and you'll see how the mask is drawn and how it all works.

Looking back over the script, you'll notice that the code to describe and manipulate the blocks is well separated from the code that draws them onto the screen. We could have done the same thing by attaching, moving, and removing movie clips in the `canvas` clip. However, as you'll see in some of the iterations, this way of doing things allows more flexibility when we want to change the way it looks (and it's arguably more efficient too).

Iterations

Now that we have a basic video effect in place, we're going to spend the rest of the chapter looking at some variations and iterations. Although code is shown for each one, you may want to skip straight to the FLAs on the CD and start playing around with them.

> *The following iterations tend to involve making changes to the initialization and modification code blocks in* processFrame.. *Most of these changes are fairly self-explanatory though, so we won't spend too much time discussing them.*

lookin_it1.fla

The human brain is extremely good at picking out faces with very little information. This is the reason for the man on the moon, and why cloud formations seem to have expressions. Let's alter the code so that each new `Block` is more likely to be tall and narrow (than wide and flat), so that we get vertical stripes and make the face easier to spot.

Here's how we can make that change:

```
this.processFrame = function() {
    var b = this.blocks;

    if (Math.random() < 0.5) {
        var nB = new Block(0, Math.random() * this.height,
            ➥ 5 + (Math.random() * 10), 2 + (Math.random() * 60));
        b.push(nB);
    }
    for (var i=0; i<b.length; i++) { // modification
        b[i].w *= 1.01;
        b[i].h *= 1.06;
        b[i].x += b[i].w * 0.8;
```

```
              if (b[i].x > this.width) {
                 b.splice(i, 1);
                  i--;
              }
          }
      }
      this.drawAll();
  }
```

I also wanted to have the effect going both ways – the easiest way to achieve this was to put all the code into a movie clip called effect, and put two instances of it on the stage, in a new layer called effects.

Do this for yourself, and name the instances movie1 and movie2. Place one at (0, 0) and the other at (470, 0). Now add this code on the main timeline:

```
movie2._xscale*=-1;
```

Multiplying the _xscale of a clip by -1 effectively flips it horizontally.

lookin_it2.fla

This one uses two masked videos, playing slightly out of time with each other. Again, the simplest way to achieve this was with two instances of the whole effect.

Within the initialization function, I added an extra line of code, which makes the video start playing at a random frame:

```
this.attachMovie("myMovie", "mmov", 9, {_x:this.xPos, _y:this.yPos});
    this.width = this.mmov._width;
    this.height = this.mmov._height;
    this.mmov.gotoAndPlay(Math.ceil(Math.random() * this.mmov._totalframes));
    this.mmov.setMask(c);
    this.blocks = new Array();
    this.onEnterFrame = this.processFrame;
};
```

This means that the two instances of the mymovie movie clip will start at different frames, so they will not play entirely in sync.

The `processFrame` function has been changed again to alter the appearance of the blocks:

```
this.processFrame = function() {
  var b = this.blocks;

  if (Math.random()<0.200000) {
    var nB = new Block(0, Math.random()*this.height,
           ➥ 2+Math.random()*1, 60+Math.random()*20);
    b.push(nB);
  }

  for (var i = 0; i<b.length; i++) {
    b[i].w = b[i].w*1.300000;
    b[i].y = b[i].y*0.960000;
    b[i].x = b[i].x+b[i].w*0.200000;
    if (b[i].x>this.width) {
      b.splice(i, 1);
      i--;
    }
  }

  this.drawAll();
};
```

There's now just a one in five chance that the `if` condition will be met, so blocks will be generated less frequently.

The drawing code has been tweaked to give a slight impression of depth:

```
this.drawBlock = function(cvs, x, y, w, h) {
  cvs.moveTo(x, y);
  cvs.beginFill(16711680);
  cvs.lineTo(x+w, y);
  cvs.lineTo(x+w, y+h+10);
  cvs.lineTo(x, y+h-5);
  cvs.lineTo(x, y);
  cvs.endFill();
};
```

It's a simple example of the flexibility gained by separating the logic (keeping track of the blocks) from the presentation (drawing them out) mentioned a few pages back. All we've done is alter how the blocks are represented on screen. As far is Flash is concerned, it's working with exactly the same `Block` objects as it was in the main effect.

In fact, it's more common to find application programmers talking about presentation layers and such – but it's a handy paradigm to keep in mind even for simpler coding tasks.

lookin_it3.fla

This one uses two different videos and a white background – so it doesn't need the gradient layer we put in the original lookin.fla. The building looks far away, but it's actually appearing in front of the face, creating an optical illusion.

The video lookin.flv was embedded into a movie clip called movie2, with a Linkage identifier of movie2. The new video, building.flv, was embedded into a movie clip called movie3, which I gave a Linkage identifier of movie3.

We also have two new movie clip symbols: movie2container and movie3container. These are both variations on the mymovie symbol, with very similar code in each one.

First, let's look at the init function for movie2container:

```
this.init = function() {
  this.createEmptyMovieClip("canvas", 10);
  var c = this.canvas;
  c._x = this.xPos;
  c._y = this.yPos;
  this.attachMovie("movie2", "mmov", 9, {_x:this.xPos, _y:this.yPos});
  this.mmov.setMask(c);
  this.blocks = new Array();
  this.onEnterFrame = this.processFrame;
};
```

And here's the equivalent for movie3container:

```
this.init = function() {
  this.createEmptyMovieClip("canvas", 10);
  var c = this.canvas;
  c._x = this.xPos;
  c._y = this.yPos;
  this.attachMovie("movie3", "mmov", 9, {_x:this.xPos, _y:this.yPos});
  this.mmov.setMask(c);
  this.blocks = new Array();
  this.onEnterFrame = this.processFrame;
};
```

The only difference here is the Linkage identifier that each one uses to attach its video-containing movie clip.

The other changes in the code from the `lookin.fla` ActionScript occur in the `processFrame` function.

For movie2container:

```
this.processFrame = function() {
  var b = this.blocks;
  if (Math.random()>0.8) {
    b.push(new block(0, 50+Math.random()*250, 10, 600));
  }
  for (var i = 0; i<b.length; i++) {
    b[i].x += b[i].w*0.3;
    b[i].w *= 1.01;
    b[i].h *= 1.01;
    if (b[i].x>300) {
      b.splice(i, 1);
      i--;
    }
  }
  this.draw();
};
```

And for movie3container:

```
this.processFrame = function() {
  var b = this.blocks;

  if (Math.random()>0.4) {
    b.push(new block(0, Math.random()*250,
➥          20+Math.random()*10, 20+Math.random()*10));
  }

  for (var i = 0; i<b.length; i++) {
    b[i].x += b[i].w*0.3;
    b[i].w *= 1.01;
    b[i].h *= 1.01;
    if (b[i].x>300) {
      b.splice(i, 1);
      i--;
    }
  }

  this.draw();
};
```

As you can see, the only difference between the two is in the parameters passed into the new block. This means that the blocks drawn on each container will be different shapes.

lookin_it4.fla

This is what happens if we don't always clear the canvas each frame before we redraw the blocks in their new position – they leave trails:

```
this.drawAll = function() {
  var c = this.canvas;
  var b = this.blocks;

  c.lineStyle();

  if (Math.random() < 0.2) {
    c.clear();
  }

  for (var i=0; i<b.length; i++) {
    this.drawBlock(c, b[i].x, b[i].y, b[i].w, b[i].h);
  }
}
```

Basically, on average the old blocks will be cleared one in every five frames.

We've actually got three instances of effect on the stage here, and a line of code we used in lookin_it2.fla is included within the init function to make them start playing at a random frame of the video:

```
this.mmov.gotoAndPlay(Math.ceil(Math.random() * this.mmov._totalframes));
```

We're also changing the height of each frame here, which along with the trails gives a kind of 'torn strips' look:

```
this.processFrame = function() {
  var b = this.blocks;
  if (Math.random()<0.2) {
  var nB = new Block(0, Math.random()*this.height,
          ➥      2+(Math.random()*1), 15+(Math.random()*20)));
    b.push(nB);
  }
```

We're only drawing a new block approximately one in every five frames, as they are hanging around for longer.

Then there are a few changes to the w, h, x and y parameters:

```
for (var i=0; i<b.length; i++) {
    b[i].w *= 1.1;
    b[i].y += (Math.random() < 0.8) ? 1 : -1;
    b[i].x += b[i].w * 0.3;
    b[i].h -= 2;
    if (b[i].x > this.width + 50) {
        b.splice(i, 1);
        i--;
    }
}
this.drawAll();
}
```

The main change here is that y will increase by one 80% of the time, and the rest of the time it'll decrease.

lookin_it5.fla

Here, two instances of the clip are overlaid, and the top one is given an alpha value of 50%.

First, we change the x and y coordinates of the video to (0,0):

```
this.xPos = 0;
this.yPos = 0;
```

As we're going to be starting our blocks from the extreme left-hand side of the stage, we want the video to be visible from there.

Again, we add the extra line of code into the init function, so that each instance of effect starts at a random point on its respective timeline:

```
this.mmov.gotoAndPlay(Math.ceil(Math.random() * this.mmov._totalframes));
```

Then we have some changes to the `processFrame` function:

```
this.processFrame = function() {
  var b = this.blocks;
  if (Math.random() < 0.4) {
  var nB = new Block(-50, Math.random() * this.height,
      ➡     15 + (Math.random() * 15), 15 + (Math.random() * 50));
    b.push(nB);
  }
```

We now have a 40% chance of a new block being generated each frame.

Starting the `block` x value at -50 prevents the new blocks from seeming to 'jump' into existence on the left-hand side, and contributes to a smoother progression.

The h property of each block is drastically decreased in each frame, so it quickly attains a negative value. The block is still drawn without any problems though, and we get the effect of blocks enlarging upwards rather than downwards (remember that Flash's y axis is, for some reason, reversed).

Again, there are some changes to the values of the `block` parameters:

```
for (var i=0; i<b.length; i++) {
  b[i].w *= 1.1;
  b[i].y += (Math.random() < 0.2) ? 1 : -1;
  b[i].x += b[i].w * 0.15;
  b[i].h -= 10;
  if (b[i].x > this.width + 50) {
    b.splice(i, 1);
    i--;
  }
}
this.drawAll();
};
```

lookin_it6.fla

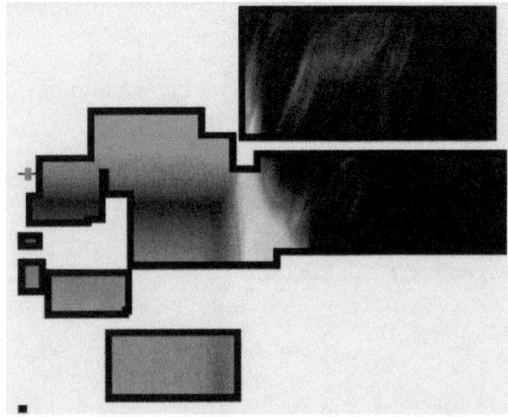

In this version, what appear to be outlines are really just the same blocks drawn slightly bigger on a secondary background canvas (bg). This is a useful trick in many situations, especially for making shadows and outlines for groups of objects without getting in between the objects themselves. (An offset and setting bg._alpha to a lower value would create a drop shadow.)

First make some alterations to the drawAll function:

```
this.drawAll = function () {
    var c = this.canvas;
    var bg = this.bg;
    var b = this.blocks;
    c.clear();
    bg.clear();
    for (var i=0; i < b.length; i++) {
        this.drawBlock(c, b[i].x, b[i].y, b[i].w, b[i].h);
        this.drawBlock(bg, b[i].x-10, b[i].y+10, b[i].w+20, b[i].h-20);
    }
};
```

As you can see, we just re-use the drawBlock function – this time asking it to use the bg movie clip as a canvas and draw to coordinates 10 pixels outside those it's drawing to in the mask.

Because now it looks messy where we draw outside the borders of the movie clip (it doesn't matter when it's a mask as it isn't visible), we apply yet another mask to the background layer when we initialize the clip:

```
this.init = function () {
    this.createEmptyMovieClip("canvas", 10);
    this.createEmptyMovieClip("bg", 7);
    this.createEmptyMovieClip("bgMask", 8);
    var c = this.canvas;
    this.bg._x = this.bgMask._x = c._x = this.xPos;
    this.bg._y = this.bgMask._y = c._y = this.yPos;
    this.attachMovie("myMovie", "mmov", 9, {_x:this.xPos, _y:this.yPos});
    this.width = this.mmov._width;
    this.height = this.mmov._height;
    this.mmov.setMask(c);
    this.drawBlock(this.bgMask, this.xPos - 10, this.yPos - 10,
    ➡                            this.width + 20, this.height + 20);
    this.bg.setMask(this.bgMask);
    this.blocks = new Array();
    this.onEnterFrame = this.processFrame;
};
```

We use the drawBlock function to draw a simple block, just larger than the stage, on the bgmask clip.

If you comment out the last two new lines, where you set the mask, you'll see why this extra mask is necessary. Once the black blocks are not hidden by the video, you can see they are solid shapes, and the illusion of outlined blocks of video is lost.

And once again, we've tweaked the block parameters inside the `processFrame` function:

```
this.processFrame = function() {
    var b = this.blocks;
    if (Math.random()<0.400000) {
    var nB = new Block(-50, Math.random()*this.height,
                        15+Math.random()*15, 15+Math.random()*50);
        b.push(nB);
    }
    for (var i = 0; i<b.length; i++) {
        b[i].w = b[i].w*1.100000;
        b[i].y = b[i].y+3;
        b[i].x = b[i].x+b[i].w*0.100000;
        b[i].h = b[i].h-6;
        if (b[i].x>this.width+50) {
            b.splice(i, 1);
            i--;
        }
    }
    this.drawAll();
};
```

Oh, one final thing to remember. When we originally wrote the `drawBlock` function, it didn't matter what color we drew in, as the drawing would be used as a mask. But now we want to see the blocks, so unless you want your outlines to be red (which I think changes the mood slightly) amend the `beginFill` method within the `drawBlock` function:

```
this.drawBlock = function(cvs, x, y, w, h) {
    cvs.moveTo(x, y);
    cvs.beginFill(0);
```

lookin_it7.fla

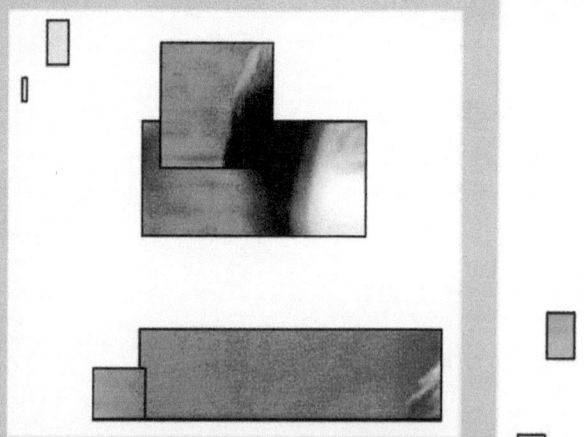 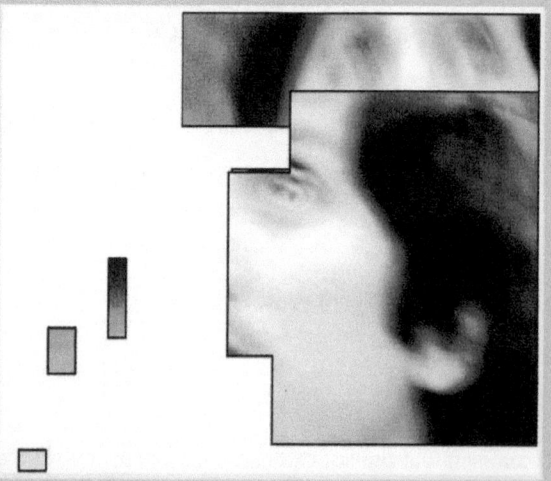

In this version, based on `lookin_it6.fla`, the borders are slimmed down to two pixels and three instances of the effect are overlaid, with the line of code added to randomize the frame that the video starts playing in each of them, so they play out of sync.

To achieve the almost insectoid block-lurching movement, x motion for each frame is partly based on the sin of the y position (which itself is somewhat randomized). Block height is increased in a similar way, but to a lesser extent.

First, the changes to the init function:

```
this.init = function() {
    this.createEmptyMovieClip("canvas", 10);
    this.createEmptyMovieClip("bg", 7);
    this.createEmptyMovieClip("bgMask", 8);
    var c = this.canvas;
    this.bg._x = this.bgMask._x=c._x=this.xPos;
    this.bg._y = this.bgMask._y=c._y=this.yPos;
    this.attachMovie("myMovie", "mmov", 9, {_x:this.xPos, _y:this.yPos});
    this.width = this.mmov._width;
    this.height = this.mmov._height;
    this.mmov.gotoAndPlay(Math.ceil(Math.random() * this.mmov._totalframes));
    this.mmov.setMask(c);
    this.drawBlock(this.bgMask, this.xPos-2, this.yPos-2,
        ➥                      this.width+4, this.height+4);
    this.bg.setMask(this.bgMask);
    this.blocks = new Array();
    this.onEnterFrame = this.processFrame;
};
```

Next, the usual tweaks to the block shape:

```
this.processFrame = function () {
    var b = this.blocks;
    if (Math.random() < 0.06) {
        var nB = new Block(-15, Math.random() * this.height,
            ➥                  1 + Math.random() * 15, 1 + Math.random() * 10);
        b.push(nB);
    }
    for (var i=0; i<b.length; i++) {
        b[i].w *= 1.1;
        b[i].y -= 6 * Math.random();
        b[i].x += 6+ Math.sin(b[i].y *0.1) * 6;
        b[i].h += 4+ Math.sin(b[i].y *0.1) * 2;
        if (b[i].x > this.width + 2) {
            b.splice(i, 1);
            i--;
        }
    }
    this.drawAll();
}
```

The parameters passed to the drawBlock function for bg are changed so that the blocks drawn here will only be slightly bigger than those drawn on the canvas movie clip:

```
for (var i = 0; i<b.length; i++) {
    this.drawBlock(c, b[i].x, b[i].y, b[i].w, b[i].h);
    this.drawBlock(bg, b[i].x-2, b[i].y-2, b[i].w+4, b[i].h+4);
}
};
```

lookin_it8.fla

In this iteration, based on the last one, we only have one instance of the effect on the stage. By replacing the `drawBlock` function with a `drawCircle` one (in this case, one swiped from Casper Shuirink and modified slightly – thanks!) and doing a couple of other tweaks, we have a stylish bubble effect.

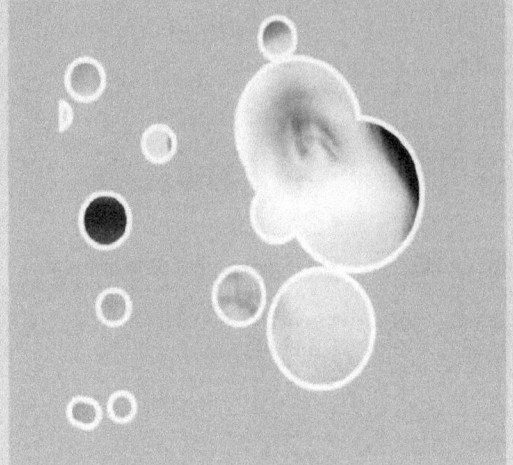

First, let's change the parameters passed to `drawBlock` within the `init` function to make the outlines look a bit more substantial:

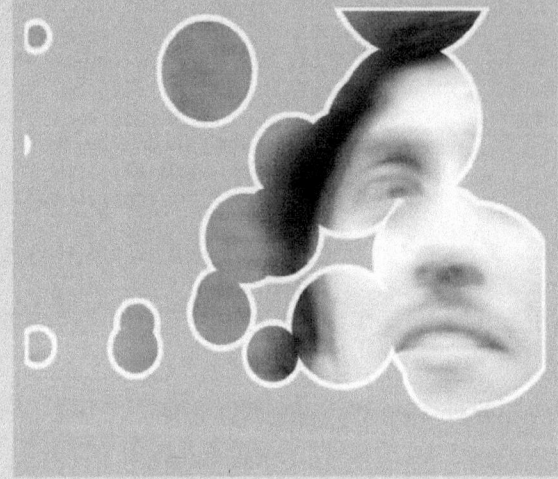

```
this.init = function() {
    this.createEmptyMovieClip("canvas", 10);
    this.createEmptyMovieClip("bg", 7);
    this.createEmptyMovieClip("bgMask", 8);
    var c = this.canvas;
    this.bg._x = this.bgMask._x=c._x=this.xPos;
    this.bg._y = this.bgMask._y=c._y=this.yPos;
    this.attachMovie("myMovie", "mmov", 9, {_x:this.xPos, _y:this.yPos});
    this.width = this.mmov._width;
    this.height = this.mmov._height;
    this.mmov.gotoAndPlay(Math.ceil(Math.random() * this.mmov._totalframes));
    this.mmov.setMask(c);
    this.drawBlock(this.bgMask, this.xPos-5, this.yPos-5,
        ➥                  this.width+10, this.height+10);
    this.bg.setMask(this.bgMask);
    this.blocks = new Array();
    this.onEnterFrame = this.processFrame;
};
```

Now some alterations to the `processFrame` function:

```
this.processFrame = function() {
    var b = this.blocks;
    if (Math.random()<0.14) {
    var nB = new Block(-15, Math.random()*this.height,
        ➥              15+Math.random()*25, 1+Math.random()*10);
      b.push(nB);
    }
```

```
        for (var i = 0; i<b.length; i++) {
          b[i].w *= 1.02;
          b[i].y -= 2*Math.random();
          b[i].x += 5+Math.sin(b[i].y*0.1)*5;
          if (b[i].x-b[i].w/2>this.width) {
            b.splice(i, 1);
            i--;
          }
        }
        this.drawAll();
      };
```

Now let's look at the `drawAll` function:

```
      this.drawAll = function () {
          var c = this.canvas;
          var bg = this.bg;
          var b = this.blocks;
          c.lineStyle();
          c.clear();
          bg.clear();
          for (var i = 0; i < b.length; i++) {
            this.drawCircle(c, b[i].x, b[i].y, b[i].w*0.5);
            this.drawCircle(bg, b[i].x, b[i].y, b[i].w*0.5 + 8);
          }
      };
```

The same block-moving code as before is used – we're just ignoring the `h` property of each and passing the `w` property divided by two when the `drawCircle` function needs a radius parameter.

Even though we are now going to draw circles rather than blocks, don't forget that the `drawBlock` function is still needed for the large mask.

And now for the last, vital extra function: `drawCircle`.

```
      this.drawCircle = function(cvs, x, y, r){
        cvs.moveTo(x+r, y);
        cvs.beginFill(0xffffff);
        cvs.curveTo(r+x, -0.4142*r+y, 0.7071*r+x, -0.7071*r+y);
        cvs.curveTo(0.4142*r+x, -r+y, x, -r+y);
        cvs.curveTo(-0.4142*r+x, -r+y, -0.7071*r+x, -0.7071*r+y);
        cvs.curveTo(-r+x, -0.4142*r+y, -r+x, y);
        cvs.curveTo(-r+x, 0.4142*r+y, -0.7071*r+x, 0.7071*r+y);
        cvs.curveTo(-0.4142*r+x, r+y, x, r+y);
        cvs.curveTo(0.4142*r+x, r+y, 0.7071*r+x, 0.7071*r+y);
        cvs.curveTo(r+x, 0.4142*r+y, r+x, y);
        cvs.endFill();
      } // (Casper Schuirink)
```

Don't worry too much about this. While there are much more elegant-looking ways of drawing a circle, sometimes the performance gains of hard-coding numbers are a good enough excuse for ugly code!

lookin_it9.fla

A bit of a departure... Since we already had circles happening, here's a strange rippling distortion effect made with only a few modifications to the code from lookin_it8.fla.

We need to make some changes to the initialization function:

```
this.init = function() {
    this.createEmptyMovieClip("canvas", 10);
    this.createEmptyMovieClip("bg", 7);
    this.createEmptyMovieClip("bgMask", 8);
    var c = this.canvas;
    this.bg._x = this.bgMask._x=c._x=this.xPos;
    this.bg._y = this.bgMask._y=c._y=this.yPos;
    this.attachMovie("myMovie", "mmov", 9, {_x:this.xPos, _y:this.yPos});
    this.attachMovie("myMovie", "bgmov", 1, {_x:this.xPos, _y:this.yPos});
    this.attachMovie("myMovie", "mmov2", 2, {_x:this.xPos, _y:this.yPos});
    this.width = this.mmov._width;
    this.height = this.mmov._height;
    this.mmov.setMask(c);
    this.mmov2.setMask(bg);
    this.mmov.gotoAndPlay(4);
    this.mmov2.gotoAndPlay(2);
    this.blocks = new Array();
    this.onEnterFrame = this.processFrame;
};
```

We're overlaying three movies here from within the ActionScript - one remains unmasked (bgmov), and the other two (mmov and mmov2) are masked by canvas (as usual) and bg, which is where our circles were being drawn anyway.

mmov and mmov2 are started on frames 2 and 4 respectively, and these slight offsets from bgmov are what make the visual effect work.

rebecca video masking

lookat_it16.fla

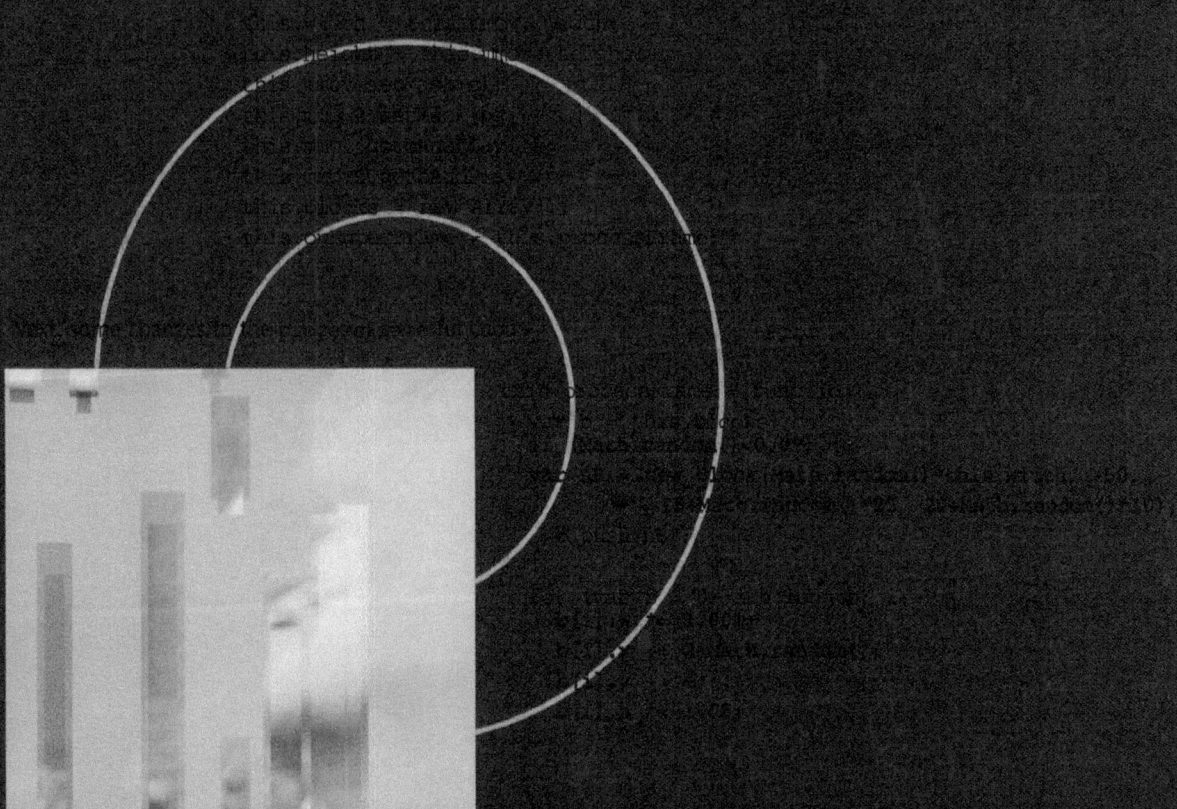

```
        if (b[i].y>this.height) {
                b.splice(i, 1);
                i--;
            }
        }
        this.drawAll();
    };
```

We start the blocks at a random position along the x axis and 50 pixels above the video - the reverse of what we've been doing before.

Then in each frame, y is incremented by 4, so blocks move down the screen at a constant rate.

Also, obviously, we've switched back to blocks again, because those circles were just way too exciting:

```
    this.drawAll = function() {
      var c = this.canvas;
      var bg = this.bg;
      var b = this.blocks;
      c.lineStyle();
      c.clear();
      bg.clear();
      for (var i = 0; i<b.length; i++) {
        this.drawBlock(c, b[i].x, b[i].y, b[i].w, b[i].h);
        this.drawBlock(bg, b[i].x-10, b[i].y-40, b[i].w+20, b[i].h+20);
      }
    };
```

lookin_it11.fla

Finally, we've a bit of a bizarre variation, continuing from `lookin_it10.fla`. In the init function, we got rid of the background and made mmov fully opaque again:

```
    this.init = function() {
      this.createEmptyMovieClip("canvas", 10);
      this.createEmptyMovieClip("bg", 7);
```

```
            var c = this.canvas;
            this.bg._x = c._x=this.xPos;
            this.bg._y = c._y=this.yPos;
            this.attachMovie("myMovie", "mmov", 9, {_x:this.xPos, _y:this.yPos});
            this.attachMovie("myMovie", "mmov2", 2,
                ➥                      {_x:this.xPos, _y:this.yPos, _alpha:50});
            (new Color(this.bgmov)).setTransform({ra:'70', rb:'20', ga:'30', gb:'50',
                ➥                      ba:'20', bb:'20', aa:'10', ab:'100'});
            this.width = this.mmov._width;
            this.height = this.mmov._height;
            this.mmov.setMask(c);
            this.mmov2.setMask(bg);
            this.mmov.gotoAndPlay(4);
            this.mmov2.gotoAndPlay(2);
            this.blocks = new Array();
            this.count = 0;
            this.onEnterFrame = this.processFrame;
        };
```

Now some changes to the `processFrame` function:

```
        this.processFrame = function() {
            var b = this.blocks;
            if (Math.random()<0.15) {
            var nB = new Block(Math.random()*this.width, -50,
                ➥              25+Math.random()*50, 30+Math.random()*50);
                b.push(nB);
            }
            for (var i = 0; i<b.length; i++) {
                b[i].x += 5+10*Math.sin(i+this.count*0.12);
                b[i].y += 11+12*Math.cos(i+this.count*0.4);
                if (b[i].y>this.height+100) {
                    b.splice(i, 1);
                    i--;
                }
            }
            this.count++;
            this.drawAll();
        };
```

We increased the block-generation frequency and made the blocks bigger, because we also removed the code that makes them grow over time.

As well as that, we made use of the Math.sin and Math.cos functions with a counter variable to make the blocks move around in erratic little ellipses on their way from the top of the screen to the bottom.

The only change in drawAll is to make the blocks masking mmov2 a bit bigger:

```
        for (var i = 0; i<b.length; i++) {
            this.drawBlock(c, b[i].x, b[i].y, b[i].w, b[i].h);
            this.drawBlock(bg, b[i].x-10, b[i].y-10, b[i].w+20, b[i].h+50);
        }
    };
```

Now, the change to the `drawBlock` function is where it gets interesting:

```
this.drawBlock = function(cvs, x, y, w, h) {
   var m = x+(w*0.5);
   var n = y+(h*0.5);
   var z = n*Math.sin(this.count*0.1);
   x *= 0.5;
   y *= Math.sin((this.count+x)*0.03);
   cvs.moveTo(x, y);
   cvs.beginFill(0xffffff);
   cvs.curveTo(m+z, n+z, x+w, y);
   cvs.lineTo(x+w, y+h);
   cvs.curveTo(m-z, n-z, x, y+h);
   cvs.lineTo(x, y);
   cvs.endFill();
};
```

We create three new variables from the standard ones that get fed into it.

m is halfway across the x axis, n is halfway down the y axis, and z is a pretty meaningless number based on n and a sine wave. We also change the values of x and y, which really distorts the output.

Then we replace the top and bottom lineTo commands with curveTo, using combinations of our new variables as control points. Now the shapes seem to bounce around somewhat.

I think the most important thing to take away from all these iterations is a sense of how easily a piece of code can be tweaked to produce quite different results – and maybe how spending a bit more time fiddling can yield something you wouldn't have thought of to begin with. So, if you haven't started playing with these FLAs already, open them up and get tweaking.

Hoss founded award winning new media agency Flammable Jam back in that sunny summer of 2000, and currently works for MMI (www.mmiweb.com) and Limone Media (www.limonemedia.com). In addition to talking at seminars such as Flash Forward and Milia, Hoss also takes on personal commissions such as the Life of Pi promo at www.canongate.net/pi. He lists his inspirations as Paul Daniels, Ron Jeremy, and the number 69. His personal site www.h69.net acts as a showcase for his antics and proves you can't offend all of the people all of the time.

Focus
Hoss Gifford

I hate watching people doing magic tricks. It's the most frustrating thing – I just can't handle not knowing how it was done. We all know magicians rely on sleight of hand and clever props to fool their audience that one thing is happening when the reality lies elsewhere, but I'm not content with this. I can't enjoy the trick without the closure of discovering the technique that's been used.

That's one of the reasons I liked Paul Daniels' telly show, because even as a youngster I could still see enough rough edges to work out how most of it was done. Nowadays though, everything is so slick that if you don't know, you'll not work it out.

The flip side of this is that I love creating tricks – making my own props, developing my own sleight of hand. I don't have a top hat and work children's parties though. My tricks are all Flash-based.

The first step is to really get a grasp on the limitations. Not just the limitations of Flash, but of the medium itself. For example, while Flash can move, scale, rotate, even shift the colors of an imported bitmap, it can't (yet) modify the bitmap's individual pixels. There's no Gaussian blur filter for example.

Next, I look for treatments for my concepts that push Flash beyond those limitations...

Eyes wide shut

A few years back, a guy called Nikola Tosic contacted me to see if I would be interested in contributing to a project called Kubrick.org, where I could take one of Stanley's films and create an online piece to represent my interpretation of that film. I saw this as a great opportunity, as films have always been a great passion for me, and I was only just getting into using Flash as a creative medium and this could be a great project to try some new techniques out.

I chose the film "Eyes Wide Shut", partly because it contained quite a lot of erotic imagery (which is nice) and partly because I wasn't very sure whether I liked the film or not. I wanted to avoid going with Clockwork Orange or 2001: A Space Odyssey because they were too obvious to me. I love both these films and I wanted something that would challenge me to think in a way that straight tribute wouldn't.

I developed quite a few concepts and at one point had quite an elaborate series of interweaved animations showing the relationships between the various narratives. But as I refined these ideas, I kept coming back to one image that I had grabbed from the film – an image that showed Tom Cruise and Nicole Kidman with their backs to the camera, looking into a mirror in which we see their fronts reflected.

This image summed up the film for me beautifully. It shows the couple in a naked embrace, but continually self-referential. The two sets of couples created by the mirror image reminds me of the two sides of each character's personality, and of the intensity of both betrayal and loyal passion that they have for each other. Finally, the positioning of Cruise's hand on the back of Kidman's neck with his wedding band on view seems like a visual metaphor for his infidelity.

I decided to drop my other concepts and develop this one. Because of the voyeuristic nature of the image (we're peering over their shoulders into a private moment) I wanted to have 'blinds' that covered the image, with the user having to drag them out of the way in order to see what was going on.

Since this would be my only piece for Kubrick.org, I was able to put more work into it than this. I figured that if I'd been working with video, I'd have wanted to play with the depth of field – starting with the foreground in focus (and a blurred reflection), and then pulling the mirror image into focus (blurring the characters' backs).

Of course, interactive bitmap blurring is still beyond the limitations of Flash, so I needed a little sleight of hand to make it work. You can see the finished piece at www.h69.net/eyeswideshut.

Wondering how I did it? Well read on, and all will be revealed!
In fact, just as with all the best magic tricks, the solution was a simple one. Using Photoshop, I created two copies of the original image: one with foreground blurred (shown below on the left), and one with the background blurred (on the right).

I brought both these modified images into Flash and placed one on top of the other. I put the top one into a movie clip, and added some code that would vary its alpha transparency with the x position of the cursor – from 0 (when the cursor is all the way to the left) to 100 (when it's all the way to the right). This meant that Flash would dynamically fade between two bitmaps, giving a very realistic impression of a video change of depth of field.

I've always loved the simplicity of this project. It's a subtle image transition and I was surprised how simple it was to create a convincing effect. That was in the days of Flash 4: now that Flash MX has added video to our palette, I decided it was time to revisit this technique, and see if I can come up with some more props.

Homeless part 1 – alpha fade

So, I decided to try out the fading technique I'd used in the Eyes Wide Shut project, but this time on video rather than a still bitmap. I did a video shoot in my local park and this time imported the footage into After Effects to create the two versions.

If you've never used After Effects, it's essentially Photoshop with a timeline – that's the easiest way to think about it, making it ideal for the task in hand.

I'll be honest: it was a disaster. There was too much overlap between the foreground and background, making it extremely difficult to create the two different versions of the video – especially where the chains of the swing are in front of the trees in the distance. The other thing that struck me was that this was really just going to end up being a technology demo, which isn't really my bag. I much prefer to produce concept rather than technology-driven projects. So, both the execution and the concept needed work. For me, it was back to the drawing board.

Don't be afraid to fail. It's not a bad thing. It's by far the fastest way to learn stuff.

On my way to work the next day, I saw an advert on the front page of the local newspaper with a very strong headline. It read, 'Spend a little less to give a little more.' It was for a homeless shelter in Glasgow and with consumer excess of Christmas starting to build up, the message was very poignant.

Later that same day, I walked to the supermarket up the street to get something for lunch. As I was waiting to cross the road I noticed a guy selling 'The Big Issue' outside the shop. I'd actually tuned him out as I see and hear him there every day and was focusing on the shop behind him, thinking about what to buy for lunch.

That's when it struck me. I'd found a great execution for a strong concept, and had reminded myself in the process that buying 'The Big Issue' for a quid doesn't hurt my finances much, but can make a real difference to the homeless guy freezing his backside off in the rain.

I explained to the guy what I was planning doing and would he be interested in helping out. He told me he'd love to do it as long as I gave him money to make up for the sales he'd lose out on during the ten minutes of filming. Shrewd. Very shrewd.

My idea was to get him in the foreground and the checkouts of the shop through the window in the background. The street was very noisy so I didn't pick up much of his voice, so after filming a few minutes I got him to speak into the camera's microphone so that I could record some clear dialog. I then went into the shop with the camera in my jacket pocket and let it record the sound of the checkouts. Covert stuff.

Preparing the video

Once my video footage was in the can, I had to pick out a section that could be looped effectively. I used Adobe After Effects (www.adobe.com) to apply a simple technique that involves using duplicate layers of the same video, but offset from each other, so that the end of one layer fades out onto the start of the next. This allows us to take a section of the new composition that will loop perfectly.

Now I had my source loop, it was time to create the two versions. If this were a still image in Photoshop, I'd draw a path around the Big Issue vendor, feather its selection and then use the result as a mask to do my blurring. As I said earlier, After Effects is basically Photoshop with a timeline, so I did exactly this but I also animated the path over time as he moved about a bit.

As a finishing touch, I reduced the saturation of the foreground shot, making it feel cold (as it was), and increased the saturation of the background shot, making it feel nice and cosy.

I exported the two clips to 100% quality Sorenson 3 encoded QuickTime movies, which I then ran through Sorenson Squeeze to create FLV files that I could bring back into Flash.

My final movie size was to be 748x420 pixels, but to keep file size down I created the FLVs at 374x210 and selected 'Image Smoothing' from the Playback options. Then I scaled up the video by 200% in Flash. This technique produces smaller file sizes for the same quality as if you used a video clip at the full size. The downside, however, is that it gives the processor more work, which in this project became so much of an issue that I had to reduce the amount of scaling in the final version to 125%.

Preparing the sound

Since I'd recorded the sound separately from the video, I exported raw WAV files from the video and took them into Acid Pro (www.sonicfoundry.com), using the same technique as I had for the video to create the loops.

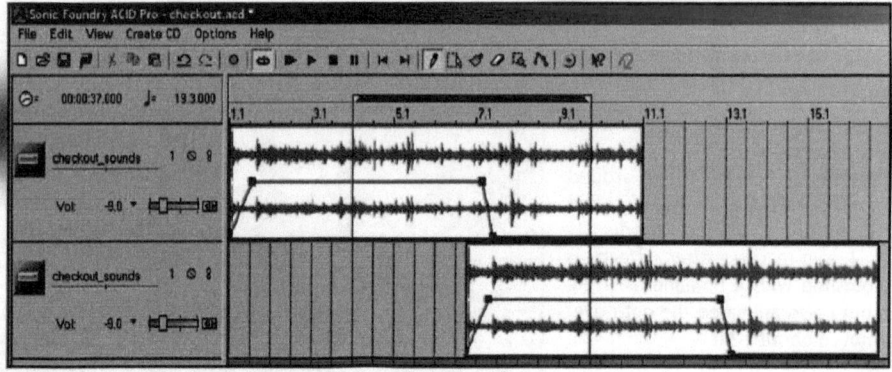

Now that I had all my assets ready, it was time to dive into Flash.

The basic prototype in Flash

I created a Flash file that was effectively a duplicate of the Eyes Wide Shut file, but with the two video clips instead of stills. Open homeless_alpha-fade.fla to see the finished file.

I rewrote the code from scratch because the original was Flash 4, and hey, we've come a long way, baby. I put each of the videos in a movie clip so that I could have a nice, neat, one-frame-long root timeline. I named the clip at the back shop and the one on top issue.

Check out the code in the actions layer of `homeless_alpha-fade.fla`. It's actually a lot simpler than it looks. Let's go through it now:

```
stop();

initObjects();
triggerLeft = 188;
triggerRight = 414;
mouseOnVendor = 1;
```

We start by setting up some variables and running the function `initObjects`, which looks like this:

```
function initObjects () {
  _root.createEmptyMovieClip('fader',2);
  _root.createEmptyMovieClip('mouseTrigger',3);
  mouseTrigger.onEnterFrame = function () {
    triggerMouse ();
  }
}
```

This creates a couple of empty movie clips, `fader` and `mouseTrigger`, which we'll use to monitor and control the user interaction. Right away, we attach an `onEnterFrame` handler to the `mouseTrigger` clip, which contains a call to `triggerMouse` – a function that will check where the user's mouse is and (if necessary) trigger the fading animation.

Here's what that function looks like:

```
function triggerMouse () {
  if ((_root._xmouse > triggerLeft)
      && (_root._xmouse < triggerRight)) {
    if (!mouseOnVendor) {
      mouseOnVendor = 1;
      triggerFade (99, 1000);
    }
```

We start by checking to see if the user's mouse is over the Big Issue vendor. If it is, we check the value of `mouseOnVendor` to determine whether the mouse has *just* rolled over the vendor – that being the case, we call the `triggerFade` function to fade the foreground video clip's alpha up to 99%. We also set the `mouseOnVendor` toggle, so that next time through this function Flash will know that we've already triggered the fade animation.

```
  } else {
    if (mouseOnVendor) {
      mouseOnVendor = 0;
      triggerFade (0, 1000);
    }
  }
}
```

The `else` statement basically does the inverse of this, causing the foreground video to fade out when the mouse rolls off the vendor.

Now let's look at `triggerFade` in a little more detail, as it's going to form the basis of our code as we build on this file.

```
function triggerFade(alf, time) {
```

The first thing to spot is that it expects to have a couple of arguments passed to it: `alf` is the alpha transparency level (between 0 and 100) that `issue` should fade down to, while `time` is the time (in milliseconds) it should take to do so.

Next, we set up some initial variables within the `fader` movie clip:

```
fader.fadeTime  = time;
fader.dAlf  = alf - _root.issue._alpha;
fader.initAlf  = _root.issue._alpha;
fader.onTime  = getTimer();
```

We store the requested duration of the fade in `fadeTime` and the difference between the current `_alpha` and the requested final `_alpha` goes into `dAlf`. The initial `_alpha` of `issue` is stored in `initAlf` and we take a note of the current time in `onTime`.

Now it's time to attach the `onEnterFrame` handler function, telling Flash to run the following code every time `fader`'s playhead enters a new frame.

```
fader.onEnterFrame = function() {
```

This is the really clever line of code: it divides the time passed so far by the total fade duration, and stores the result in a variable called `perc`:

```
perc = (getTimer() - this.onTime) / this.fadeTime;
```

So, perc now contains a value (somewhere between 0 and 1) that can tell us how far through the fade transition we are. A value of 0 signifies that no time has passed (so we must be right at the start of the fade) whereas 1 indicates that the full time has passed and it's about time the fade was over.

This allows us to carry out transitions and animations that are independent of the movie's framerate. Later on in the chapter, we'll spend a bit of time looking at why this is such a handy thing to be able to do. For now though, let's just see how it works:

```
if (perc < 1) {
    var alfOffset = perc * this.dAlf;
    _root.issue._alpha = this.initAlf + alfOffset;
```

We check that perc is less than 1, in which case the fade hasn't finished yet. Remember the variable dAlf, which stores our target _alpha value for the movie clip issue during this fade transition? Well, at the start of the transition we want 0% of this target value (that is, _alpha is 0 and issue is invisible), while at the end of the transition we want 100% of the target value (so _alpha has the same value as dAlf).

Well, that's exactly what we do. We multiply dAlf by the current value of perc and store the result in the local variable alfOffset. Now all we need to do is add this value to the starting value initAlf and we have the required current value of _alpha for the movie clip issue.

```
    } else {
        _root.issue._alpha = this.initAlf + this.dAlf;
        this.onEnterFrame = null;
    }
  }
}
```

The else code only runs if perc is *not* less than 1, which only happens when the full time for the transitions has passed. There's no need to use perc in calculating how much _alpha needs to be added – we know that the full amount is now required. So, we simply add dAlf to initAlf to get the final required _alpha value. Since the transition has now finished, we no longer want the fader movie clip's onEnterFrame code being triggered. We therefore get rid of this code by setting it to null.

This may seem like a lot of hard work just to fade out a movie clip when you could so easily do it manually using keyframes and tweening on a timeline, but it has the advantage of being able to fade at different speeds and to any value of _alpha.

That's it. I told you it was simple! All we basically have is three sets of 'props' to perform our trick: the video clips themselves, the function containing the knowledge of how to fade one video out to reveal the other, and some buttons to trigger the effect.

Frame rate-independent animation

There are almost as many opinions on what frame rate to use in a Flash movie as there are frame rates. Traditional cell based animators working in Flash will argue for 10 or 12 fps. Sandro Corsaro, author of "The Flash Animator", believes that most designers who think they need higher frame rates to achieve fluid animation simply *don't know* how to animate well.

When using video it's best to stick to the frame rate of the source video (I use PAL video and therefore 25fps). However, if I'm creating an animation that's code-based (a navigation menu for example, I may use up to 101 fps.

Many people will argue that such a high frame rate is bad practice as few users have computers powerful enough to run the movie at full speed, or even monitors with a fast enough refresh rate to show each frame if they did.

Of course, if your animations and transitions are Frame Rate Independent (FRI), it isn't so important what frame rate your end user's computer can achieve. The `triggerFade` function explored in this chapter gives us an FRI transition: it calculates how far it is through the transition by measuring how much *time* has passed rather than how many *frames* have passed. Likewise, the buttons tell Flash to fade the movie clip over the course of a thousand milliseconds, not over twenty-five frames.

In a movie running at 25fps, both equate to a second of animation. Okay then. Let's say we chose to hand-tween this fade over twenty-five frames of a timeline in a Frame Rate Dependent (FRD) animation. The problem starts when the animation's played back on a computer that can't keep up, and only manages, say, 10fps. This means that the second-long transition will take two-and-a-half (25 divided by 10) times longer than it ought to: 2.5 seconds.

A notable exception to this is when a streaming sound is playing which will force the timeline to skip frames if necessary.

The FRI animation will *always* take one second to complete, but in this example where the user only achieves 10fps, they'll only see ten frames of animation during the transition. In the same respect, if we ramp up a movie's frame rate to 101fps, those people who can get the higher frame rates will see the same thing as everyone else – only much smoother, as the second-long transition contains many more frames.

FRI for multiuser Flash

With robust socket servers like Unity (www.moock.org/unity) and Macromedia Flash Communication Server (www.macromedia.com/software/flashcom) making an impact on the Flash scene, networked multiplayer Flash gaming has become extremely viable, and FRI techniques are fundamental to the creation of these games.

Take a driving game for example. A user with a really old computer that can only manage 10 fps should still have a car that moves at the same speed as someone with a computer cranking out the intended 61 fps.

In this case, instead of the code moving the car by a set number of pixels per frame, it should move it by its current speed multiplied by the time it took to get from the last frame to the current frame. This means that although the person with the faster computer sees a much smoother game, their car will still move at the same speed as the one on the slow computer.

The only significant downside of FRI animation rears its ugly head if you're exporting your Flash work to video using Pete Barr-Watson's very clever export-through-Director technique. This requires a movie to play very slowly without skipping frames. Of course, if you don't plan to export to video then you needn't worry about this.

Transforming color

The concept was now strong but it needed a punchline – what marketing folk describe as a 'call to action'. I decided that after a set time, the video should become brighter and lighter, allowing me to overlay some big heavy black type.

I created a new Flash file and imported a video clip. Its size, content, and duration aren't important, as I'm simply planning to develop a function that can do the color transition I'm after; I'll then apply it to the Homeless file. Check out `homeless_coltran.fla` for the finished file.

The Color object

As we saw earlier in this chapter, we can use ActionScript to fade a movie clip in and out by changing the value of its `_alpha` property. This is all very well, but as soon as you start modifying a clip's color settings manually (using the drop down on the Property Inspector) you realize there's a lot more to play with besides the `_alpha`. If you select Advanced and hit the Settings... button, you'll see the Advanced Effect dialog:

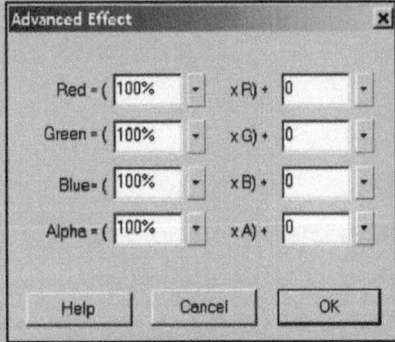

Playing about with the settings in this dialog can produce some really wild visuals. If only these settings were available through ActionScript. Well, they are – but they're not quite as straightforward to use as the `_alpha` setting.

Imagine our movie clip (containing the video footage) as a television. It has a control panel that lets us adjust things like the position of the image (using the `_x` and `_y` buttons), the size of the image (using the `_scale` buttons) and the `_alpha` button that we've been using thus far.

There's actually a bunch of other buttons to play with, which affect the color of the clip. The standard television has a panel over these to stop the inexperienced user from tampering with them. If, however, you can lay your hands on a special `Color` object that clips onto the telly's control panel, you can then access all these extra properties by using a special TV remote control called a **color transform** object.

The remote contains all the same settings as we saw the Advanced Effect dialog box, but calls them ra, rb, ga, gb, ba, bb, aa, and ab. You just need to set them as you want them, and press the `setTransform` button to apply the new settings.

Homeless part 2 – color transition

That's enough analogies for one day – let's look at how it works for real. You can find this version of the project in the file `homeless_coltran.fla`. Once again, I've placed the actions in a layer called actions on the root timeline:

```
stop();

initObjects();
initColor();
initButtons();
```

We start by running a few functions to set up all the bits and bobs the animation needs to run.

The first function we call is `initObjects`, which once again creates a couple of empty movie clips for us. This time though, they're called `colTrans` and `setColClip`.

```
function initObjects () {
  _root.createEmptyMovieClip('colTrans',4);
  _root.createEmptyMovieClip('setColClip',5);
}
```

Next, we have a new function called `initColor`, which sets up all the objects we're going to need for the color transformations:

```
function initColor () {
  issueCol = new Color(issue);
  issueColTrans  = new Object();
  issueColTrans.ra = issueColTrans.ga
                        = issueColTrans.ba
                        = issueColTrans.aa = 100;
  issueColTrans.rb = issueColTrans.gb
                        = issueColTrans.bb
                            = issueColTrans.ab = 0;
}
```

This is all we need to control the movie clip's extra color properties. The first line creates a `Color` object called `issueCol`, which grants us access to these properties. The next line creates our remote control: a 'color transform' object that we use to store all the settings we want to apply.

The next two lines apply default values to each of the object's properties, corresponding to the default settings in the Advanced Effects dialog: 100% with 0 shift. We now have all the code needed to represent our remote button for applying the color transform settings – and apply them is precisely what we do next:

```
setColClip.onEnterFrame = function () {
  issueCol.setTransform(issueColTrans);
}
```

To keep things simple, we apply the color settings every frame – it would actually be better practice to apply them only when there's a change made to the settings. Note that we don't apply setTransform to the movie clip itself, but to the Color object we attached to it.

Now we need a few buttons to test out the effect. I've added three movie clips to the bottom right corner of the stage, with the instance names warpBut, invertBut, and resetBut.

The initButtons function contains all their code.

```
function initButtons () {
```

warpBut is the first button to have its code attached.

```
warpBut.onRelease = function() {
    _root.triggerColTrans(100, 100, -100,
                          204, 0, 213, 750);
}
```

We're calling the function triggerColTrans with the parameters required to transform the video's colors to the purple and yellow version that we created manually earlier.

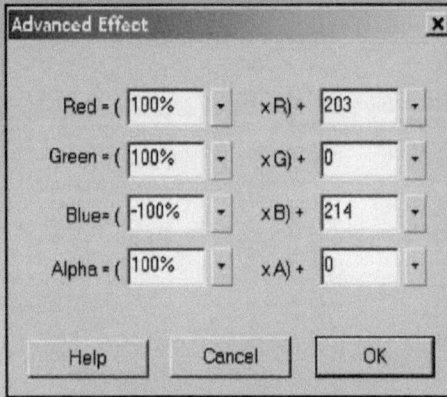

If you look closely at the numbers we're passing in, you'll notice they correspond to the values we'd set in the Advanced Effects dialog box to manually adjust the color.

The seventh (and last) argument our buttons pass to the triggerColTrans function is the period over which the transition should take place.

The `initButtons` function continues to set the other buttons' actions in the same way. The second set of values creates a blue-tinted inverted version:

```
invertBut.onRelease = function() {
  _root.triggerColTrans(-70, -35, 100,
                             255, 255, 255, 750);
}
```

The final set gives us a default 'reset' version of the video, which takes 5000 milliseconds (or five seconds to you and me) to complete:

```
resetBut.onRelease = function() {
  _root.triggerColTrans(100, 100, 100, 0, 0, 0, 5000);
}
}
```

Finally, we have the function that calculates values for the color transform object over time. This means that we'll get a color transition rather than a straight switch.

```
function triggerColTrans (ra, ga, ba, rb, gb, bb, time) {
  // SET INITIAL VALUES FOR FADE ENGINE
  colTrans.colTime  = time;

  // SET DELTAS
  colTrans.dra      = issueColTrans.ra - ra;
  colTrans.dga      = issueColTrans.ga - ga;
  colTrans.dba      = issueColTrans.ba - ba;
  colTrans.drb      = issueColTrans.rb - rb;
  colTrans.dgb      = issueColTrans.gb - gb;
  colTrans.dbb      = issueColTrans.bb - bb;

  // SET INITIAL VALUES
  colTrans.ira      = issueColTrans.ra;
  colTrans.iga      = issueColTrans.ga;
  colTrans.iba      = issueColTrans.ba;
  colTrans.irb      = issueColTrans.rb;
  colTrans.igb      = issueColTrans.gb;
```

```
colTrans.ibb     = issueColTrans.bb;

// TAKE A NOTE OF THE TIME THE TRANSITION STARTS
colTrans.onTime    = getTimer();

// ADD COLOR TRANSITION ENGINE TO ISSUE VIDEO CLIP
colTrans.onEnterFrame = function () {

  // CALCULATE HOW FAR WE ARE THROUGH TRANSITION
  perc = (getTimer() - this.onTime) / this.colTime;

  // PERFORM THE COLOR TRANSITION
  if (perc < 1) { // STILL DURING TRANSITION
    _root.issueColTrans.ra =
      ➥                  this.ira - (this.dra * perc);
    _root.issueColTrans.ga =
      ➥                  this.iga - (this.dga * perc);
    _root.issueColTrans.ba =
      ➥                  this.iba - (this.dba * perc);
    _root.issueColTrans.rb =
      ➥                  this.irb - (this.drb * perc);
    _root.issueColTrans.gb =
      ➥                  this.igb - (this.dgb * perc);
    _root.issueColTrans.bb =
      ➥                  this.ibb - (this.dbb * perc);

  } else {

    // TIME IS UP - END TRANSITION
    _root.issueColTrans.ra = this.ira - this.dra;
    _root.issueColTrans.ga = this.iga - this.dga;
    _root.issueColTrans.ba = this.iba - this.dba;
    _root.issueColTrans.rb = this.irb - this.drb;
    _root.issueColTrans.gb = this.igb - this.dgb;
    _root.issueColTrans.bb = this.ibb - this.dbb;

    // MY JOB HERE IS DONE
    this.onEnterFrame = null;
  }
}
}
```

This looks pretty scary, but it's really just an adaptation of the triggerFade function that we looked at earlier. Go back a few pages, have another look at the original triggerFade function and compare it to this huge wallop of code. They are pretty much the same.

This time, instead of adjusting one variable across time (for the _alpha), we're adjusting six variables (for each of the six settings of the Color object). So it's no more complicated, it's just a bit more repetitive. Easy, eh?

> I'm only calculating the values for six of the parameters, as I only want this code to change the video color. We therefore leave the last two properties (aa and ab) at their default values as they control the _alpha.

Homeless part 3 – color transform fade

Now it's time to add our shiny new color warping code to the interactive depth of field video file. I'm afraid it's not as simple as you might think though. Feel free to go ahead and integrate the code, but you'll quickly discover that it doesn't work. Why?

Well, in our first file, we dynamically adjust the _alpha property of the top video movie clip to fade between the different videos. The problem with integrating the new color warping code is that it *also* sets the alpha transparency – but via the color transform object. In fact, it currently sets the alpha to 100% on every frame, overriding any attempts to fade out the video.

We need to rewrite our original code to set the alpha using a color transform object, instead of accessing the _alpha property directly. Starting again may initially seem frustrating but it's an essential part of this type of work. Build it, break it, fix it, build it again – that's how it goes.

> *This approach to development isn't the only way to do things. My technical reviewers suggest that the more normal approach is 'plan, plan, document, plan, plan, document, go do it'.*
>
> *In my experience, this is the approach favored by managers as it makes their jobs easier, as it reduces the risk of missing deadlines and ensures that the client knows exactly what they are going to get before production commences.*
>
> *'Build it, break it, build it again' requires a client with a lot a faith in the development team, but the huge advantage is that this approach is much more likely to produce a more innovative solution, as you can propose to try something out that might not work. Some clients aren't prepared to take these risks. Fortunately, I don't work for them.*

Check out `homeless_coltran_fade.fla` for the finished file. It does exactly the same as `homeless_alpha_fade.fla`, except that we're now using the Color object to adjust the _alpha.

Compare the two files and you'll see that they're actually very similar. Here's the code for `homeless_coltran_fade.fla` with the new and changed code highlighted.

```
stop();
initObjects();
initColor();
triggerLeft = 188;
triggerRight = 414;
mouseOnVendor = 1;
```

We add the `initColor` function at the start:

```
function initObjects () {
  _root.createEmptyMovieClip('fader',2);
  _root.createEmptyMovieClip('mouseTrigger',3);
  _root.createEmptyMovieClip('colTrans',4);
  _root.createEmptyMovieClip('setColClip',5);
  mouseTrigger.onEnterFrame = function () {
    triggerMouse();
  }
}
```

We now need the two extra empty movie clips from homeless_coltran.fla.

```
function triggerFade (alf, time) {
  fader.fadeTime  = time;
  fader.dAlf  = alf - issueColTrans.aa;
  fader.initAlf  = issueColTrans.aa;
  fader.onTime  = getTimer();
  fader.onEnterFrame = function () {
    perc = (getTimer() - this.onTime) / this.fadeTime;
    if (perc < 1) {
      var alfOffset = perc * this.dAlf;
      _root.issueColTrans.aa = this.initAlf + alfOffset;
    } else {
      _root.issueColTrans.aa = this.initAlf + this.dAlf;
      this.onEnterFrame = null;
    }
  }
}
```

This time round we're adjusting the aa parameter of the color transform object, as opposed to the _alpha property of the clip directly.

```
function initColor () {
  issueCol = new Color(issue);
  issueColTrans  = new Object();
  issueColTrans.ra = issueColTrans.ga
           = issueColTrans.ba
           = issueColTrans.aa = 100;
  issueColTrans.rb = issueColTrans.gb
           = issueColTrans.bb
           = issueColTrans.ab = 0;
}

setColClip.onEnterFrame = function () {
  issueCol.setTransform(issueColTrans);
}
```

The `initColor` and `setColClip.onEnterFrame` functions have been copied and pasted from homeless_coltran.fla – no changes required. The new file still has the `triggerMouse` function from homeless_alpha_fade.fla – also copied and pasted with no changes required.

Now that we have a version of the FLA that can perform color and alpha transitions, we need to make use of this feature. That means combining our two most recent files so that we have a movie that doesn't just fade between the two videos, but will also warp their color while doing so.

Homeless part 4 – color and fade

Open homeless_col_and_fade.fla to see the finished file. It looks like a lot of code, but we're not adding that much to our previous incarnations of this file – let's see what's new.

```
stop();
initObjects();
initColor();
triggerLeft = 188;
triggerRight = 414;
mouseOnVendor = 1;
resetMessageTimer();
```

We start by adding in a call to the function resetMessageTimer – we'll check that out in just a minute. First though, we add another empty movie clip for use in the next function. This will be responsible for triggering the color warping of the video after a set amount of time.

```
function initObjects () {
    _root.createEmptyMovieClip('fader',2);
    _root.createEmptyMovieClip('mouseTrigger',3);
    _root.createEmptyMovieClip('colTrans',4);
    _root.createEmptyMovieClip('setColClip',5);
    _root.createEmptyMovieClip('timer',6);
    mouseTrigger.onEnterFrame = function () {
        triggerMouse ();
    }
}
```

Now, our new function resetMessageTimer sets up some variables, including the length of time to wait until triggering the color warp.

```
function resetMessageTimer () {
    timer.onTime   = getTimer();
    timer.colTranOn  = 11000;
    timer.messageOn  = 13000;
```

Once the time specified in colTranOn is up, we call triggerColTrans, passing in the appropriate parameters to give us the blue-tinted inverted image.

```
timer.onEnterFrame = function () {
    this.now = getTimer() - this.onTime;
    if (this.now > this.colTranOn) {
        _root.triggerColTrans (-70, -35, 100,
                                255, 255, 255 , 750);
```

The timer waits a little longer (until the time specified in messageOn has passed) and then plays the movie clip containing the call to action:

```
timer.onEnterFrame = function () {
    this.now = getTimer() - this.onTime;
    if (this.now > this.messageOn) {
        _root.message.gotoAndPlay('on');
        this.onEnterFrame = null;
    }
  }
 }
}
```

Once the call to action (movie clip message) has run through, the blank_button instance on frame 184 presents an onRelease handler that calls the restart function:

```
function restart () {
    triggerColTrans (100, 100, 100, 0, 0, 0, 5000);
    resetMessageTimer();
    message.gotoAndPlay('off');
}
```

This transforms the video colors back to normal and runs resetMessageTimer to reset everything, ready to run again from the start.

```
setColClip.onEnterFrame = function () {
    setCol ();
}
```

The empty movie clip setColClip gets the job of running setcol in its onEnterFrame.

```
function setCol () {
    shopColTrans.ra = issueColTrans.ra;
    shopColTrans.ga = issueColTrans.ga;
    shopColTrans.ba = issueColTrans.ba;
    shopColTrans.rb = issueColTrans.rb;
    shopColTrans.gb = issueColTrans.gb;
    shopColTrans.bb = issueColTrans.bb;
    _root.issueCol.setTransform(issueColTrans);
    _root.shopCol.setTransform(shopColTrans);
}
```

The main point to note is that we now have two Color objects (one for each video clip) and two color transform objects (for the same reason). The setCol function (which applies the color transforms) copies all but the two alpha parameters into the color transform object for the bottom video movie clip. We don't actually need the alpha values, as this video should always be totally opaque.

The rest of the code in homeless_col_and_fade.fla is the same as we used in previous files, but with some of it duplicated, allowing for the extra Color and color transform objects.

Homeless part 5 – sound

You could be forgiven for beginning to think that I'd forgotten all about the sound effects that we created earlier. In actual fact, it's the most straightforward part of the project, so I integrated sound into the first prototype when I started developing this project for myself. For purposes of clarity in this book though, I've left it until the end.

Before diving into the code, we need to think about what we want to achieve. We need to write ourselves a mini brief. Here are my objectives:

- When the Big Issue vendor is in focus, we should hear his sound at 85% volume, with the sound effect of the shop at 15% volume.

- When we pull focus to the shop, the sound should fade to reflect this, with the volumes being inverted (so 15% volume for vendor, and 85% for the shop).

The final file is called homeless.fla, and contains this additional code:

```
stop();

initObjects();
initColor();
initSound();
triggerFade(100,1000);
triggerLeft = 188;
triggerRight = 414;
mouseOnVendor = 1;
resetMessageTimer();
```

At the start, we call a couple of new functions to initialize the sound.

```
function initObjects () {
  _root.createEmptyMovieClip('fader',2);
  _root.createEmptyMovieClip('mouseTrigger',3);
  _root.createEmptyMovieClip('colTrans',4);
  _root.createEmptyMovieClip('setColClip',5);
  _root.createEmptyMovieClip('timer',6);
  _root.createEmptyMovieClip('shopSC',7);
  _root.createEmptyMovieClip('issueSC',8);

  mouseTrigger.onEnterFrame = function() {
    triggerMouse();
  }
}
```

We create another two empty movie clips to hold our Sound objects. We need one for each of the sound effects – we'll use the following function to create them:

```
function initSound() {
    issueSound = new Sound(_root.issueSC);
    issueSound.attachSound ('issueWav');
    issueSound.setVolume(85);
    issueSound.start(0,696969);

    shopSound = new Sound(_root.shopSC);
    shopSound.attachSound ('shopWav');
    shopSound.setVolume(15);
    shopSound.start(0,696969);
}
```

The initSound function creates two sound objects for the two sound effects. It sets them up by attaching the relevant sound file, setting their volume to zero, and starting playback (looped plenty of times).

```
function setVol (v) {
    v = Math.min(v,85);
    v = Math.max(v,15);
    issueSound.setVolume(v);
    shopSound.setVolume(100 - v);
}
```

The setVol function looks for a passed argument v, which it uses to set the volume of the two clips. When v is at 100, the vendor's sound is set to its maximum of 85%, while the shop sound is set to its minimum of 15%. The opposite is true when v is 0.

Now we need to insert some calls to this function, so that the volume will change as we fade from one video to the other:

```
function triggerFade (alf, time) {
    fader.fadeTime  = time;
    fader.dAlf      = alf - issueColTrans.aa;
    fader.initAlf   = issueColTrans.aa;
    fader.onTime    = getTimer();
    fader.onEnterFrame = function () {
        perc = (getTimer() - this.onTime) / this.fadeTime;
        if (perc < 1) {
            var alfOffset = perc * this.dAlf;
            _root.issueColTrans.aa = this.initAlf + alfOffset;
            setVol (this.initAlf + alfOffset);
        } else {
            _root.issueColTrans.aa = this.initAlf + this.dAlf;
            setVol (this.initAlf + this.dAlf);
            this.onEnterFrame = null;
        }
    }
}
```

All we need to do is add the two highlighted lines of ActionScript – another really simple solution. By tying the volume to the alpha setting of the top video movie clip, we have a ready-made sound level for the fade.

Conclusion

To me, this project really underlines how important it is to not be afraid of failing. More than once things simply didn't work out – I had to go back a step or two and try doing things in a different way. Although this is true of most innovative projects, it becomes even more evident when you add video to the equation.

Even as I sit typing this, I have to admit to myself that the final animation is just too processor-intensive. My development computer is a very fast PC with a disgusting amount of RAM, and even that only just manages to keep everything going smoothly.

Testing on an average Mac will show this up to be practically unwatchable. So my next step is to reduce the size of the animation. It means I'll be able to use smaller video, and therefore smaller file sizes (which is nice), but it won't have the impact of the current large format.

Then again, if you're reading this five years on from now you'll be laughing at my whinging, as even five-year-old computers will be able to play it okay!

What did you get out of this? Hopefully, I've inspired you to go and try something experimental that's never been done before. Hopefully, you won't be put off by the fear that it might not work. So what if it doesn't? It's what you learn in the process that's more important.

And if you get a chance, e-mail me a link to your new stuff at hoss@h69.net. That's what makes me tick. Isn't that what makes us all tick?

Ken Jokol   www.pinderkaas.com

(Remembered) Lost Things

A hardback copy of Give Me Liberty signed by Frank Miller and Dave Gibbons, CD2 of American Breakbeat compilation, the first CD single by the More Fire Crew, three Stray Bullets comics, the contents of one hard drive, a cassette of home acoustic recordings, friends, the front brakes of my bmx, a red mobile phone, a cheap microphone, various passwords, Commando BBC Micro cassette, two plastic bullets, The Sea & Cake (S/T) CD, photographs, a variety of Magic: The Gathering cards, the sleeve of How to Say Llanfairpwllgwyngyllgogerychwyndrobwyllllantysyliogogogoch 7", Match Day II Spectrum cassette, jobs, four rechargeable batteries, an electric shaver power cable, money, a floppy disk with a homemade brown parcel tape label, a hi-fi remote control, family, Rampage Spectrum cassette, the egg-timer and/or dice for various board games and, record 2 of the Shaft soundtrack by Isaac Hayes.

If anybody reading this has found or 'acquired' any of the above, then I would dearly love to hear from them, and maybe get them back. E-mail kenj@pinderkaas.com.

Thanks to Pete for modelling and Katy for camerawork.

A moving video mannequin
Ken Jokol

When the video object first arrived in Flash, I must confess I had a few niggling worries. I was pleased and excited of course, but I couldn't help wondering if Flash was about to enter a bloat period where every SWF on the net would contain a couple of MB worth of video? I had nightmares of the first CD games, where developers suddenly realized that even though their new game took up the equivalent of 40 floppies, there were still 600 MB free on their shiny disk. What did they do with all of this space? Fill it with an hour's worth of bad, slow-loading video of course. Ah, those were the days!

To my surprise though, this hasn't been the case at all – quite the opposite in fact. On my travels around the net, I've seen very little interesting work done with video. Of course, a few innovators have done some amazing work, but the average Flash user doesn't seem that bothered by the new avenues available to him. So, high ideals in hand, I thought I'd set out to see what this new video object could do.

Evolving ideas

Things often come a long way from where they started. In fact, the experiment we're going to look at in this chapter began life as an idea for a video game – something like Mortal Kombat or Toonstruck. Admittedly, I much preferred Street Fighter 2's kinetic cartoon style to Mortal Kombat's digitized fighters, but the idea was there. I thought about taking that digitized ethic, and putting it into a platform game. Maybe against photographed obstacles such as evil dogs that chase you, or maybe against traditional vector backgrounds to give it that 'Tron' feel.

Then I got to thinking about how this might realistically be achieved. I'd originally thought of having the whole character as one object, and filming different movement states, for example walking, running, and jumping.

Next, I thought that rather than filming a whole new body animation for each action, I might be able to film separate limbs, and then link them together with ActionScript to create the actions.

After pondering this for a while, I decided to take a step back, and that it would be easier to film complete single limb actions than to try and smoothly construct them from smaller parts that would probably never quite fit together anyway. After thinking of a few possible actions that would suit this method, it occurred to me that rather than a platform game, I could create some kind of hybrid beat-'em-up / RPG. Different actions could have different attributes – a fast, but light rabbit-punch animation, a slow, but heavy haymaker, a high-blocking arm, a fast-walking, but weak leg, and so on. Each fighter would be constructed using a number of limbs, and then set against each other. The victor could then claim one of the loser's limbs as his own at the end of the match.

That sounded like great fun, but it also sounded like a logistical nightmare. Fighting games live or die by their collision detection, and Flash isn't renowned for its speed or accuracy in that department. I loved the idea of being able to drag animations onto a character though, kind of like a video dress-up doll. I also liked the idea of having multiple limbs all moving at once in different directions, making an insane Swiss army knife man.

That then was the idea: to film a number of limb movements, bring them into Flash, and mask them somehow. These animations could then be positioned on a body and displayed. I also had in the back of my mind that if this proof-of-concept worked, then I could always save the finished creature I'd built, and bring it into my still-evolving beat-'em-up.

So, it's now a dress-up doll with a difference: rather than trying out new outfits on a static body, you can try new limbs instead. Drag limb animations out of a standard interface, and drop them into position on the body. Rotate them into the arrangement you desire, or drop the ones you don't like and watch them fall away.

When you're happy with your creation, hit the Display button to see it in all its glory against the background of your choice. If it's still not to your liking, then switch back to edit mode and carry on working. When everything's as good as it's going to be, hit the SAVE button and record your simulacrum in a text file ready to share with your friends.

The creative process

Although this application was actually created over three days (with bouts of writing in-between), I started thinking about how it would all work for a few days beforehand. Once I'd got away from the computer game idea, and started thinking in terms of an application, I noted down all the elements that I wanted from the movable limbs and the manipulations available to each of these. Some of the things that I decided upon (like drag'n'droppable limbs) are tried and tested elements that are familiar to most users.

It won't surprise you at all to see that the creative process for this application can be split into two definite sections: creating the video clips of moving limbs, and designing and coding the interactive elements. Both processes benefited from a lot of thinking and some planning before even getting to the desk.

I decided to do the video and graphic elements first as this felt like the obvious way to begin testing and building the application. If anything went wrong at this stage, I would have saved myself a great deal of coding time and could try and find another direction to take the project. I also tried to think ahead by planning very carefully how this part of the process would go, and this definitely made it go much more smoothly than if I had jumped straight in.

The scripting part required that I lock myself in a room and code like a demon. Because I had a preconceived idea of how the application would look and function, this part of the process went pretty well too, but inevitably there were some bumpy patches...

Okay, enough about all of this, let's get down to it – starting with the insane process of creating the disembodied limbs.

Creating the limb video clips

I planned to shoot twenty-five separate limb actions: twenty arm movements and five leg movements. These could then be flipped horizontally to provide me with equivalent clips for the opposite side. The filming itself would be tricky, but it was quickly apparent that the greatest challenge would be bringing the video into Flash so that it would appear as clips of moving disembodied limbs, removed from their background. This would have to be achieved by masking. Now masking one or two bitmaps is one thing, but when you have over twenty video clips of between forty and a hundred frames each, then hand-drawing vectors doesn't sound that much fun, unless you have an incredible amount of time and patience.

To get around this factor, I needed to automate the whole process. Working this out gave me a minor headache, but I figured out how to do it in a few steps, using a few applications to help me along the way.

The process of creating the video clips can be broken down into a number of stages:

- filming the video sequence
- editing it into a continuous loop
- exporting the frames of the video to an image sequence
- running a Photoshop batch action on each image of the sequence to create a monotone image sequence
- batch vectorizing each image
- importing the vector images into Flash
- importing the video and masking it with the vector image layer

Although it sounds quite easy now I've got it down like that, the experimentation involved was considerable. There was a great deal of hit and miss while I refined this process, and there might have been an easier way. Overall though, it was relatively quick and simple once I'd done a few limbs. I'll go through the process in detail here so you can avoid the mistakes I made along the way.

Shooting the video

Before the shoot began, I'd already determined that the best possible scenario would be to work with a great deal of contrast during the filming, so that the desired part of the video – the limbs – stood out over the background. This would then help when it came to the later stages, as there would be a distinct way for Photoshop to select the limbs over the unwanted background.

Essentially, this is a little like bluescreening – a feature that's built into software like Adobe After Effects for masking off certain colors – just on a much more lo-fi level. Not having access to a studio and adequate lighting equipment meant that I filmed against a black background to hide the shadowing from my house lighting. I chose black because it offers good contrast with the white of my skin.

The video was then shot using a DV-PAL camera at 25fps. I quickly realized the difficulty of filming individual limbs in awkward positions, especially in a small camera space. It was quite good fun, but it's hard work being a hyperactive hand model!

Once a friend and I had finished making idiots of ourselves on camera, I took the footage into iMovie to edit.

Editing the video

I chose Apple's iMovie 2 for editing because it's easy, free, and (best of all) very fast to get work done with. As iMovie is only available for Macs, PC users will need to use some alternative software: the obvious candidate is Movie Maker, which is also free, fast, and easy to use. What's more, you'll be glad to know that the new version 2 finally has some functionality!

I imported the DV video into iMovie through a FireWire connection, and edited it into short loops as best I could. In some awkward cases, I had to place two copies of the same video sequence back to back, and reversed the second clip to make it look like one looped movement. This would often result in some pretty crazy results, but it's a pretty good trick considering I didn't have time to reshoot any footage.

Given more time to work on this, I would reshoot (or at least re-edit) a lot of the footage because I can see the flaws; no doubt you can too. One thing that did annoy me (and I'd dearly love to go back and rectify this) is the ay that we filmed wearing t-shirts. Originally, it was just my friend in front of the camera, but later on I decided to do some juggling and kept my t-shirt on.

If I was to reshoot, I think I'd remove my t-shirt altogether and shoot everything wearing next-to-nothing. At least this would make for better limb integration, and it would also allow me to easily create a Leonardo da Vinci...

After editing the video, I stripped out the sound and exported it as a QuickTime MOV at full quality (no compression) and 25fps. The arms were exported at 150x113, maintaining 4:3 ratio, with the legs just a little bigger.

Checking da loops

Before I went ahead and split the videos into an image sequence, I decided to check that the loops ran okay. QuickTime (Pro and standard) allows you to loop a video file continuously using Movie > Loop – great for testing if something runs okay over and over.

If the loops weren't working, I trimmed them in QuickTime Pro, opening two copies of the same clip and checking the first and last frames back to back. I had another task to perform in QuickTime Pro while I was working on the legs. Because of the impossibility of filming one leg only on camera, I decided to film both legs at once, and to mask out the unused one. Filming in portrait, this is what I started out with:

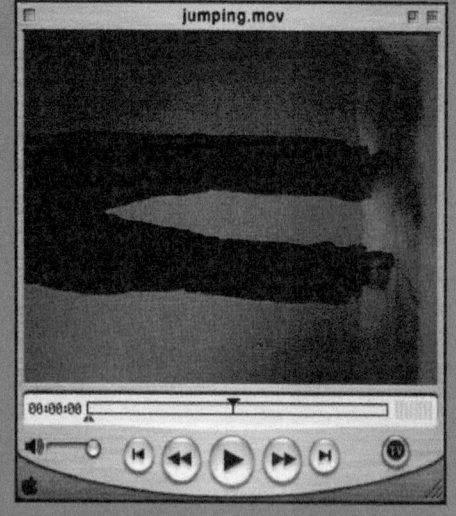

I then needed a black and white image that I could apply to the clip as a mask. QuickTime would mask black areas and show white areas. Each clip required a slightly different mask; the one shown below (jumping.mov) used a white image with a horizontal black bar to mark out the part of each frame I wanted to use. Here's how it looked with the mask:

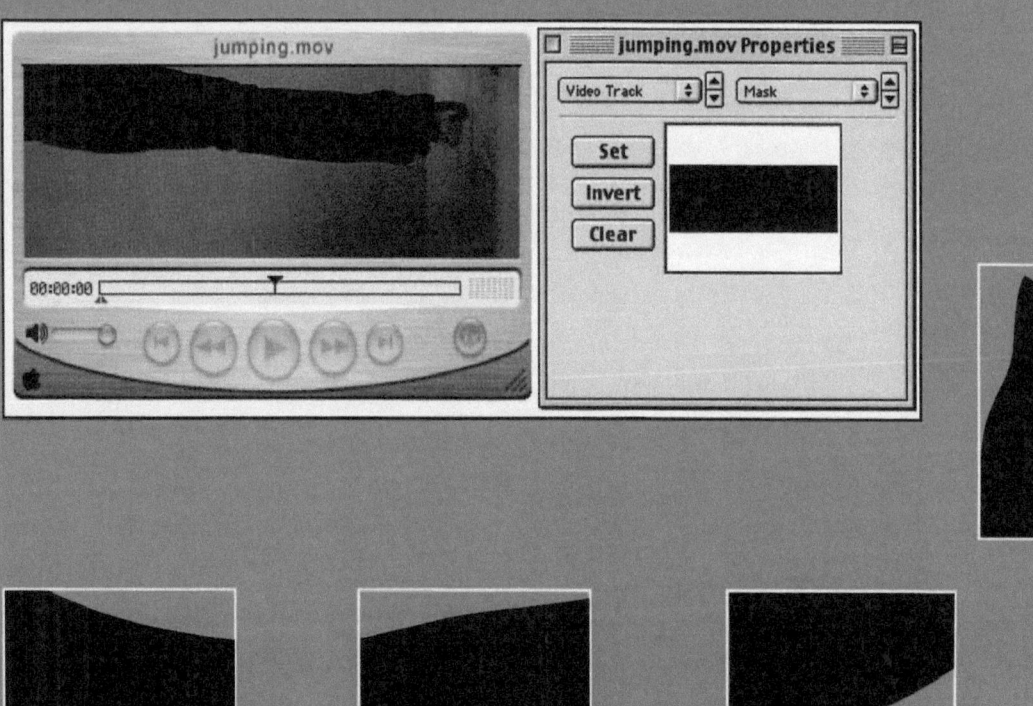

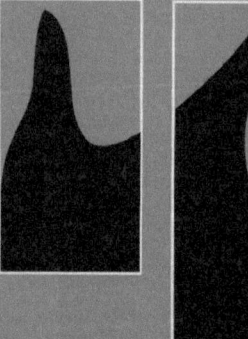

All that then remained was to rotate the clip in QuickTime Pro – and presto! The leg clips were sorted:

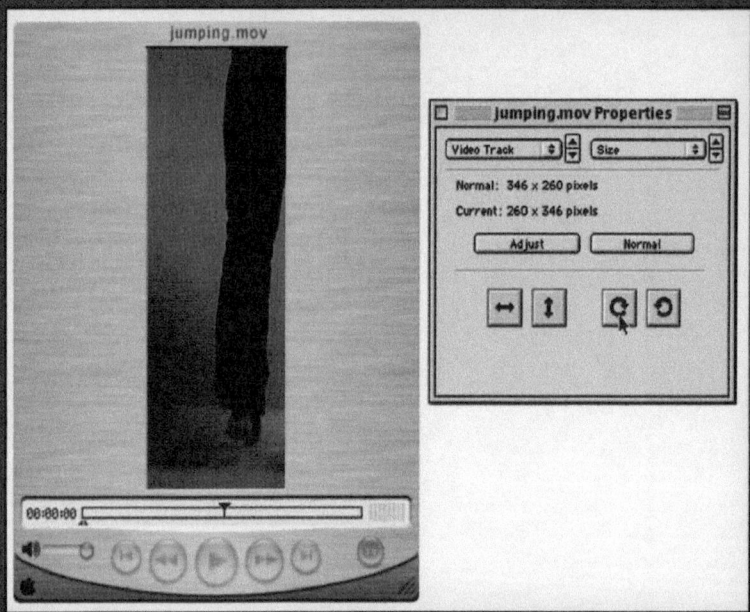

At this point, I needed to strip all the limb videos into image sequences.

Creating an image sequence from video

Splitting a video into individual images can be done in many applications (free and otherwise), but I decided to do it with QuickTime Pro. Although Flash MX can easily do this, I find QuickTime a little quicker because it does what I need in fewer steps (and speed is of the essence...).

With the MOV files in QuickTime Pro, I exported them all as image sequences (File > Export > Export as Image Sequence). I chose the PICT format here because it keeps them at a decent uncompressed quality.

All of the limbs were split in this way, with each sequence saved in its own folder. With all the images created in this way, it is on to the most important step in the process: batch processing the images in Photoshop.

If you want to do this in Flash, import the video, extend the timeline to show all the frames you want to show, and choose File > Export Movie. Then select a format for your images from the menu – I'd recommend PICT for the Mac and BMP for Windows, as both are uncompressed and adequately reproduce the source quality.

Batch processing images in Adobe Photoshop

Okay, let's recap what we have so far. Well, we have a number of folders full of PICT images, and a load of MOV files. Well, the MOV files can sit out for a while because they won't feature until we get to working in Flash.

The image files though need to be processed ready for vectorization. The reason we do this is to make the vectorization as easy as possible, eradicating as many mid-tones as possible. Creating a contrasted image from what we already have is the kind of task Photoshop gobbles up for breakfast.

Image editing powers aside, Photoshop has the ability to record Actions – sort of like macros, if you've not seen them before – and can run these on a batch of files at once. Photoshop 7 has some scripting abilities too, but that's another

The general task we need to perform is to select the void background space, change it to white, invert the selection and fill the selected area to black. Here's the before and after:

 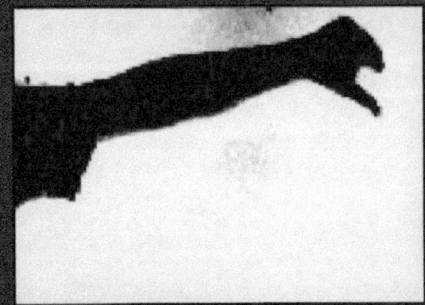

Here's an outline of the action that I recorded:

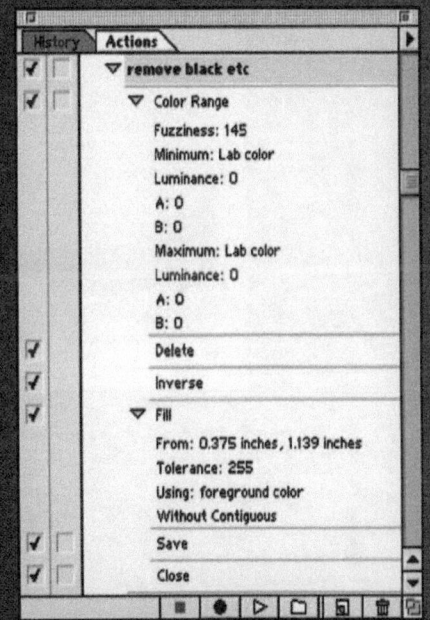

The first step uses Select > Color Range to select the image's black background, and the next step then deletes this selection. The default background color in Photoshop is white, so gives us a white background for the image.

The next step inverts the selection, leaving the limb selected. This is filled with the foreground color, black, giving us a contrasted black and white image that's ready for vectorization.

Finally, Photoshop saves over the original file and closes the image so that it's ready to work on the next one.

As you can see, there isn't much to this, and there are other ways to do it (I came up with a few), but it works perfectly for what we need here. Contrast is the key when it comes to vectorizing images.

The action is then set to run on a folder of images using File > Automate > Batch. When doing this, you just need to select the action you want to run, and specify source and destination folders. This will then leave us with many folders of processed images, ripe for vectorizing.

Batch vectorizing the image sequence

When it comes to batch vectorizing images, you have a few possible applications available to work with. The best known of these is Adobe Streamline, available for both Mac and PC, but unfortunately no longer updated.

Unless you're intending to batch covert a lot of images to vectors, it's probably not worth putting out for a $100+ application. Fortunately, there are quite a few shareware applications around that you might want to try, so these might be of more benefit to you for occasional or sporadic vectorizing. If you don't need to batch a load of images at once, Flash's trace bitmap might just do the trick and will save you some cash in the bargain.

The application I've used here is called Silhouette (www.silhouetteonline.com), a Mac-only program by FreeSoft. It's not particularly cheap, but it is very powerful and fast. It also has the bonus of exporting to SWF format, which makes it ideal for use with Flash. All in all, it was ideal for this project.

After a little experimentation, I decided on the following settings:

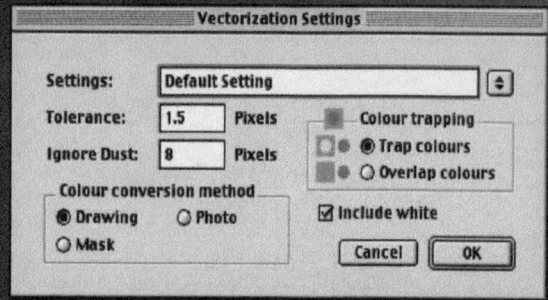

The important setting to know about here is Include White. During early testing, I noticed that I needed to keep the white area to maintain the position of the limb in context to the space, so that I wouldn't need to go through and reposition everything. If the shape is imported alone, then Flash will place them near the registration point according to the height of the vector objects.

These examples below might both look okay, but the next frame of the animation – with the ball at a higher point – would move the arm down a little bit and ruin the animation.

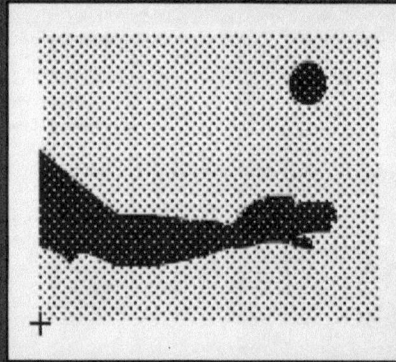
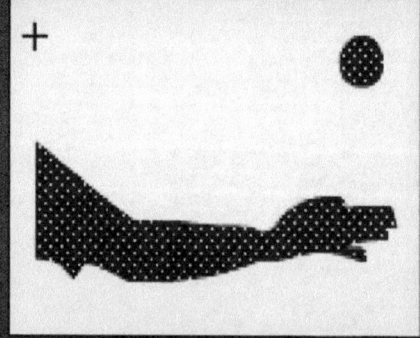

However, there's a downside to including the white area in the animation: all the white has to be deleted before the masking will work – after all, we only want to mask the limbs. In fact, I did find a way to speed through this; I'll let you in on it in the next section.

When it came to the batch vectorizing, I opted to export to the EPS format (as opposed to SWF) because it made batch importing a little easier in Flash and produced a better end result.

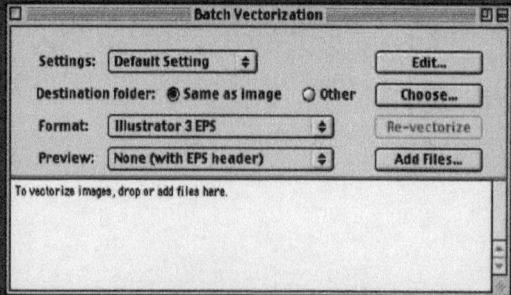

To begin the batching process, just drag and drop a load of files into the bottom part of the Batch area (as shown above). Silhouette is extremely quick at working through a load of images, so before you know it, you should be ready to import the vector shapes into Flash.

Importing the vector masks and video into Flash

You'll be glad to know that this is the final step in the whole import process. We have all the relevant files correctly formatted and all that remains to do is to pull them into a Flash movie (called `mannequin.fla`) and construct them in the right way.

To quickly recap, we have the following files to use in Flash:

- A QuickTime MOV for each limb. These will be used as the imported video for each limb.
- A series of EPS files for each limb. These will mask the imported video.

The PICT files are no longer needed at this point as they were only used for the conversion process from bitmap to vector.

Each limb is contained in its own movie clip. The first thing to do with each limb is to import the EPS files. This process is made easier because Flash offers to import files that it recognizes as making up a sequence. A dialog like this is certainly welcomed:

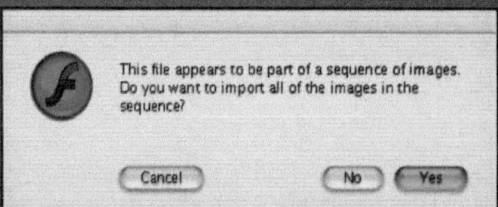

A word of warning here: Flash will only recognize files as a sequence if they're named properly. A list of vector files like these – with each name ending in a number, followed immediately by the file extension – should be okay with Flash:

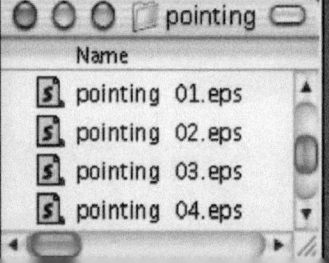

However, Flash will not recognize the following list as a sequence, since the file names (minus the `.eps` extension) all end with the same characters:

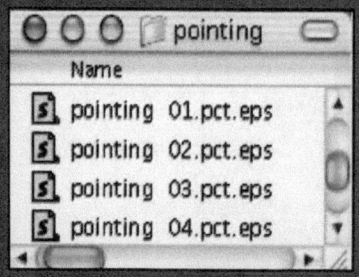

So, if you don't get the dialog offering to do it, try renaming your files to look more like the first example above.

Once the images have been imported as a sequence, they're placed in consecutive key frames on a single layer:

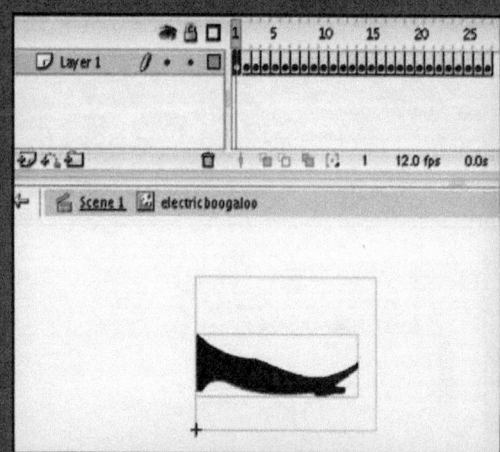

All the vector objects on each keyframe now need to be ungrouped so that we can delete all the white, and leave just the black shape. Done manually, this would be a long, tedious affair; fortunately though, it can be automated using Edit Multiple Frames.

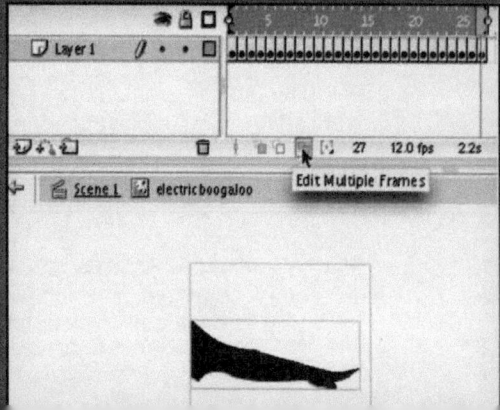

Switch on this option and onion-skin all the frames. Then press CTRL/APPLE+A to select all the grouped vectors.

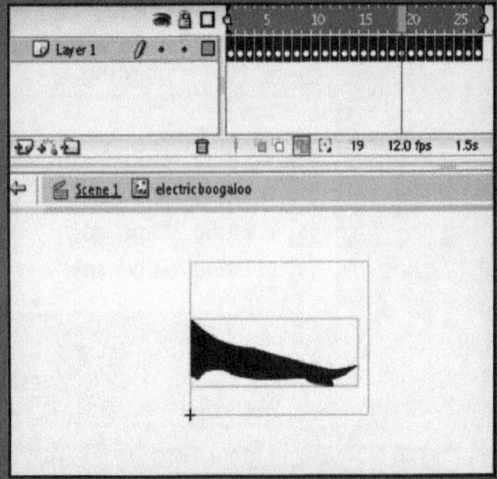

Ungroup them using Modify > Ungroup or CTRL/CMD+SHIFT+G. Do this twice to make sure that all the groups are broken up, and you'll end up with a sequence of raw vector shapes.

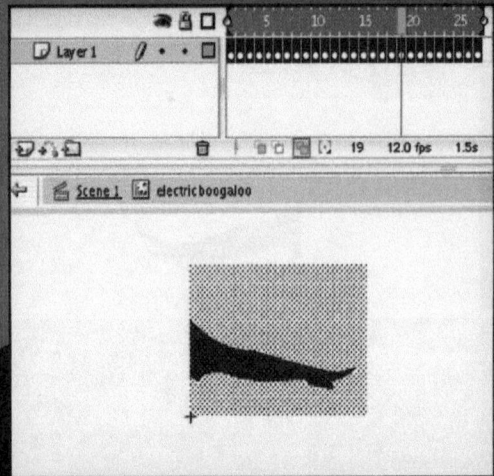

To delete the white, unselect all and then click on the white area and delete it. You'll notice that this has acted on the last frame – this is because of later frames having a greater depth using Edit Multiple Frames. If you select the white area again, the last but one frame will be selected – repeat this step until you have deleted all the white areas and are on frame 1.

This is usually a pretty flawless exercise, but sometimes white areas do tend to get away from you, so you need to manually kill any extra bits.

Once this is done, rename the layer as vectors; now the mask is ready for the video. Add a new layer called video below vectors – this is the layer we'll import the video into.

A few things to note here: the video is 25fps, so I've upped the frame rate to 25fps in the Flash movie; I've imported the video at 50% quality, with a keyframe interval of 48 (this seemed to perform better), synced to the Flash movie and at full size (150 x 113).

Once the video is imported, it needs to be positioned correctly: an x position of 0 and a y position of -113 for the arm movies. This coordinates the video with the imported EPS files. The last thing to do now that they are correctly positioned together is to move them as a unit, making the registration mark the center of the limb point of the arm:

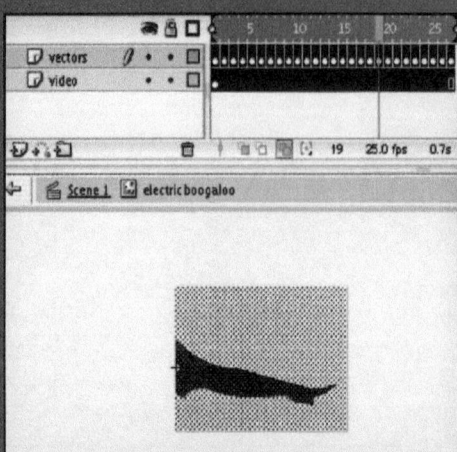

Once this is done, set the vectors layer as a mask layer and the video layer is masked. Lock both layers to have a preview of the masking:

To test the animation, hit ENTER or drag a copy onto the main stage and publish it. That's it for our first limb! Now you need to do the same for each of the others; while this might seem like a chore, it's amazing how quickly you can get through them all once you've done a couple and got the hang of it.

That's the end of our semi-automated process masking our video in Flash. A few of you might have thought of different ways to achieve the same end. One alternative might be to import a transparent PNG sequence instead of video. It would be a pretty good bet because you can avoid all the masking stuff.

Although PNGs of photo-like content might be large, you can set them to use JPEG compression instead to squeeze some more out of it. I think video gives us a smaller file, but the performance might be smoother with PNGs.

Of course, if you have any other suggestions, then please let me know!

Creating the assets for the movie

I don't want to go into too much detail about the individual components of the movie, as most of them are pretty self-explanatory when you look at the FLA. Let's just take a quick look at the folders in the library, to familiarize ourselves before we come to the code.

The alert boxes folder

I've designed this project so that users can save and share creations by cutting and pasting text settings into a text file.

Our first folder contains all the assets required to manage this: the exportAlert movie clip symbol contains a dynamic text field that Flash will use to display the settings used when you want to save them for posterity.

Meanwhile, the loadAlert movie clip symbol contains an input box into which you can type the name of a text file that contains settings you'd like to load in.

The arms folder

This folder contains the video clips and movie clips to display the arm animations, along with the arm dropper movie clip, which is used as a drop target area.

The arm movie clips are set up as we saw earlier, with the video clip playing underneath a vector mask layer. In addition to this, there's an instance of a movie clip called limbpoint on the top layer of each – we'll look at this in more detail later.

Each movie clip has been given a linkage identifier so that we can call it from the code, in the format a1, a2 and so on.

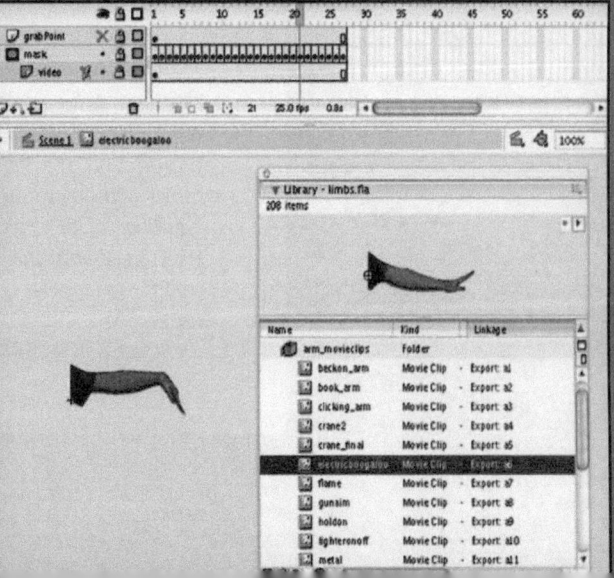

The bgrnds folder

This contains the assets to display the scenic backgrounds of our movie. The bg movie clip is a very simple five-frame movie, containing a different JPEG on each frame, apart from the last one which is empty. This will be called upon from within the ActionScript to change the background.

The body folder

This contains the body movie clip - basically a picture of our rather handsome model, presently limbless, for the user to adorn with as many appendages as he sees fit. The movie clip contains all three of the drop areas we'll be using in the code, with instance names of `dropper17`, `dropper18`, and `dropper19`.

Flash UI Components

There's not much to say about this folder really - it just contains the UI components (and their assets) that I used to build the movie interface.

The legs folder

This contains the movie clips for the leg movement videos, set up in exactly the same way as the arm movie clips, with linkage identifiers following on in the series, from `a21` to `a25`. It also contains the leg drop area.

The library_silhouettes folder

This contains single-frame movie clips representing each of the video clips, using a shape taken from one of the vector masks from the relevant clip. These are used later to make our buttons, which are dynamically attached using ActionScript.

The OTHER folder

This folder contains most of the other important assets we need for the functionality of our movie:

- buttonback is a simple single-frame movie clip, which is used as a button.

- flipTest is a two-frame movie clip, which highlights which mode the user is currently in: Display or Edit.

- libraryStore is perhaps the most important movie clip in this folder, as it's used within the ActionScript to create our buttons. It's a 25-frame movie that consists of two layers: the top layer contains an instance of backbut, which is used to define button functionality; each frame in the bottom layer contains a silhouette movie clip, with the frame number corresponding to the relevant movie clip's linkage identifier.

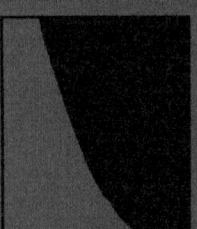

This was designed so that we can use the same counter within the code to refer to the button and the video. For example, the movie clip electricboogaloo *has a linkage identifier of a6; meanwhile the silhouette that represents the rather groovy electric boogaloo movie is in frame 6 of the* libraryStore *movie clip (whose linkage identifier is* grabButtons*).*

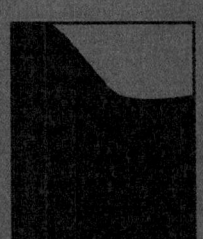
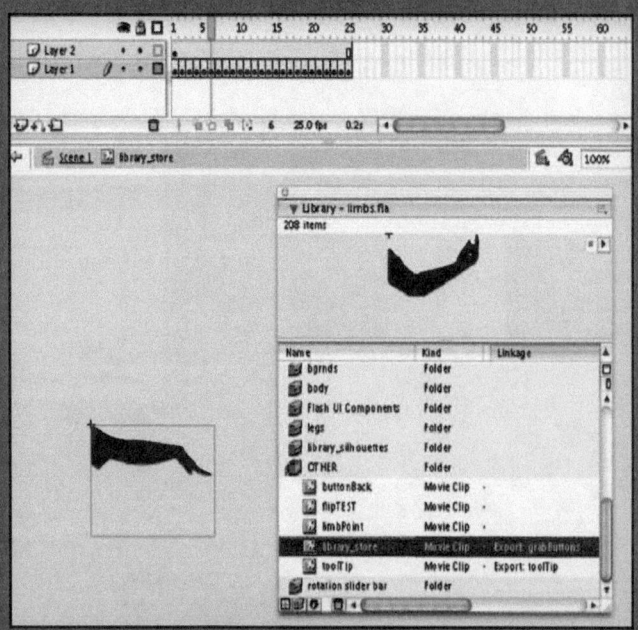

- Limbpoint is a two-frame movie with a `stop` action in each frame. It is attached to each video clip to allow the user to drag and drop the limbs, and the two frames represent whether the limb is currently selected or not.

- Tooltip is a single-frame movie clip containing a non-selectable dynamic text field. This is used to display the name of each limb clip when the relevant button is rolled over.

The rotation slider bar folder

This contains the assets for... yes, you guessed it: the rotation slider bar. We will allow users the ability to change the rotation of the limb(s) once attached, by moving this slider from left to right.

Dissecting the code

Now that we've looked at all our assets, let's examine the engine of our project - the ActionScript.

When scripting, I attempted to be modular, coding the application so that adding new limbs or assets isn't much of a nightmare. The limb palettes, for instance, are dynamically attached using ActionScript, allowing them all to be easily repositioned, manipulated or removed by changing a few figures.

All of the code in the movie is placed on frame 1 of the actions layer on the main timeline.

Initializing the movie

The first function sets up a number of essential things in the movie. The call to this function will take place right at the very end of the code, and will start the ball rolling. Besides setting a few essential variables, it also performs a system check and creates the limb buttons or palettes.

```
initFunc = function() {
  fscommand("allowscale", "false");
  stageWidth = 700;
  stageHeight = 600;
  exportStr = "";
```

This fscommand stops the published movie from being scaled out of proportion, and the stage's size is stored in the following two variables.

The next piece of code in the file is actually one of the last pieces that I added. I work on both a Mac and a PC, and I know how much slower the Mac Flash player can be. To try and compensate a little for this fact, I decided to run a quick system test to determine the host system, and then set the movie's quality accordingly. This can be done using the new System Capabilities object. When you check the current operating system, Flash will return a full system string, for example, "Windows XP", or "Mac OS 10.1.5".

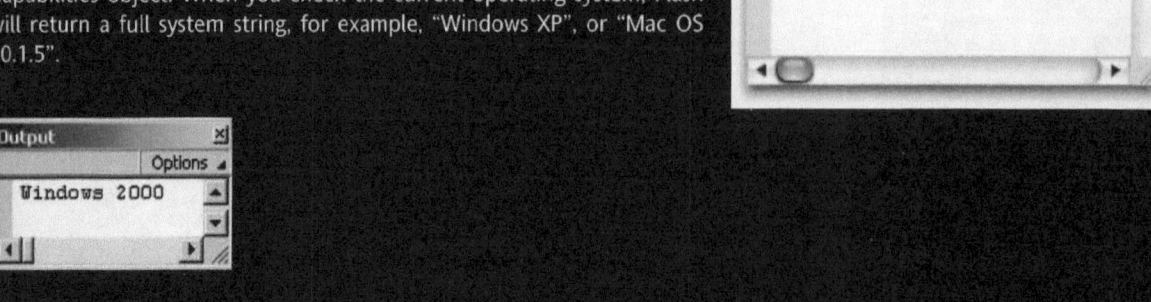

All we need from this string are the first three characters ("Win" or "Mac") to tell the difference between them. Okay, so we could have just used the first letter, but this makes it more readable. We use a substring to read just the first three characters, and then set the quality accordingly. Here's the code:

```
sys = System.capabilities.os;
  if (sys.substring(0, 3) == "Win") {
    _quality = "high";
  } else if (sys.substring(0, 3) == "Mac") {
    _quality = "medium";
  }
```

After determining the quality that the movie will play at, it's time to turn to the content itself. The following code sets up the limb library palettes.

First up, some basic variables:

```
limbDepth = 2000;
currentLimb = "";
```

limbDepth is the initial depth of the limbs. Every time a new limb is created, this number is incremented to ensure that each limb is on its own level.

currentLimb will contain the name of the currently selected limb. It's blank until we start bringing limbs onto the stage.

Then a textArray to hold the names of all of our animations:

```
textArray = new Array("", "beckoning", "reading",
      "clicking", "scooping", "patting", "boogaloo",
      "waving lighter", "shooting", "stopping",
      "lighting lighter", "rocking", "flexing",
      "juggling", "warning", "punching",
      "waving lighter", "drinking", "catching",
      "disagreeing", "agreeing", "forward kick",
      "kicking back", "jumping", "kicking", "swanning");
```

It's used when we display the tool tips. It's a pretty no-frills array, the only vaguely noteworthy feature being the blank first entry because the index of animations begins at 1, but the array begins at 0.

Next, we set the buttons for each of our limb animations.

To lay out our buttons, we need to set a number of variables for the arms and legs individually. We start though with a variable for both:

Left Arm Palette

```
count = 1;
```

The `count` variable is used to keep track of which button we're making. Now onto the variables for the different limb types, starting with those for the arms.

We firstly set the number of `columns` and `rows` that we want in each set of buttons – there are two sets of buttons, one for right-handed limbs, and one for left-handed limbs:

```
columns = 2;
rows = 10;
```

Next, we have some variables to position the button sets:

```
armlefttypos = 283;
armleftxpos = 60;
armrighttypos = 283;
armrightxpos = 578;
armxmult = 50;
armymult = 30;
```

The first four variables here set the x and y positions of the two grids – one for right arms and one for left. (It's worth noting here that where the code says left, we're talking about *our* left: that's our model's *right*-hand side. The variables `armxmult` and `armymult` set the multiplication or spacing for the grid.

Next, we have a variable to determine how small the buttons will be compared to the actual movie clip that we're using:

```
armButtonPercent = 30;
```

Now it's time to position the buttons, starting with the left-hand set. We set up a set of simple nested `for` loops for the `rows` and `columns` of our buttons:

```
for (i=0; i<rows; i++) {
    for (j=0; j<columns; j++) {
```

Next, we attach our movie clip from the Library, and set a variable, `current`, to store its path:

```
current = _root.attachMovie("grabButtons",
                    ➥"grabButton"+count, count);
```

This attaches an instance of the libraryStore movie clip (whose linkage name is grabButtons) for each button.

Then comes more code for our buttons' positioning and display:

```
                current._x = (j*armxmult)+armleftxpos;
                current._y = (i*armymult)+armleftypos;
                current.gotoAndStop(count);
                current._xscale = armButtonPercent;
                current._yscale = armButtonPercent;
                current.hFlip();
                limbBut.call(current.butBack, count, true);
                count++;
            }
    }
```

We position each button, and set its image to the correct frame in the movie clip. We also set the button's size, and attach the `hFlip` function to it. We'll come to this function a little later, but basically it flips the silhouettes horizontally, as in the library we only have left-handed clips.

We use the `call` method to attach the `limbBut` function to current.butBack. Again, we'll look at this function later, but it basically controls what happens when we click on a button. We ▓▓▓▓▓▓▓▓ of parameters to the function – the first holds the number of the limb that we need to attach, and the ▓▓▓▓▓▓▓▓ f the limb is reversed. Again, we need the limb movie clips to be reversed when they are attached to th▓▓▓▓▓▓▓▓ e moment they are all left arm clips, and this is the palette for the right arm, on the left hand side.

The code for the right-hand set of buttons is almost exactly the same:

```
        for (i=0; i<rows; i++) {
            for (j=0; j<columns; j++) {
                current = _root.attachMovie("grabButtons",
                                     "grabButton"+count, count);
                current._x = (j*armxmult)+armrightxpos;
                current._y = (i*armymult)+armrightypos;
                current.gotoAndStop(count-20);
                current._xscale = armButtonPercent;
                current._yscale = armButtonPercent;
                limbBut.call(current.butBack, count-20);
                count++;
            }
        }
```

The only differences this time a▓▓▓▓▓▓▓▓llows:

■   We place the buttons on the ▓▓▓▓▓▓▓▓ of the stage.

■   We subtract the total number of ▓▓▓▓▓▓▓▓ 20) from the current `count` value. This ensures that we get the correct image for the button, along with the correct limb animation when we press it.

■   We don't need to flip the button images or the attached video clips.

The code for the legs is very similar, with a number of declared variables to start:

```
legsNum = 5;
leftlegxpos = 395;
leftlegypos = 553;
rightlegxpos = 145;
rightlegypos = 553;
legxmult = 35;
legButtonPercent = 25;
```

There are no column, row, or y multiplier variables here, since we want the legs laid out in a single row. The following chunk of code now lays out both right and left leg sets, and closes the initialization function:

```
for (j=0; j<legsNum; j++) {
    current = _root.attachMovie("grabButtons",
                        ➡ "grabButton"+count, count);
    current._x = (j*legxmult)+leftlegxpos;
    current._y = leftlegypos;
    current.gotoAndStop(count-20);
    current._xscale = legButtonPercent;
    current._yscale = legButtonPercent;
    current.hFlip();
    limbBut.call(current.butBack, count-20, true);
    count++;
}
for (j=0; j<legsNum; j++) {
    current = _root.attachMovie("grabButtons",
                        ➡ "grabButton"+count, count);
    current._x = (j*legxmult)+rightlegxpos;
    current._y = rightlegypos;
    current.gotoAndStop(count-25);
    current._xscale = legButtonPercent;
    current._yscale = legButtonPercent;
    limbBut.call(current.butBack, count-25);
    count++;
}
};
```

Flipping methods

Next, we need to define a couple of prototype methods. Once defined, these methods will become a part of every movie clip on the stage. So in this example, we're creating a method to flip a movie clip along an axis.

The first method, hFlip, (which you'll remember from the button layout code) flips along the horizontal axis, and the second method, vFlip, flips along the vertical axis. Once these prototypes are defined, we can use them to flip any movie clip on the stage.

The simplest way to flip a movie clip over is to multiply its _xscale (or _yscale) property by -1:

```
MovieClip.prototype.hFlip = function() {
    this._xscale *= -1;
};
MovieClip.prototype.vFlip = function() {
    this._yscale *= -1;
};
```

I know we've already seen one use for the `hFlip` function, but I also wanted to assign these functions to two movie clip buttons on the stage (hFlipBut and vFlipBut) so that the user has the ability to click them and flip the currently selected limb animation (`currentLimb`):

```
hFlipBut.onRelease = function() {
  _root[currentLimb].hFlip();
};
vFlipBut.onRelease = function() {
  _root[currentLimb].vFlip();
};
```

Centering methods

In the same way as the flip methods were created, there are also two methods to center movie clips according to the stage size (as defined in the initialization function). These methods are used particularly with the load and save dialog boxes, which you will see a little later. Here's the code for the centering methods:

```
MovieClip.prototype.hCenter = function() {
  this._x = (stageWidth/2)-(this._width/2);
};
MovieClip.prototype.vCenter = function() {
  this._y = (stageHeight/2)-(this._height/2);
};
```

A movie clip is then centered horizontally using the method like so:

```
MyMovieClip.hCenter();
```

Now let's take a look at how the buttons get their abilities.

Placing the limbs on the body

The `dropFunc` function is the main engine for determining the placement of limbs on the body. It's attached to the `limbPoint` movie clip on every limb. This means that whenever we refer to _parent within this function, we are talking about the whole limb, and not just the `limbPoint`.

First of all, we stop the limb animation from playing when it's being dragged:

```
dropFunc = function() {
  this._parent.stop();
```

This helps prevent the movie seeming too busy when you're arranging limbs, and also gives the processor a break from animating and dragging at the same time.

Next, we apply a new function, `dropDetect`, to the `limbPoint`:

`_root.dropDetect.apply(this);`This function contains code that *detects* when we've dropped a limb – we'll take a proper look at it shortly.

Next, we set up an `onPress` event:

```
this.onPress = function() {
  this._parent.stop();
  _root.dropDetect.apply(this);
```

This simply repeats the previous code, but this time it takes effect when we click on an existing limbPoint (rather than when we're just dragging a limb from a button). Once we've clicked on a limb, we need to start dragging it around with the mouse:

```
this._parent.startDrag();
```

In the initialization function at the beginning of this code, we defined a variable called currentLimb. We'll now use that to help keep track of which limb we've selected. As we saw when we looked at the limbPoint movie clip earlier, each limbPoint has two states: the first is a small gray circle; the second is a larger, brighter circle that indicates the limbPoint is selected. So, we now want to make sure that the previously selected limbPoint is set back to its gray 'off' state, while the newly selected one is set to its colored 'on' state:

```
_root[currentLimb].limbPoint.gotoAndStop(1);
_root.currentLimb = this._parent._name;
_root[currentLimb].limbPoint.gotoAndStop(2);
```

So, these three lines basically reset the old limbPoint, change currentLimb to reflect the limb we're currently dragging, and then set its limbPoint to the 'on' state.

Next, we send some settings to our rotation slider on the stage:

```
_root.angler = _root[currentLimb]._rotation;
_root.sliderBar.slideDrag._x =
        ➥ _root.angler/(fullrotation/100);
    };
};
```

We want the slider to reflect the rotation of the currently selected clip, so that you can see the changes applied in real time. We'll cover the rotation in more detail a little later on.

Listening out for a dropped limb

When a user picks up a limb they can do two things with it – place it somewhere on the body, or drop it elsewhere on the stage where it will drop off the screen and be removed. The dropDetect function defines all the code that kicks in when you release a limb that you're currently dragging.

I initially had a few problems with this functionality, because limbs are attached to the mouse when the appropriate silhouette button is pressed on the stage. We need to detect when the limb is released so that we can check its drop target, but because the initial press was on the button, not the limb, we can't detect an onRelease event on the limb. I thought about using a two-click system – where you click once on the limb silhouette to attach it to the mouse, and click again to release it onto the body – but this system didn't feel at all natural.

How was I going to get Flash to detect when a limb had been dropped on the stage? In the end, I got around the problem by using onMouseUp instead of onRelease. This approach came with its own problem though: onMouseUp events are global, so the event will fire every time the mouse button is released – whether or not the user's currently dragging a limb. Solution: only define the onMouseUp handler when we start dragging a limb, and undefine it as soon as the limb's dropped.

So, the first thing to do when dropDetect is called is to define the onMouseUp handler function. This has to do several things: first and foremost, it stops the limb getting dragged about:

```
dropDetect = function() {
   this.onMouseUp = function() {
      this._parent.stopDrag();
```

After that, it uses the parent's _droptarget to detect whether we've dropped the limb on the body, or just on the stage:

```
tempStr = eval(this._parent._droptarget);
```

Note that I've used eval to check the target path. Flash will return the drop target using slash notation (to preserve Flash 4 compatibility), so we use eval to convert the path to dot notation. We then store it in the variable tempStr.

All our defined drop areas have the name dropperXX, where XX is a two-digit number. Rather than running a loop to check through all of the drop areas on the stage, we can instead simply cut the last two characters from the end of the path, so that every instance effectively has the same name of just dropper.

This may seem like overkill for only three drop points, but the original idea was to have dynamically user-added points, and the functionality was left in just in case it was decided to go back down that route.

Next, we define a new String object containing our path:

```
s = new String(tempStr);
```

Next, we use the slice method to cut the last two characters from the string:

```
tempStr = s.slice(0, -2);
```

> By using a minus number for the end point of a slice, you effectively count backwards from the end of the string, rather than going forwards from the start.

Once that's done, we check to see if we've dropped the limb on any of our drop areas, no matter which one it is:

```
if (tempStr == "") {
    return;
}
```

If the limb has been dropped anywhere but on a drop point, we return nothing from the function.

If we've dropped it on a defined drop area, we remove any onEnterFrame events that might be running (we set one initially to attach the limb to the mouse after clicking the silhouette button), and start the limb animation playing again:

```
if (tempStr == "_level0.tshirt.dropper") {
    this.onEnterFrame = undefined;
    this._parent.play();
```

Otherwise, we clearly haven't dropped the limb on a defined drop area. We therefore set up an onEnterFrame event that will move the limb down the screen until it drops off the bottom, and then we remove it:

```
} else {
    this._parent.onEnterFrame = function() {
        this._y += 10;
        if (this._y>650) {
            this.removeMovieClip();
        }
    };
}
```

Finally, we remove the onMouseUp event to stop it from firing whenever the mouse is clicked:

```
            this.onMouseUp = undefined;
        };
    };
```

Functionality for the buttons

The next thing we need to do is define a function to apply to the silhouette buttons on the main stage. We pass two parameters to this function when we call it: numb and reverse. numb is the number of the button (so that we can attach the correct video clip to it) and reverse determines whether the video clip should be displayed normally (if it's on our right-hand side) or in reverse (if it's on our left-hand side):

```
    limbBut = function (numb, reverse) {
```

The first thing we define in the function is an onRollOver event:

```
    this.onRollOver = function() {
        _root.attachMovie("toolTip", "toolTip", 999999);
        _root.toolTip._x = -100;
        _root.toolTip._y = -100;
        _root.toolTip.onEnterFrame = function() {
          this._x = _xmouse;
          this._y = _ymouse;
        };
```

This event attaches a tool tip text field (called toolTip) to the mouse. The text field inside the movie clip is set below-left of center so that it won't impinge on the mouse cursor when it's displayed.

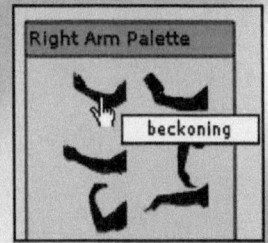

Another thing that I found was that if the movie clip was attached, and then positioned in an onEnterFrame event, it would appear briefly in the top corner of the screen before being repositioned at the mouse cursor. I solved this by positioning the movie clip off-screen directly after it was attached, and then running the onEnterFrame action afterwards.

Next, we pull the correct descriptive text out of the array that we defined earlier (in the initialization function), and place it into our tool tip:

```
        _root.toolTip.Hint.text = _root.textArray[numb];
    };
```

Finally, we define an onRollOut event to remove the tool tip:

```
    this.onRollOut = function() {
        _root.toolTip.removeMovieClip();
    };
```

The next bit of code to add is what happens when the button is clicked.

First of all, we no longer need the tool tip to be displayed, so we remove it:

```
    this.onPress = function() {
        _root.toolTip.removeMovieClip();
```

Next, we increment our `limbDepth` counter and attach the appropriate animation:

```
_root.attachMovie("a"+numb, "limb"+_root.limbDepth,
                                  ➡ _root.limbDepth);
```

We also need to set the state of `limbPoint` to indicate that our new limb is the currently selected one. We do this in exactly the same method as we did before:

```
_root[currentLimb].limbPoint.gotoAndStop(1);
_root.currentLimb = "limb"+_root.limbDepth;
_root[currentLimb].limbPoint.gotoAndStop(2);
```

Following that, we also reset the rotation slider accordingly:

```
_root.angler = _root[currentLimb]._rotation;
_root.sliderBar.slideDrag._x =
          ➡ _root.angler/(fullrotation/100);
```

Next, we set up a variable, `limbName`, to hold the path to our limb. We do this both as a means of shorthand, and so that if we change the name at any point in the life of the code, we only need to change this variable:

```
limbName = _root["limb"+_root.limbDepth];
```

The next line of code stores the number of the current limb – as taken from the linkage for this limb. This will be used much later on when it comes to exporting and importing the creation.

```
limbName.frame = numb;
```

We now need to set the orientation of the left-hand limbs using our previously defined `hFlip` method:

```
if (reverse) {
  limbName.hFlip();
}
```

After setting the type and orientation of our limb, it's time to position it. We set it to the mouse position, and then start dragging it:

```
limbName._x = _xmouse;
limbName._y = _ymouse;
limbName.startDrag();
```

Finally, we attach the `dropFunc` function to the `limbPoint` of our current limb:

```
_root.dropFunc.apply(limbName.limbPoint);
_root.limbDepth++;
    };
  };
```

Edit and display modes

Now that we've got our main code up and running, we can add some extra features. The first of these is a couple of buttons to switch between an edit mode and a display mode. In edit mode, we can attach new limbs to the body, and interact with the limbs that are already there.

In display mode however, the body comes to the fore, giving a cleaner view of our animation.

The code for the buttons is fairly simple:

```
editBut.onRelease = function() {
  _root.tshirt.swapDepths(1500);
  _root.tshirt.dropper17._visible = true;
  _root.tshirt.dropper18._visible = true;
  _root.tshirt.dropper19._visible = true;
  this.gotoAndStop(2);
  _root.displayBut.gotoAndPlay(1);
};
_root.editBut.gotoAndStop(2);
```

We just change the depth of the body movie clip, and hide or show the drop areas. We then toggle the state of the currently selected button and its opposite number, so that when it's 'on' the background color of the button changes.

The code for the Display button is placed within a function, because it's not only called by `displayBut`, but also whenever the user loads in a saved creation:

```
displayMode = function() {
  _root.tshirt.swapDepths(6004);
  _root.tshirt.dropper17._visible = false;
  _root.tshirt.dropper18._visible = false;
  _root.tshirt.dropper19._visible = false;
  _root[currentLimb].limbPoint.gotoAndStop(1);
  _root.displayBut.gotoAndStop(2);
  _root.editBut.gotoAndPlay(1);
};
displayBut.onRelease = function() {
  displayMode();
};
```

The only other point to note is that there's an extra line in the Display button code, which sets the currently selected `limbPoint` to its 'off' state. We do this to make sure that it's not visible when we display our animation.

Limb rotation

Our final addition is to code a slider that we can use to alter the rotation of the selected limb.

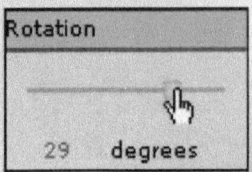

First, we set a variable defining the total degree of rotation that we want people to be able to apply to a limb. Your average human limb has about 180 degrees of movement (from side of head to side of body on the y-plane – we don't want to cross the body yet), but this seemed a little too much in testing, so it was limited to 120 degrees:

```
fullrotation = 120;
```

We set up a simple slider by locking its movement to a fixed range along one axis, and then translating its position to a rotation amount for the currently selected limb:

```
sliderBar.slideDrag.onPress = function() {
  this.startDrag(true, -50, 0, 50, 0);
  this.onEnterFrame = function() {
    _root.angler = Math.round(this._x*(fullrotation/100));
    _root[currentLimb]._rotation = _root.angler;
  };
};
```

When we're done with changing the rotation, we simply release the slider, and the `onEnterFrame` event is removed:

```
sliderBar.slideDrag.onRelease = function() {
  this.stopDrag();
  this.onEnterFrame = undefined;
};
```

Exporting the creation

I thought it would be cool for people to share their creations with others, so I decided to add some saving functionality. Normally, for web-based projects, I'd have the option of saving to a database or creating a new XML document, but to save on all the preparation jazz that comes with those avenues, I've opted to use the somewhat arcane method of dumping an export string to the screen. The exported string can then be copied and pasted and saved in a text file in a text editor like NotePad on Windows or TextEdit on the Mac.

Here's an export of a favorite of mine – I call it rocking gently (pre-saved for your pleasure as `rocking_gently.txt`):

```
&limbXpos1=365.95&limbYpos1=246.95&limbRot1=0&limbXsize1=-100&limbYsize1=100&limbFrame1=25
&limbXpos2=316&limbYpos2=247.95&limbRot2=0&limbXsize2=100&limbYsize2=100&limbFrame2=24&limbXp
os3=294.05&limbYpos3=131&limbRot3=41&limbXsize3=-100&limbYsize3=100&limbFrame3=11&limbXpos4
=384.1&limbYpos4=138.05&limbRot4=-32&limbXsize4=100&limbYsize4=100&limbFrame4=17&limbsTotal=5
```

If this looks alien to you, and if you've never imported a text file into Flash, fear not: there isn't much to it. The previous string is simply a list of variables, separated by the & symbol, which are imported into Flash. It might make it easier if you look at a shorter example:

```
&name=Ken Jokol&age=25&website=pinderkaas
```

There are three variables here to extract:

```
name = "Ken Jokol"
age = 25
website = "pinderkaas"
```

Remember that each variable is separated by the ampersand (&) symbol. In fact, Flash will only load in files starting with this symbol.

When a text file of this format is loaded into Flash – we'll see how in the next section – Flash extracts the variables and places them within the Flash movie. These can then be used as can any other variable in the Flash movie.

A note here – exporting or writing information to a txt file or a database on a server requires use of a server-side script, such as PHP, ASP, Perl or ColdFusion. If you'd like to store information on the users machine, take a look at Flash MX's shared object. The shared object acts like a giant cookie, allowing vast storage.

Before we actually get to the script, it's probably worth looking at the information that needs to be dumped for each creation. Firstly, each limb will need to be exported, and for each of these there is a list of properties to store:

- the limb type (for example 'rocking', 'pointing')
- the x and y position of the limb
- the limb's rotation
- the horizontal and vertical flip of the limb

The export functionality is attached to the exportButton instance:

```
exportButton.onRelease = function() {
    exportCount = 1;
```

exportCount is used here to number the variables during dumping. Before we get on to specific properties, we need to check that each limb exists. Why do this? Well, to cover up for limbs that we removed during creation. This saves us keeping an array of the objects, which would need to be reshuffled after every released limb.

```
for (i=2000; i<_root.limbDepth; i++) {
    exportLimb = _root["limb"+i];
    if (exportLimb) {
```

Here, we begin by setting up a for loop to run from the base depth level (2000) to the maximum limbDepth. The next line of code sets exportLimb to be a limb object using the counting variable i. Of course, if a limb object no longer exists – say the first limb dragged on (aka _root.limb2000), was removed – then this would equal nothing or be undefined. The next line of code then checks if it does exist, looking for a true to proceed to the code where it fetches the properties.

Then we have some code that grabs the properties of the current existing limb:

```
xpos = exportLimb._x;
ypos = exportLimb._y;
rot = exportLimb._rotation;
xsize = exportLimb._xscale;
ysize = exportLimb._yscale;
exframe = exportLimb.frame;
```

The first five of these actually check directly from the object itself; the last takes its value from the variable stored during the object's creation.

These lines of code then add the stored properties to the `exportStr` string:

```
exportStr += "&limbXpos"+exportCount+"="+xpos;
exportStr += "&limbYpos"+exportCount+"="+ypos;
exportStr += "&limbRot"+exportCount+"="+rot;
exportStr += "&limbXsize"+exportCount+"="+xsize;
exportStr += "&limbYsize"+exportCount+"="+ysize;
exportStr += "&limbFrame"+exportCount+"="+exframe;
//
exportCount++;
}
}
```

At this point, it's worth pointing out how the variables are written. Basically, each variable name has to be different. Even though we're dealing with values stored for different limbs, if there are two variables called `limbXpos`, the second one will over-write the first.

Let's look at one of our limbs again:

```
&limbXpos1=365.95&limbYpos1=246.95&limbRot1=0&limbXsize1=-100&limbYsize1=100&limbFrame1=25
```

Each variable name is suffixed with a number, making each one unique. This makes life simpler when it comes to importing, since each variable is easily referenced.

These next lines of code simply stop the user pressing the SAVE or LOAD buttons while they're performing one or the other:

```
_root.importButton._visible = false;
_root.exportButton._visible = false;
```

Once the `for` loop is finished, we check to see if there's any data to dump by finding out whether `exportStr` is equal to nothing:

```
if (exportStr == "") {
exportStr = "No data to export";
```

If `exportStr` has some data, then the string is suffixed with the number of limbs being exported:

```
} else {
exportStr += "&limbsTotal="+(exportCount);
}
```

This makes the importing procedure easier as Flash will know how many limbs to import.

In light of all this, let's remind ourselves how `rocking_gently` looks in dumped form:

```
&limbXpos1=365.95&limbYpos1=246.95&limbRot1=0&limbXsize1=-100&limbYsize1=100&limbFrame1=25&
limbXpos2=316&limbYpos2=247.95&limbRot2=0&limbXsize2=100&limbYsize2=100&limbFrame2=24&limbXpo
s3=294.05&limbYpos3=131&limbRot3=41&limbXsize3=-100&limbYsize3=100&limbFrame3=11&limbXpos4=
384.1&limbYpos4=138.05&limbRot4=-32&limbXsize4=100&limbYsize4=100&limbFrame4=17&limbsTotal=5
```

Now that we have all the data gathered, it needs to be presented so that the user can copy and paste it. I've decided to go for a standard pop-up window within Flash so that it stands out from the rest of the interface.

EXPORTED DATA. Copy and paste into a text document and save as .txt

&armXpos1=295&armYpos1=132.95&armRot1=44&armXsize1=-100&armYsize1=100&armFrame1=&armXpos2=388.95&armYpos2=130.95&armRot2=-208&armXsize2=100&armYsize2=100&armFrame2=&armXpos3=316.05&armYpos3=235.1&armRot3=0&armXsize3=100&armYsize3=100&armFrame3=&armXpos4=363.05&armYpos4=246.05&armRot4=0&armXsize4=-100&armYsize4=100&armFrame4=&armsTotal=5

OK

This window has the linkage name of exportLinkage and is attached from the library:

```
_root.attachMovie("exportLinkage", "exportWin", 9768);
_root.exportWin.outputStr = exportStr;
_root.exportWin.hCenter();
_root.exportWin.vCenter();
```

`outputText` is a dynamic text box that displays the data, so the `exportStr` data is sent to it. The last two lines here use the aforementioned `hCenter` and `vCenter` methods to center the window according to the stage size.

The last thing left to do in our export code is to provide the OK button with some code:

```
_root.exportWin.okButton.onRelease = function() {
  removeMovieClip (_root.exportWin);
  exportStr = "";
  _root.importButton._visible = true;
  _root.exportButton._visible = true;
}
};
```

This simply removes the window from the screen (using `removeMovieClip`), clears the `exportStr` variable ready for the next save, and brings back the SAVE and LOAD buttons so they can be used again.

That's it for the export code. Now we need a way to get the data back in – via the import window.

Loading data

As mentioned earlier, Flash saves us a lot of effort when it comes to importing data – converting text files (or data from other sources) into variables ready for use. Because the data is presented to us, we need to write a function to parse (or run through) each of the variables and redraw the creation. This isn't too difficult to do because all the hard work was done during our export.

The user can request to load a file by clicking the LOAD button:

A window will appear on screen asking for a URL or text filename. This is accompanied by OK and CANCEL buttons. The contents of the input text box you see here are hooked up to the variable `importFilename`.

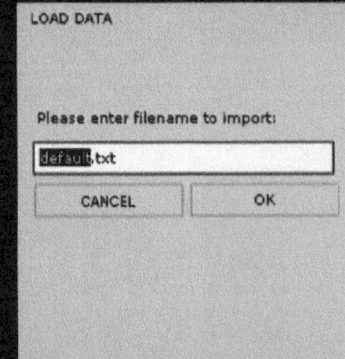

We now set up the OK button, storing the user input in the variable `filename`:

```
_root.loadWin.okButton.onRelease = function() {
    filename = _root.loadWin.importFilename;
```

The next line sets up a new `loadVars` object called `importData`:

```
importData = new LoadVars();
```

This will be used to store all the variables that need to be loaded in.

We now set up a function to run in the event that the data's been received by Flash:

```
importData.onLoad = function() {
```

We need to set this up before we actually load the data in.

Then we set up a `for` loop, which just runs through all the clips and removes them – whether or not they still exist:

```
for (i=2000; i<_root.limbDepth; i++) {
    current = _root["limb"+i];
    removeMovieClip(current);
}
```

We could use a check to see if the current instance exists as we did with the export data, but `removeMovieClip` isn't fussy, so we don't really need to bother.

These next few lines prepare the movie to recreate the loaded data:

```
_root.limbDepth = 2000;
removeMovieClip(_root.loadWin);
_root.onEnterFrame = undefined;
```

Firstly, we initialize the `limbDepth` variable, then remove the pop-up window and clear the `onEnterFrame` handler function.

The next section of code concentrates on importing and drawing from the data. This line creates a `for` loop using the `limbsTotal` variable from the `importData` object:

```
for (i=0; i<importData.limbsTotal; i++) {
```

This will run through the data for every limb saved in the text file, creating it and positioning it:

```
framenum = importData["limbFrame"+i];
limbName = _root.attachMovie("a"+framenum, "limb"+ _root.limbDepth,
                                                    _root.limbDepth);
```

The first line of code here extracts the limb type from the loaded data. `framenum` is set to a value fetched from any of the numbered `limbFrame` variables (for example, `limbFrame1` or `limbFrame2`) using `i` as a suffix number.

Although square-bracketed referencing is usually used for instances and objects, it can also be used for variables, as we've done here.

The last line then sets a variable to reference the currently created limb. This is used as a shortcut here to set its properties:

```
limbName._x = importData["limbXpos"+i];
limbName._y = importData["limbYpos"+i];
limbName._rotation = importData["limbRot"+i];
limbName._xscale = importData["limbXsize"+i];
limbName._yscale = importData["limbYsize"+i];
```

All these values are set to variables taken from the loaded data. This is the most important part of the code, as it's responsible for recreating all the user's superb creations.

All that now remains to be done is to apply dragability to the limbs, and increase the limbDepth ready for the next item in the list:

```
_root.dropFunc.apply(limbName.limbPoint);
limbName.play();
_root.limbDepth++;
}
}
```

Once the loop has finished and all the limbs have been placed, the onLoad function is closed.

We bring back the SAVE and LOAD buttons, and change to displayMode to show our creations in their best light:

```
_root.importButton._visible = true;
_root.exportButton._visible = true;
displayMode();
```

The final line of code actually loads our text data into the importData object. Once the data's loaded in, the onLoad function we created a second ago will kick in.

```
importData.load(filename);
};
};
```

The last piece of code for the loading is the script for the CANCEL button. Most of this should be familiar by now:

```
_root.loadWin.cancelButton.onRelease = function() {
removeMovieClip (_root.loadWin);
_root.importButton._visible = true;
_root.exportButton._visible = true;
}
};
```

That's it for the saving and loading code for now. It's not the best method of storage in the world, but it's a quick, easy, and effective way to let users share their Frankenstein creations.

Changing the background image

Background images were included in the Flash movie to provide a little depth and context to the creations. I've provided a series of four JPEG images contained within the bg movie clip.

There are two other options on the menu: cycle all and clear. The former runs through all of the images in succession, while the latter gives us a blank canvas.

I toyed with the idea of providing a loadMovie option to dynamically load in a JPEG image from a URL or file location, but decided against it, as I didn't want to overcomplicate things. If you're interested in dynamically loading a JPEG into Flash, try something like this:

```
// create a blank movie clip to store the loaded image
_root.createEmptyMovieClip("jpegHolder", 1);

// specify where a JPEG image file can be found
imageUrl = "http://www.pinderkaas.com/image.jpg";

// use loadMovie to load an image from the set location
jpegHolder.loadMovie(imageUrl);
```

If you want to read more about loading JPEGs dynamically into Flash, take a look at the chapter I wrote for "Flash MX Application & Interface Design" (ISBN 1-904344070).

The easiest way to place a list neatly within the interface is to use a drop-down style menu, usually popular in HTML web pages. Flash MX has several built-in interface components like the drop-down menu (called a ComboBox), which are fully customizable and easy to work with.

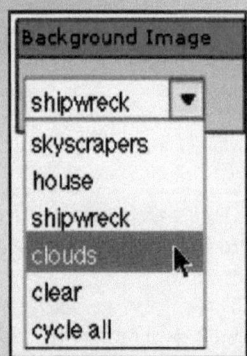

The code to set this drop-down and to change the image is quite painless. Firstly, the menu items need to be set; I used an array for this.

```
imageArray = new Array ('skyscrapers', 'house', 'shipwreck',
➡                                'clouds', 'clear', 'cycle all');
```

The next section writes these array values to the ComboBox menu – which I gave an instance name of dropdown. The addItem method of the ComboBox is used here to apply two things:

- a label for the menu item ("skyscrapers" or "clouds")
- a data value (1, 2)

Here's the code:

```
for (i=0; i<imageArray.length; i++) {
  dropdown.addItem (imageArray [i], i+1);
}
```

The data value stored here is a number that we'll extract in the next function:

```
getImageSelection = function() {
    selectedImage = dropdown.getSelectedItem().data;
```

The `getSelectedItem` method here allows us to read the data value of the selected element of the ComboBox so that we can send the `bg` timeline to that particular frame:

```
if (selectedImage == imageArray.length) {
    bg.gotoAndPlay (1);
} else {
    bg.gotoAndStop (selectedImage);
}
}
```

The `if` statement here checks to see if the dropdown is set to the 'cycle all' element, in which case it sends the `bg` timeline playing wildly. If any other drop-down selection has been made, the `bg` timeline is sent to the retrieved frame.

These next few lines of code do a number of things, like resizing the ComboBox.

```
dropdown.setSize (100);
dropdown.setChangeHandler("getImageSelection");
```

The second line of code calls the function to be performed when the user changes the value of the drop-down menu.

This next lot of code selects a random image to show when the Flash movie starts up:

```
rndImage = random (imageArray.length-1);
dropdown.setSelectedIndex (rndImage);
getImageSelection();
```

Once a random number is selected, the `setSelectedIndex` method of the ComboBox is used to change the default value to the randomly selected figure. Calling the function then updates the image selection.

That's it for the background image changing. As you can see, using components makes things pretty simple, and the pre-built methods are ace.

Iterations

So, where can we take the video puppet from here? One thing that immediately springs to mind is to give him a life of his own. Once we've built him, we want to be able to let him go in the real world (well, our badly simulated version of the real world anyway), and see how he fares for himself. This opens up a whole new spectrum of iterations – how will he interact with objects? How will he interact with the other inhabitants of his crazy world? Will he get into fights with them? Dance for them? Share a cup of tea with them?

Before we go too far into these slightly mad ideas, let's get right back to the basic building blocks of what we'll need to be able to achieve our dream. The first thing that we need if we want him to interact with things is a simple physics engine.

I'm not going to go into any great detail here, but my commented FLA is included as `gravity.fla` if you want to take a look at it. It's only a fudged version rather than an implementation using real physics, but it just about does the job as a proof of concept. The created creature simply falls down the screen, rotating depending on limb bias, and then lands in a heap. The undulating motions of the creature seemed to make him better suited to moving through water, so I added the worst animated wave you'll ever see to give him the semblance of swimming. You can move the creature with the cursor keys, and pick it up again with the mouse. This isn't much by itself, but it could be the beginnings of something more.

The ultimate aim of these implementations would be to have the creature moving properly, depending on the limb animations – something like the sodaplay.com constructor would be a dream come true. Once this is done, you could then add other objects or creatures, and allow your own creature to interact with them in a Frankenstein meets Robot Wars fashion.

The next three iterations stem from established film and TV techniques, but use the vector mask shapes. To see these in action, you'll have to load in a pre-made creation from the standard interface.

#1 – Tales of the unexpected

Many years ago, there was a British TV anthology series called "Tales of the Unexpected". The stories were pretty scary, but eerier still was the intro sequence – silhouetted women dancing in front of flames and playing cards accompanied by the most evil circus music you ever heard.

Recurring nightmares where I see the opening sequence gave me an idea for one iteration on the mannequin movie: full body masking and flames. You can find it saved on the CD as `unexpected.fla`.

The idea here is easy enough, but took two attempts. Originally, I tried to attach many limbs into a newly created empty movie clip, and use that to mask the video. The problem here was that the overlap areas of the limbs made the shape unstable.

To get around this I went for the one-video-per-masking-limb option. I'd originally avoided this approach, for fear of overloading the processor, but it actually turned out to make very little difference.

#2 – James Bond

This iteration is just a touch different to the previous FLA, with the added bonus of a background video clip playing ten frames ahead of the masked videos. This clearly shows the masked videos as a silhouette and creates a James Bond-intro style effect. The file is called `bond.fla`.

#3 – Predator

This iteration just plays on the invisibility of the Predator in the film of the same name. This time the video is only one frame ahead (or as many as you want it to be – just change the value of the difference variable) and most of the time the silhouette is invisible. On certain occasions though, when there's greater movement between frames, the shape is revealed. This file is saved as `predator.fla`.

If I'm totally honest here, I didn't get time to finish the application fully in the sense that I wanted a breathing chest and an animated head to bring it fully alive. I did decide beforehand though that the arms and legs were the crux of the application for me, and anything else was a bonus.

Given all that, I think it's cool and it was amazing fun to make - mostly trying to get over the limitations of the awkward positions which we tried to film in. But I think the hard work paid off and although the scratchy style is very raw, I quite like it. I'd like to try out this method in some games next... and maybe it'll form part of a future chapter.

If you enjoyed this chapter, or have taken this idea somewhere else, then let me know – mail me at kenj@pinderkaas.com. Thanks for reading!

I really don't know how I came to be an experimental Flash developer, since I'm not in the business of developing websites or intros. I prefer to create visual effects and interactive Flash/ActionScript multimedia presentations by succesfully combining code and design, math and art.

For instance, this year I've coded a lot of movies using bezier splines, modulation, physics and image manipulation. I'm also busy developing complex interactive Flash applications for the United Nations and teaching ActionScript for advanced users.

Last year I started reviewing and writing advanced ActionScript articles for friends of ED, co-authoring books such as "Flash Math Creativity" and "Fresh Flash: New Design Ideas With Macromedia Flash MX".

Inspiration can come from nature, books, TV, the Internet, the city, and from relationships with other people. But we must recognize that there's another, internal source of inpiration: the voice of our heart and dreams.

Nowadays, there are so many ways to build interactive applications, that there are virtually no rules or frontiers left to hinder the creative process. The new improvements of Flash MX allow us to use video and complex math algorithms in our movies, while ever-faster processors let us create more and more elaborate experiences in real time.

Please note that I've designed the effects in this chapter with the very latest processors in mind. Some of my mutant experiments are extremely CPU intensive, and may run very slowly on older computers,

Cylindrical video component

Lifaros

When I was invited to write this chapter, I wasn't sure about my participation because I'm not primarily a video man. But then I thought about just how many interesting effects I've created using static images – so why not develop and apply something similar to a moving image?

The next step was to think of something appropriate but new – this wasn't easy, as there are lots of great ActionScripters out there, constantly coming up with interesting, effective stuff. You could already find fractals, 3D engines, mask effects, and so on. Ultimately, it's very difficult to think of something totally original.

I'm a very curious person – for example I'm always observing and trying to understand the color and texture of different kinds of insects, the shapes of clouds and mountains, the behavior of bubbles, and so on. In short, I enjoy watching the subtle forces and rules of nature in action. But I'm also a dreamer – I used to imagine the machines and devices of the future, for instance robots, spaceships, 3D plasma monitors...

Suddenly I was hit by inspiration – I asked myself: Is it possible to transform a 2D video image into a 3D video cylinder using ActionScript? Is there any useful application for this new effect?

Fortunately, the answer to the first question was yes, since Flash MX gives us all the tools we need to create interactive videos. In the course of this chapter, I'm going to show you the solution I came up with.

The second question was more difficult to answer. I spent some time browsing the Web and found a few interesting panoramic videos, some real 360 degree videos that are the perfect companion to my effect. Sure, the cameras and software are complex and expensive, but I'm sure this kind of panoramic video will be the standard of the future multimedia virtual tours.

The effect

It's time to show you this new effect that can be used to modify the surface of any kind of image or video in order to create a panoramic view. Our goal will be to modify the shape of our video using some complex math operations. We'll arrange different sections of the video around the sides of a regular polygon (a flat shape whose sides are all the same length, and are placed symmetrically about a common center), make it look as if it's a 3D object (a right prism to be exact), and then apply lighting and axis rotation control.

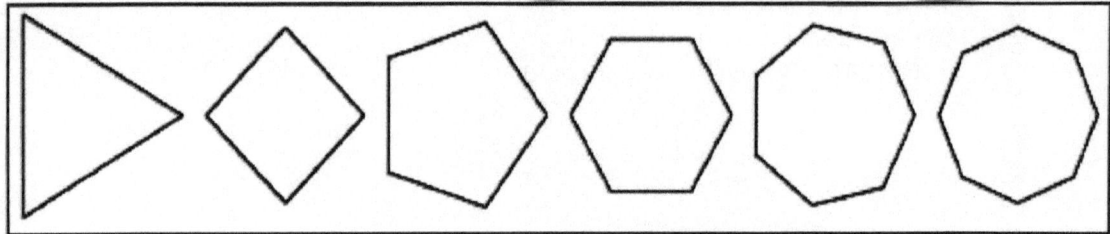

How? Well, first of all we'll need to use a little dynamic masking to chop up the source image into vertical slices.

Then we'll move, scale and skew each one to produce the effect of a 3D polygon or prism. As we add more sides to the polygon, it gets closer and closer to looking like a nice smooth cylinder – though it also puts more and more strain on the processor.

We'll see how these operations are performed when we take a look at the component's inner workings, later on in this chapter.

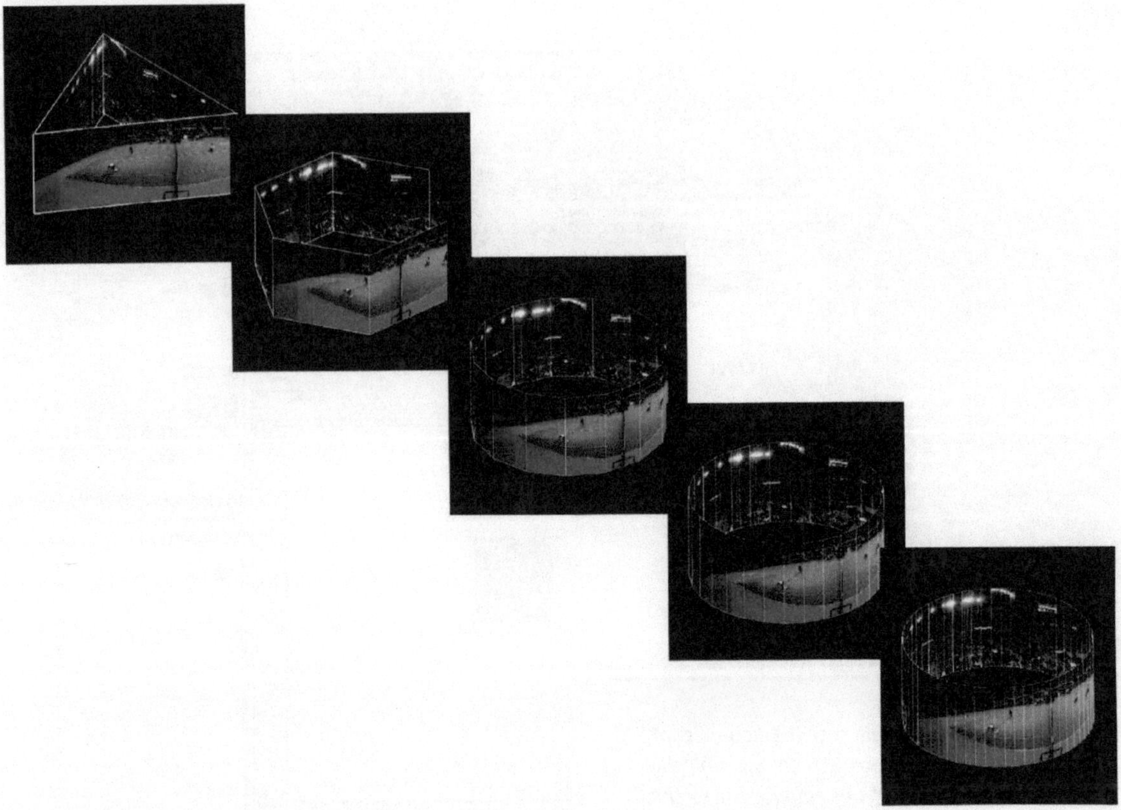

Introducing the component

It's time to install the component, and to do that you'll need the Macromedia Extension Manager. If you don't already have this on your machine, you can download it (free of charge) from www.macromedia.com/exchange/em_download/. To install it, just double click on the em_install.exe file, and follow the instructions.

Now find the file called FCylindricVideo.mxp on the CD – this is our component – and double-click on it to launch the Extension Manager. Press Accept and you're done:

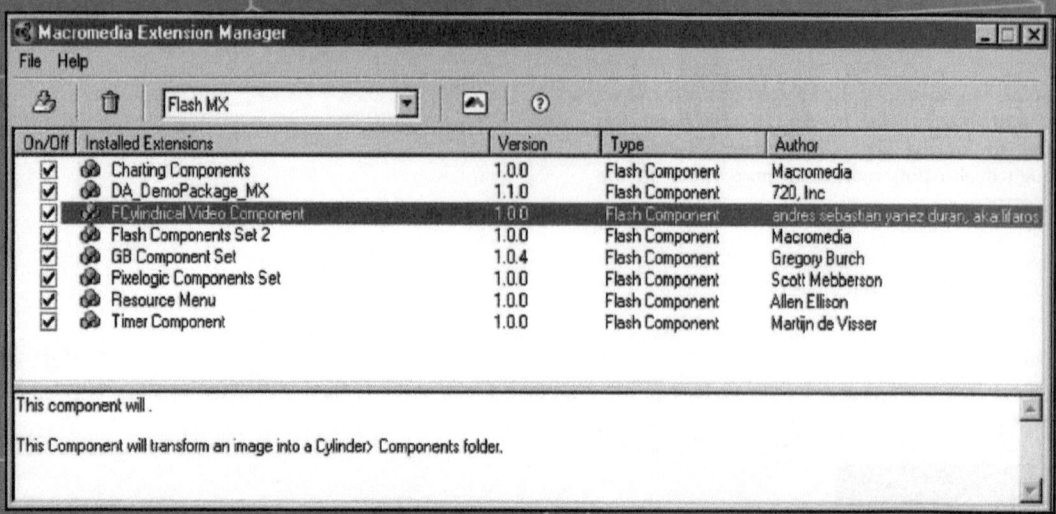

Once installed, open the Components panel (located at the Window section of the Flash interface) and select the FcylindricalVideoComponent. Drag and drop an instance onto the stage:

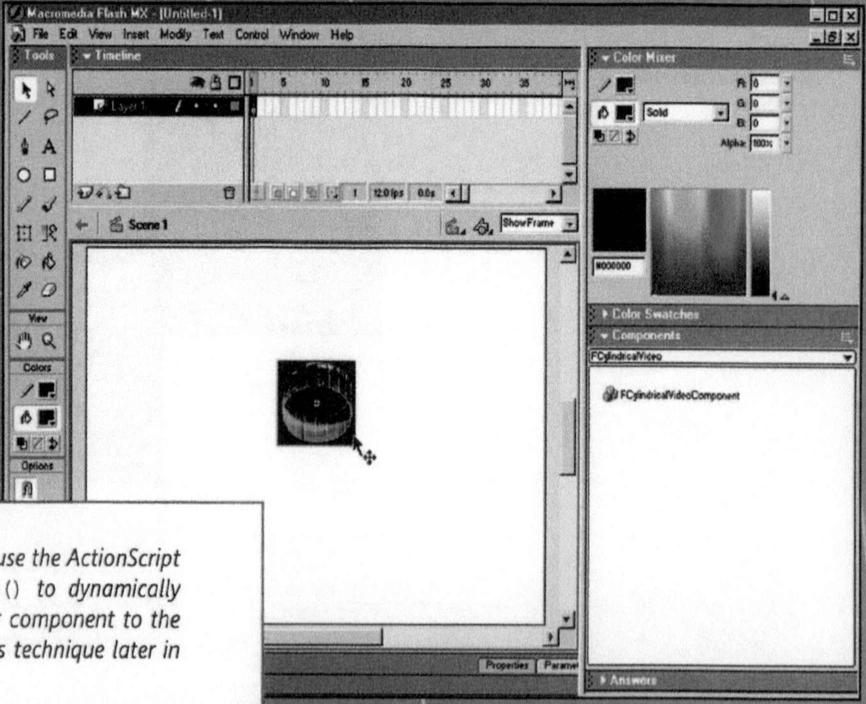

Note that we can also use the ActionScript method attachMovie() *to dynamically add an instance of our component to the stage. We'll look at this technique later in the chapter.*

Let's start by demonstrating the component with a static image. Import the file called `highres1.jpg` into the movie, and press F8 to convert it to a movie clip with the Linkage identifier `picture`.

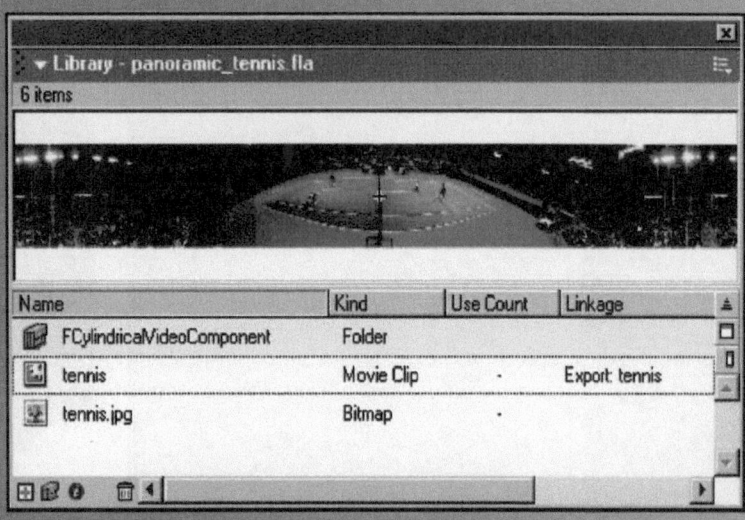

Select the component and open up the Properties inspector – you'll see the following parameters listed:

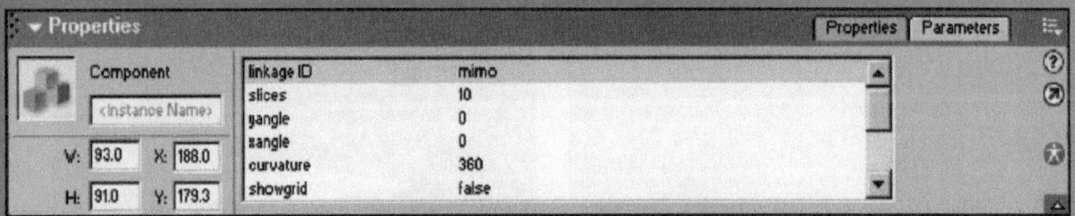

linkage ID specifies the Linkage identifier of the library object we want to wrap around the cylinder. This can be any movie clip or graphic symbol – even a text field if you like – and this may contain vector graphics, bitmaps, or even video.

We already have a suitable candidate in place, so let's set this value to `tennis` and run the movie – here's what you should see:

Okay, it's a start – believe it or not, we have actually wrapped the image around a cylinder; only trouble is, we're looking at it dead-on from the side, so it just looks like a section from the original image. We won't see the true power of the component until we look at it from a different angle.

Parameters **xangle** and **yangle** let us do just this, controlling the tilt and spin of the cylinder respectively. They both default to 0, which is why we've just been looking side-on at the cylinder. Set xangle to 20 and run the movie again – you should now see a tilted cylinder like this.

Set yangle to 180, and you can spin the cylinder round to see the other half of the picture up top.

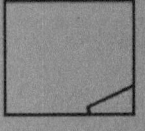

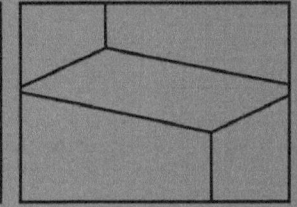

As you might expect, **slices** controls the number of slices we use to form the cylinder. It defaults to 10, giving us a slightly blocky effect. More slices will give a smoother cylinder – here's how our tennis scene looks with 50 slices.

Behind the scenes, our component's using a lot of high-powered math functions like sines and cosines – this means that as we add slices, we're putting more of a load on the CPU. Right now, we're dealing with a static image on a static cylinder – the whole thing's drawn once and then remains stationary, so processor power isn't an issue. However, once we start animating the cylinder, and particularly when we start using video (very processor-intensive in itself), we'll need to be pragmatic about the number of columns we can use – otherwise the movie will grind to a halt!

curvature lets us set the curvature of the surface (in degrees). By default, this is 360, which wraps the specified movie clip exactly once around our virtual cylinder – a curvature of 180 will wrap it round one half of the cylinder, whereas a curvature of 720 would wrap it right around twice over.

showgrid lets us activate a white grid that shows the bounds of each picture cell. You can turn it on (by setting it to true) to make the structure more obvious, but leave it turned off (false – as it is by default) to keep your animations running at top speed.

Here's the cylindrified tennis scene at 270° curvature, with showgrid set to true.

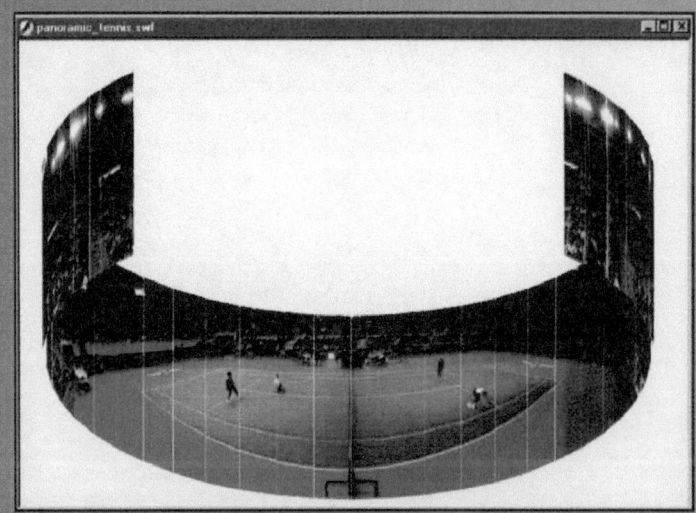

Scroll down the component's parameter list, and you can see a few more to play with:

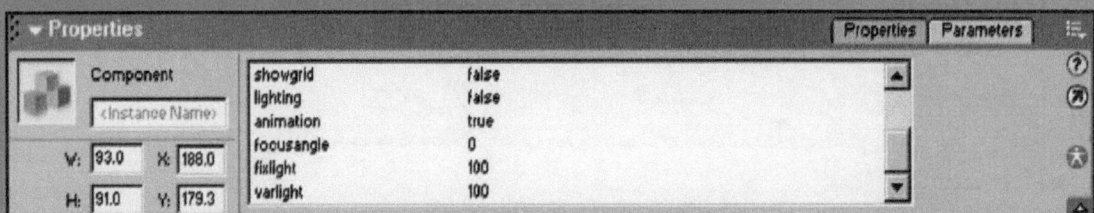

- **lighting** is a true/false setting that lets you activate a lighting effect.

- **animation** is another true/false setting that lets you animate the component.

- **focusangle** controls the direction of light.

- **fixlight** controls the overall intensity of the light, ranging from 0 to 100.

- **varlight** controls the lighting variation, again ranging from 0 to 100.

Feel free to experiment with these parameters for yourself – we'll see them in action later in the chapter.

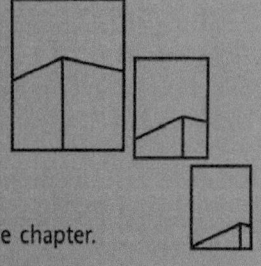

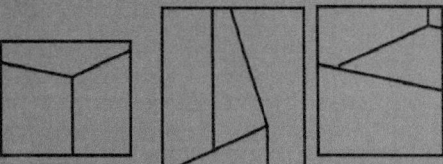

Controlling the component with ActionScript

Now let's animate the cylinder. Attach the following code to the first frame of the main timeline:

```
function yangleControl() {
    // performs y axis rotation
    var deltax= this._xmouse-img._x;
    speed += (.1*deltax-speed)/20;
    img._yangle += speed;
}

function xangleControl() {
    // performs x axis rotation
    var deltay= this._ymouse-img._y;
    img._xangle += (-.3*deltay-img._xangle)/10;
}
```

These two functions (yangleControl and xangleControl) are used to vary the two rotation parameters slowly using some very well known easing equations. We got a very nice result because the polygon appears to be a real 3D cylinder. Best of all, if you aren't a programmer, you don't need to worry about the complex math procedures going on behind the scenes!

Of course, we also need to call them both every time we enter a frame:

```
this.onEnterFrame = function() {
    this.yangleControl();
    this.xangleControl();
};
stop();
```

Reset parameters to 360 degree curvature, 20 slices, grid off.

Now let's peek inside the component and take a look at all the ActionScript that makes it tick.

> At this point, things start to get fairly involved. If you're not comfortable with advanced ActionScript, you may want to skip this explanation and jump straight on to the "Playing with the component" section – it's not the end of the world.

Inside the component

To look inside the FCylindricalVideo component, you'll need to have an instance on the stage (you can use the one from the last example if you like), and call up the Library panel. Inside, you should find a symbol folder called FCylindricalVideoComponent, containing a movie clip, a component, and a bitmap:

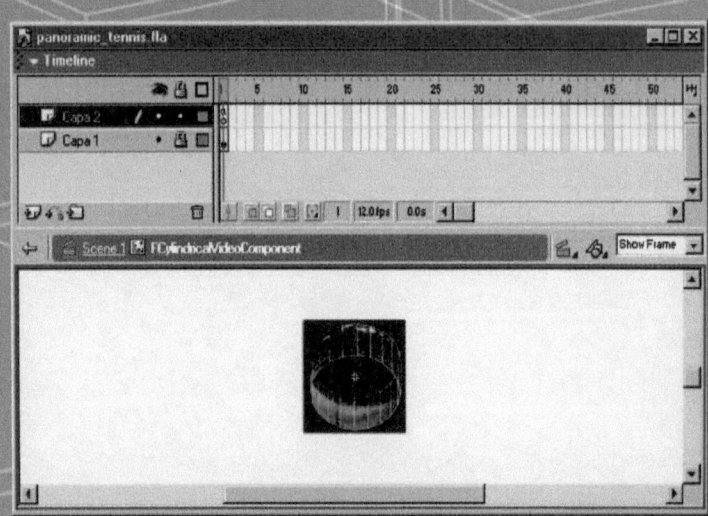

It's the component that we're interested in – notice that it's exported with the Linkage identifier FCylindricalVideoSymbol. Double-click on it, and hide the Library panel so that you can see the stage and the timeline:

All that's actually there on the stage is an instance of the small bitmap – the meat of the component is tucked away on the top layer, in the form of some 230 lines of code.

Every component's code needs to begin with #initclip and end with #endinitclip. These 'tags' enclose all the code that Flash needs to set up and control the component whenever it's used inside a movie. It also ensures that this code will be executed before any other code in the movie.

> By its nature, component programming involves quite a few object-oriented programming (OOP) techniques – whether or not this means anything to you, don't panic! I'm going to explain what each bit does and why it's there, so you shouldn't need a doctorate to follow what's going on.

We can break that code down into three main parts:

- A **class definition** sets us up with a place to bundle together all the code that defines our component's functionality.

- A load of **prototypes** that define all the properties and methods for that class.

- A single statement that **registers** the class as belonging to a particular symbol, in this case FCylindricalVideoSymbol.

> *This will give us the basics, but if you're interested in building components for yourself, there's an awful lot more you can do. Check out "Macromedia Flash MX Components: Most Wanted", also from friends of ED, Alternatively, Jonathan Kaye has written an excellent online tutorial called "Creating Flash MX Components", which you can find at the following URL: www.flashcomponents.net/tutorials.cfm?nav=4*

Initializing the component

As mentioned above, we begin with the #initclip tag, making sure that the components set up and ready for use before any other code in the movie tries using it. The #initclip tag also means that the class is created globally rather than just inside the movie clip. The 1 simply tells Flash to run this #initclip block before any others – since there's only one in this example, it's optional:

```
#initclip 1
```

We then define the constructor function for our FCylindricalVideoClass class. This function will be called whenever a video cylinder is instantiated, and we use it to simply call a method called init, which we'll define in a moment:

```
FCylindricalVideoClass = function () {
    this.init();
};
```

The next line ensures that our class inherits all the properties and methods of the MovieClip class. This means we'll be able to play, stop, move, and even resize the component, just as if it were a movie clip:

```
FCylindricalVideoClass.prototype = new MovieClip();
```

Now we set up the init method, which is responsible for setting up all the component's properties. Note that we have one property corresponding to each of the parameters we looked at earlier: linkage ID, xangle, yangle, and so on. They're all named with a _ prefix to help remind us that they're properties of the class.

The first half of the code tells Flash how to get and set values for each of the properties:

```
FCylindricalVideoClass.prototype.init = function() {
    this.addProperty("_varlight", this.getvarlight, this.setvarlight);
    this.addProperty("_fixlight", this.getfixlight, this.setfixlight);
    this.addProperty("_lighting", this.getlighting, this.setlighting);
    this.addProperty("_xangle", this.getxangle, this.setxangle);
    this.addProperty("_yangle", this.getyangle, this.setyangle);
    this.addProperty("_focusangle", this.getfocusangle, this.setfocusangle);
    this.addProperty("_curvature", this.getcurvature, this.setcurvature);
    this.addProperty("_slices", this.getslices, this.setslices);
    this.addProperty("_linkid", this.getlinkid, this.setlinkid);
    this.addProperty("_animation", this.getanimation, this.setanimation);
    this.addProperty("_showgrid", this.getshowgrid,this.setshowgrid);
```

For example, if someone tries reading the _varlight property, Flash will use a method called getvarlight to access the value. Likewise, if someone tries *changing* the value of _varlight, Flash will call the setvarlight method. This approach may seem a little contrived, but it has its uses, as we'll see shortly.

The rest of the init method assigns values to each of the properties – this is where the underscores become important: this._yangle is a property of the class, which can be seen from outside; by contrast, this.yangle is a variable *inside* the class, which *can't* be seen outside:

```
        this._yangle = this.yangle;
        this._xangle = this.xangle;
        this._focusangle = this.focusangle;
        this._lighting = this.lighting;
        this._fixlight = this.fixlight;
        this._varlight = this.varlight;
        this._linkid = this.linkid;
        this._slices = this.slices;
        this._showgrid = this.showgrid;
        this._curvature = this.curvature;
        this._animation = this.animation;
    };
```

Again, this may seem like a trivial distinction to make, but it's actually a very important part of the OOP approach: we need to respect it if we're to make a robust, reliable component. You'll see why in just a moment.

Building the cylinder

First though, we need to look at how the cylinder's built.

Generating slices

We begin with a prototype function called generate, which uses createEmptyMovieClip to dynamically create all the slices (or cells). Each one will contain a movie clip named holder whose purpose is to contain the following three elements:

the image movie clip
the rectangular mask named box
the grid.

The last two are created using some drawing API methods. Here's how the function looks:

```
FCylindricalVideoClass.prototype.generate = function() {
  this.cell = [];
  for (var i = 0; i<this.slices; i++) {
  for (var i = 0; i<this.slices; i++) {
    this.cell[i] = this.createEmptyMovieClip("ic_"+i, i);
    this.cell[i].createEmptyMovieClip("holder", 1);
    this.cell[i].holder.createEmptyMovieClip("box", 1);
    this.cell[i].holder.box.drawBox(100,100,0, 0xffffff,100, 0xff0000,100);
    this.cell[i].holder.createEmptyMovieClip("grid", 2);
    this.cell[i].holder.grid.drawBox(100, 100,0, 0xffffff,100, 0xff0000,0);
    this.cell[i].holder.createEmptyMovieClip("image", 3);
    this.cell[i].holder.image.attachMovie(this.linkid, "videoholder", 1);
    this.cell[i].holder.image.setMask(this.cell[i].holder.box);
    if (i<8) {
      this.cell[i].moviesound = new Sound(this.cell[i].holder);
      if (i == 0) {
        this.cell[i].moviesound.setVolume(100);
      } else {
        this.cell[i].moviesound.setVolume(0);
      }
    }
  }
  }
  this.sizer();
  this.display();
};
```

We start by creating an array of slices or cells:

```
this.cell = [];
```

Note that this is shorthand for the standard new Array declaration – this line could just as well be written...

```
this.cell = new Array();
```

Next, we use a `for` loop to set up each cell in turn. We dynamically create an empty movie clip inside the `i`th cell, and nest another empty movie clip (named `holder`) inside it:

```
this.cell[i] = this.createEmptyMovieClip("ic_"+i, i);
this.cell[i].createEmptyMovieClip("holder", 1);
```

Inside the `holder` clip, we create our three elements: `box`, `grid` and `image`:

```
this.cell[i].holder.createEmptyMovieClip("box", 1);
this.cell[i].holder.box.drawBox(100,100,0, 0xffffff, 100, 0xff0000, 100);
this.cell[i].holder.createEmptyMovieClip("grid", 2);
this.cell[i].holder.grid.drawBox(100,100,0, 0xffffff, 100, 0xff0000, 0);
this.cell[i].holder.createEmptyMovieClip("image", 3);
```

We now attach the movie clip that contains our video footage – as specified by the Linkage identifier variable `linkid` – and mask it with the `box` element so that Flash will only show the particular slice we're interested in:

```
this.cell[i].holder.image.attachMovie(this.linkid,  "videoholder", 1);
this.cell[i].holder.image.setMask(this.cell[i].holder.bo X x);
```

We want to make sure that the video soundtrack plays, but also need to avoid having a lot of sounds playing at the same time. Flash can play up to eight channels simultaneously, so we use the following code:

```
if (i<8) {
  this.cell[i].moviesound = new Sound(this.cell[i].holder);
    if (i == 0) {
      this.cell[i].moviesound.setVolume(100);
    } else {
      this.cell[i].moviesound.setVolume(0);
    }
  }
}
```

This effectively mutes all eight channels except for the first, which it plays at full volume.

Finally, once we've closed off the `for` loop, we call a couple of new methods, which will move/scale all the vertical slices and resize the masks accordingly:

```
this.sizer();
this.display();
};
```

Let's take a look at how these work.

Resizing slices

This method is responsible for moving and scaling each masked image according to the specified number of slices, curvature, and the height and width of the attached movie clip:

```
FCylindricalVideoClass.prototype.sizer = function() {
    for (var i = 0; i<this.slices; i++) {
        var angularratio = 360/this.curvature;
        var slicewidth = this.cell[i].holder.image.videoholder._width
                                                    /this.slices;
        this.cellxsize = angularratio*slicewidth;
        this.cellysize = this.cell[i].holder.image.videoholder._height;
        this.cell[i].holder.image._width =(100*this.slices)/angularratio;
        this.cell[i].holder.image._height = 100;
        this.cell[i].holder.image._x = 50*this.slices-50-100*i;
    }
};
```

Let's take this prototype apart. Remember that we've divided the big image into many smaller images, so once again we need a for loop to modify each cell in turn:

```
for (var i = 0; i<this.slices; i++) {
```

The slice width will be the image width divided by the number of slices, but we're going to going to scale this up (or down) according to the curvature setting. If curvature is set to 360, the angular ratio (360/this.curvature) will be 1 and each cell will have a width of slicewidth. If curvature is 180, the angular ratio will be 2, giving each cell a width of twice slicewidth:

```
var angularratio = 360/this.curvature;
var slicewidth = this.cell[i].holder.image.videoholder._width
                                            /this.slices;
this.cellxsize = angularratio*slicewidth;
```

The cell height will always be the same as the image height:

```
this.cellysize = this.cell[i].holder.image.videoholder._height;
```

Now we're ready to move and scale the image slice:

```
this.cell[i].holder.image._width = (100*this.slices)/angularratio;
this.cell[i].holder.image._height = 100;
this.cell[i].holder.image._x = 50*this.slices-50-100*i;
```

I won't go into detail about what each of these lines does – you might like to experiment with different settings for yourself to see what effects you can create. Over the years, I've seen many variations on this slicing code applied to jigsaw puzzles and other image effects – you can find lots of examples on sites like www.flashkit.com.

Displaying slices

Here's where the math gets particularly tricky, so let's have a diagram or two. We're approximating our cylinder as a 3D regular polygon (or prism), so we need to calculate its **apothem** (internal radius), **sector angle**, and **side length**. These values will allow us to calculate the exact scale, position and skew angle of each slice.

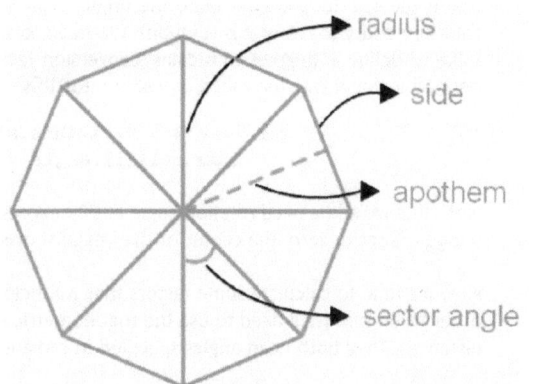

The formulae we're going to be looking at here are rather complex – however, this isn't a math book, so I won't waste time explaining every little detail. If you understand all the equations, that's great, but not essential. It's more important that you have an idea how each line affects the final outcome – again, feel free to play around with the code, and see for yourself what effects this has on the cylinder.

We start by declaring the prototype function:

```
FCylindricalVideoClass.prototype.display = function() {
```

First of all we must calculate the sector angle (`sectorangle`) of the regular polygon. This is measured in radians (not degrees as was used in the previous method). Fortunately, it's quite easy to work out, as `2*Math.PI` radians is the same as 360 degrees:

```
this.sectorangle = (2*Math.PI)/this.slices;
```

Now we're ready to calculate the apothem: the perpendicular distance from the center to a side of the regular polygon (as shown above):

```
this.apothem = (.5*this.cellxsize)/Math.tan(.5*this.sectorangle);
```

Remember that 360 degrees is the same as 2*Math.Pi radians, so I define `dtr` as Math.Pi/180. Now we can multiply any angle (expressed in degrees) by `dtr` and get the same angle expressed in radians.

Inside the `for` loop we calculate the angle, scale and position of each of our cells from the values of `xangle` (x axis rotation) and `yangle` (y axis rotation). We need to specify angles in radians (rather than degrees), and to make life easier I like to define a 'degrees to radians' conversion factor. If you scroll down to the bottom of the code, you'll see that I've defined a global variable called `dtr` to do just this – you can find `dtr` lurking in all my trigonometrical toys:

```
for (var i = 0; i<this.slices; i++) {
    this.cell[i].angle = 90*dtr + (.5+i)*this.sectorangle + this.yangle*dtr;
```

Note that we add a fixed rotation angle of 90 degrees (converted into radians with `dtr`). This helps to make sure that when `yangle` is set to zero, the center of the image shows up on the front of the cylinder.

Now it's time to calculate some factors that will help us work out the final scale, position and skew angle for each cell. In order to do this, we'll need to use the trigonometric methods `Math.sin` and `Math.cos`, which help us convert angles into distances. They both need angles specified in radians, so we need to use `dtr` again:

```
var dx = Math.sin(this.cell[i].angle);
var dy = Math.cos(this.cell[i].angle);
var sinxangle = Math.sin(this.xangle*dtr);
var cosxangle = Math.cos(this.xangle*dtr);
var dyp = Math.cos(this.cell[i].angle)*sinxangle;
```

The following diagram illustrates what these factors mean in geometric terms, shown in the context of an octagon:

Each side of the octagon corresponds to the bottom edge of one of our cells. So, each cell will appear in a different position, with a different scale, and a different skew, according to its position on the cylinder, and the orientation of the cylinder itself.

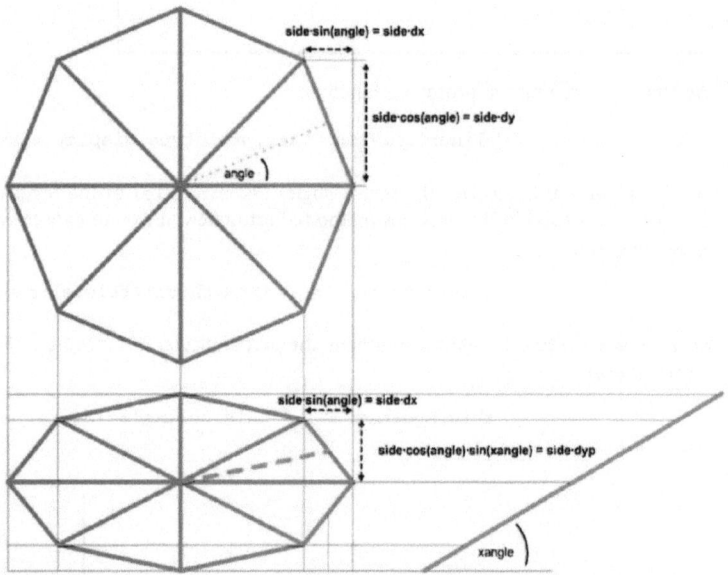

We'll use the variables `dx` and `dy` to calculate x and y projections of the cell's width according to its rotation around the y axis. If the cell is being shown right at the front of the cylinder, we're looking at it dead-on – `dx` will be 1, and `dy` will be 0. On the other hand, if it's being shown on the side of the cylinder, it'll be so thin that it vanishes – `dx` will be 0 and `dy` will be 1. Multiply these values by the cell width (as we'll do in a moment) and we'll know how wide and how skewed we need to make each cell.

Likewise, `sinxangle` and `cosxangle` are used to calculate the projections of the cell's height, according to its rotation around the x axis. Let's see how we use these to work out the scaling needed for each cell:

```
this.cell[i].holder._yscale = this.cellysize*cosxangle;
this.cell[i].holder._xscale = 1+this.cellxsize*Math.sqrt(dx*dx+dyp*dyp);
```

Note that we add an extra 1 to `xscale` – this makes it slightly wider than required, which helps us to avoid leaving gaps between adjacent slices.

Now we need to calculate the cell positions:

```
this.cell[i]._y = this.apothem*dx*sinxangle;
  if (dx*cosxangle>=0) {
    this.cell[i]._x = .99*this.apothem*dy;
  } else {
    this.cell[i]._x = this.apothem*dy;
  }
```

The purpose of the `if` statement is to detect whether an image slice is facing forward or backward. If the slice is facing backward, we multiply its x position by a factor of .99.

Assuming that lighting is enabled, we also calculate each slice's lightness according to the angle of the focus (`focusangle`) and the two lighting factors `varlight` and `fixlight`. We also need to consider whether the slice is facing forward or backward – variable s is set to 1 or -1 in each case respectively. Finally, we use the Color object and its `setTransform` method to apply the lighting:

```
if (this.lighting) {
  var s = dx*cosxangle>=0 ? 1 : -1;
  var vak = this.fixlight+s*this.varlight
    ➥*Math.cos(this.focusangle*dtr+this.cell[i].angle);
  new Color(this.cell[i]).setTransform({ra:vak, rb:0, ga:vak, gb:0,
                        ➥ba:vak, bb:0, aa:100, ab:0});
}
```

Now we use `swapDepths` to arrange the slices in the correct order – otherwise we may get slices from the back of the cylinder showing over slices from the front. Again, we need to consider whether the slice is facing forward or backward – we store this information in the variable `hh`:

```
var hh = cosxangle>=0 ? -1 : 1;
var depth = Math.floor(i*1+100000+(hh*10000*Math.sin(this.cell[i].angle)));
this.cell[i].swapDepths(depth);
```

Finally, we calculate and apply the appropriate skew to each cell, and close off the loop:

```
    this.cell[i].skew(Math.atan2(dy, -dx)/dtr, 0);
  }
};
```

The `skew` method used here is one that I've developed myself – we'll look at its prototype in a moment. It's designed to work like the skew tool in the Transform panel: skewing the sides of a movie clip, but without changing the length of those sides. Note that it expects angles to be expressed in degrees, so we have to divide the `Math.atan` value (which is in radians) by `dtr`.

Animating slices

The `loop` method simply runs `sizer` and `display` every frame, so that Flash recalculates the cell positions several times every second, allowing us to animate the cylinder. We'll only call this method if the `_animation` property is set to true, so we can still choose between obtaining a dynamic or static effect:

```
FCylindricalVideoClass.prototype.loop = function() {
  this.onEnterFrame = function() {
    this.sizer();
    this.display();
  };
};
```

Drawing the grid

The `grid` method is used to turn the cell grid on or off, simply by setting the `_visible` property of each `grid` movie clip. If necessary, you can modify the color and stroke of the grid by replacing the respective values within the `generate` method:

```
FCylindricalVideoClass.prototype.grid = function() {
  for (var i = 0; i<this.slices; i++) {
    this.cell[i].holder.grid._visible = this.showgrid;
  }
};
```

It's best to avoid using the grid if you're trying to get the best possible performance.

Cleaning up

The `clean` method is responsible for removing cells when necessary. For instance, if we reduce the number of slices while the movie's running, we'll need to delete all the surplus cells:

```
FCylindricalVideoClass.prototype.clean = function() {
  for (var i in this) {
    typeof (this[i]) == "movieclip" ? this[i].removeMovieClip() : null;
  }
};
```

Notice the `for...in` loop. This can be useful when you want to loop through all an object's children, but don't know how many of them there are.

Getter and setter functions

As we saw earlier, `Object.addProperty` lets us insulate the component's internal variables from the outside world. If someone wants to change the component's `lighting` variable from ActionScript, they have to do it by setting the `_lighting` property. Flash then uses a function called `setlighting` to actually do the deed.

This is where we define `setlighting`, along with all our component's other 'setter' functions and their 'getter' counterparts (used in a similar fashion for reading property values). Each component property has its own pair of setter and getter functions.

Why bother doing it like this? Because we can put very specific conditions into these getter and setter functions: want to make sure that the internal variable `slices` is never set to a value less than 1 or greater than 150? No problem. Write the condition into the `setslices` function, and it won't matter what illegal value the user feeds into the `_slices` property – `slices` itself will only change to a legal value.

These functions are all quite simple, and most are very similar, so there's little point in examining them all. I'm just going to explain setlighting and getlighting.

setlighting and getlighting

We use these functions to set and get new values for the internal variable lighting, and detect errors:

```
FCylindricalVideoClass.prototype.setlighting = function(newval) {
```

We simply check that the passed value exists, and make sure it's of the correct data type:

```
if (newval != undefined and typeof(newval) == "boolean") {
  this.lighting = newval;
} else {
  trace("Error: wrong _lighting value .You must enter a boolean ");
  this.lighting = false;
}
};
```

If it is, we update the internal variable. If not, we trace out an error message and deactivate the lighting.

The getter function is simpler, as there's no need for error checking. We just return the value of the internal variable:

```
FCylindricalVideoClass.prototype.getlighting = function() {
  return (this.lighting);
};
```

As you can see, the user never comes into direct contact with the internal variable. It's insulated from the outside world by getlighting and setlighting, both of which are associated with the _lighting property.

This is a fairly trivial example, but the principle's still an important one. If you don't take care to protect your component's internal settings from the wicked ways of the user, you run the risk having them break it in all sorts of subtle ways.

OOP movie clip methods

Finally, let's see a couple of movie clip methods that I use in most of my projects. Note that all the prototypes we've seen so far have been defined on the component class. These, on the other hand, are being defined specifically for MovieClip, which means they can be applied to any movie clip (including all our slices). This is good example of the power of OOP: once they've been coded, I can re-use these methods over and over again, in any project I like.

Skew

This is my famous skew engine, as mentioned earlier on. It uses some trigonometric functions to calculate the perfect scale and rotation factor for skewing a movie clip without changing the lengths of its sides:

```
MovieClip.prototype.skew = function(h_skew, v_skew) {
  for (var s in this) {
    this[s]._rotation = -45;
  }
  this._rotation = 45+(h_skew+v_skew)/2;
  this._yscale = Math.sin((90+v_skew-h_skew)*0.5*dtr)*Math.SQRT2*100;
  this._xscale = Math.cos((90+v_skew-h_skew)*0.5*dtr)*Math.SQRT2*100;
};
```

h_skew represents a horizontal skew (measured in degrees) while v_skew represents the vertical skew (also in degrees). Notice that I'm using the dtr conversion factor explained earlier in this chapter. Once again, the precise mathematical details involved here aren't easy to explain, but I can demonstrate the usage and illustrate the results.

Let's assume the movie clip we want to skew is nested inside another clip called image. The following line of code will apply a vertical skew of 30 degrees:

```
image.skew(0, 30);
```

Here's how a range of skew values will affect a square movie clip:

`image.skew(0,0);`

`image.skew(30, 0);`

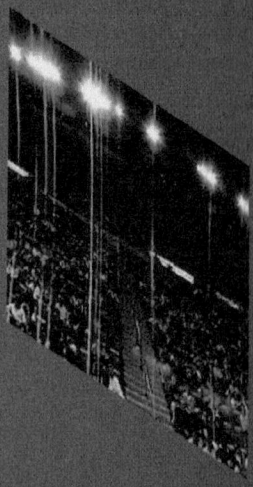

`image.skew(0, 30);`

`image.skew(30, 30);`

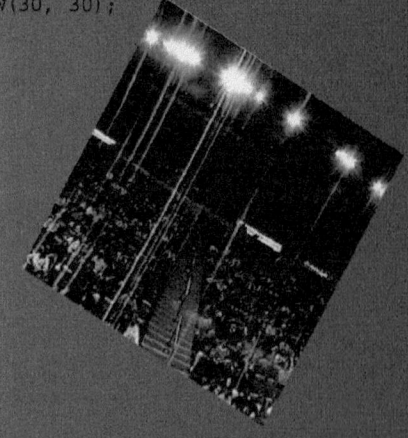

I've used this skew function to develop a lot of cool effects, such as the Image Modulator Component from friends of ED's new book "Macromedia Flash MX Components: Most Wanted". This time, I'm using it to skew the cells that make up our cylinder, giving each of the video slices the correct appearance. Feel free to copy and paste the code, and apply this method in your own projects.

DrawBox

This movie clip method uses the drawing API to draw a rectangular box centered on the point (0,0). It takes as parameters the desired width and height of the box. You can also modify the color and transparency of the stroke and the fill:

```
MovieClip.prototype.drawBox = function(mywidth, myheight,
                                       strokewidth, strokecolor, strokealpha,
                                       fillcolor, fillalpha) {
    this.beginFill(fillcolor, fillalpha);
    this.lineStyle(strokewidth, strokecolor, strokealpha);
    this.moveTo(-mywidth/2, myheight/2);
    this.lineTo(-mywidth/2, -myheight/2);
    this.lineTo(mywidth/2, -myheight/2);
    this.lineTo(mywidth/2, myheight/2);
    this.lineTo(-mywidth/2, myheight/2);
    this.endFill();
};
```

This time I'm using this method to draw the mask and the white rectangular grid.

Finishing off

Once we've defined all the class methods, we have just a few more closing lines to look at:

```
_global.dtr = Math.PI/180;

Object.registerClass("FCylindricalVideoSymbol", FCylindricalVideoClass);
#endinitclip
```

We define the fantastically useful global variable dtr for converting degrees to radians, and then use Object.registerClass to associate our new class with a particular movie clip (which we specify in terms of its Linkage ID). Finally, we use the #endinitclip tag to mark the end of the #initclip code block.

There's one more thing to do though: we don't want our dummy image (used to show the component on the stage within the authoring environment) showing up when the movie's running. No problem – we make it invisible:

```
FCylindricalVideoBody._visible = false;
```

Playing with the component

Now that we've finished poking around inside, we're ready to start a little experimentation with the component – and see how it copes with some video footage.

mimo_00.fla

Let's start by playing with a video developed by my actor friend Julio Cattani. Here he's demonstrating some facial expressions as a mime artist.

First of all, set the background color of the stage to black (not essential, but I think it looks nice), and drop an instance of the component onto the stage. Give it the instance name img.

Now create a movie clip with the Linkage ID mimo, and import the video file mimo.mov into it. A fairly short video like this is best, as it helps to keep the final file size down. You may also want to scale down the video while importing it, so as to speed up the effect.

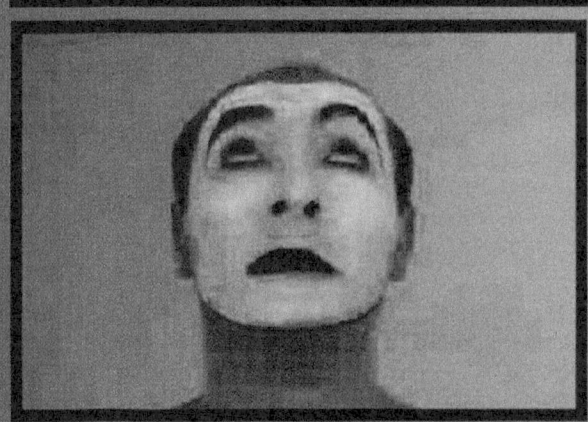

As you may have already noticed, the component's linkage ID parameter defaults to the value "mimo"; since the other default values are acceptable, we don't need to change any of the parameters at this stage.

Let's animate our video-wrapped cylinder, just as we did before with the tennis scene. Attach the following code to the first frame of the main timeline:

```
function yangleControl() {
    // performs y axis rotation
    var deltax= this._xmouse-img._x;
    speed += (.1*deltax-speed)/20;
    img._yangle += speed;
}

function xangleControl() {
    // performs x axis rotation
    var deltay= this._ymouse-img._y;
    img._xangle += (-.3*deltay-img._xangle)/10;
}
this.onEnterFrame = function() {
    this.yangleControl();
    this.xangleControl();
};
stop();
```

The following screenshots show the 3D video polygon viewed from several different x axis angle (`xangle`) rotation values, from 15 to 75 degrees.

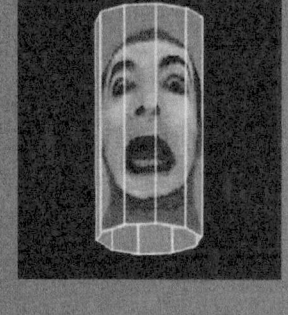

mimo_01.fla

Now let's try modifying the video curvature instead. You'll need to set the following values in the Properties inspector:

- linkage ID   mimo
- slices   20
- yangle   20
- xangle   -30
- curvature   360
- showgrid   false
- lighting   false
- animation   true
- focusangle   0
- fixlight   100
- varlight   100

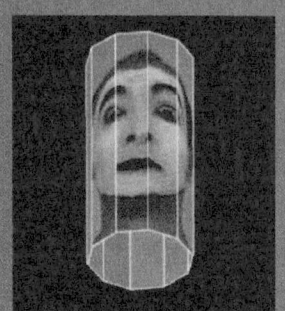

Add the following function into the first frame of the movie (main timeline) in order to modify the `curvature` and `yangle` according to the mouse position:

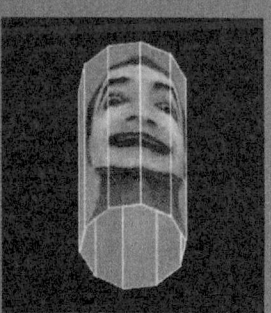

```
function yangleControl() {
  // performs y axis rotation
  var deltax= this._xmouse-img._x;
  speed += (.1*deltax-speed)/20;
  img._yangle += speed;
}
function curvatureControl() {
ymouse = (440-this._ymouse)*2;
ymouse<=135 ? ymouse=135 : null;
ymouse>=1000 ? ymouse=1000 : null;
img._curvature += (ymouse-img._curvature)/5;
}
this.onEnterFrame = function() {
  this.curvatureControl();
  this.yangleControl();
};

stop();
```

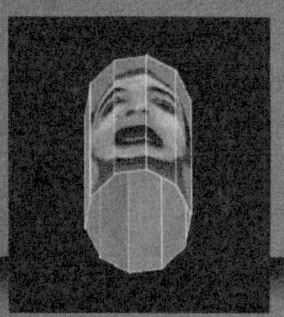

These screenshots show the 3D video polygon viewed at several different curvatures, from 360 to 180 degrees.

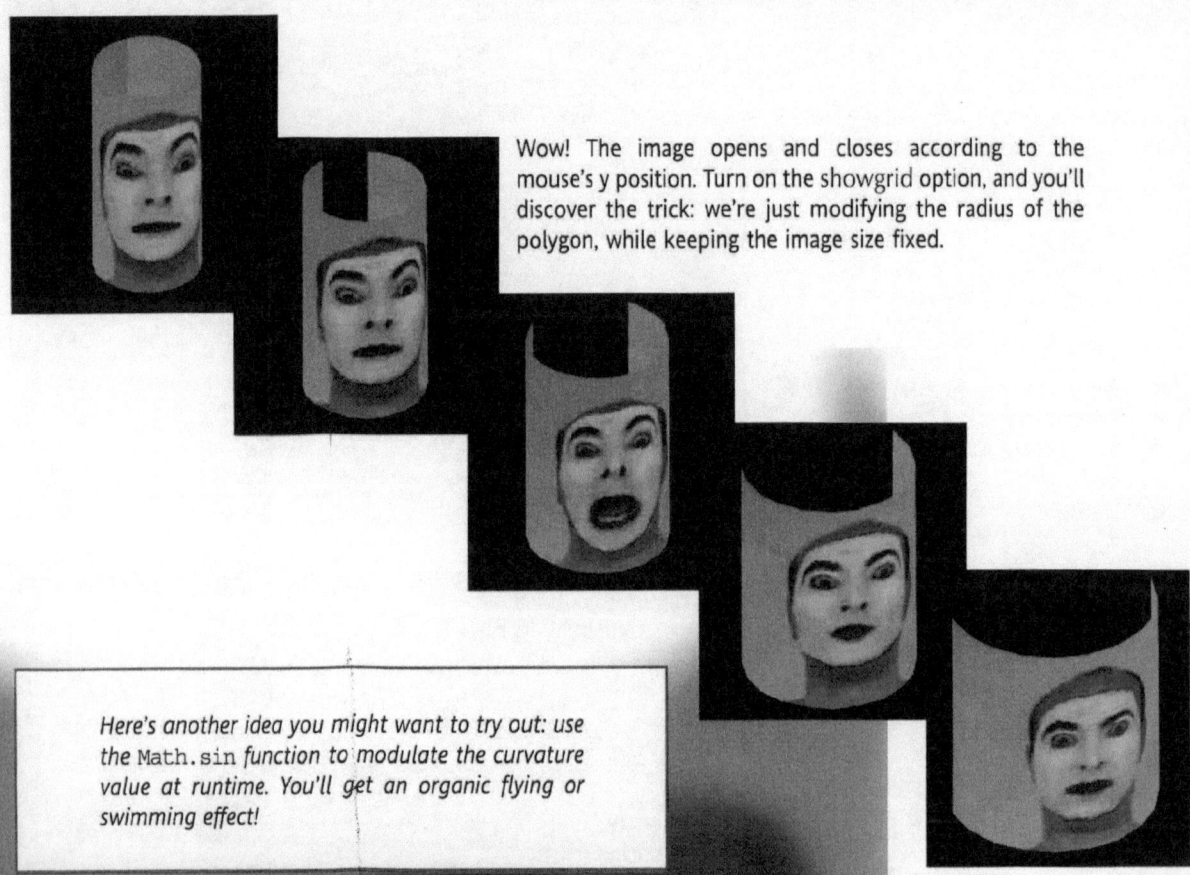

Wow! The image opens and closes according to the mouse's y position. Turn on the showgrid option, and you'll discover the trick: we're just modifying the radius of the polygon, while keeping the image size fixed.

Here's another idea you might want to try out: use the Math.sin *function to modulate the curvature value at runtime. You'll get an organic flying or swimming effect!*

mimo_02.fla

Now let's put some light on the scene, and use the mouse to control the angle of incident light on our cylinder. Select the component instance and set the following parameter values in the Property inspector:

- linkage ID   mimo
- slices   20
- yangle   -20
- xangle   45
- curvature   275
- showgrid   false
- lighting   true
- animation   true
- focusangle   0
- fixlight   100
- varlight   100

Now add the following function to the first frame, which will modify the lighting according to the mouse position:

```
function focusControl() {
  img._focusangle = -.3*(this._xmouse-img._x)+90;
  img._focusangle>=270 ? img._focusangle=270 : null;
  img._focusangle<=-90 ? img._focusangle=-90 : null;
}

this.onEnterFrame = function() {
  this.focusControl();
};

stop();
```

We're now modifying the _focusangle property, so the light beam appears to be following the mouse's x position. The focusControl function uses an easing equation and a max/min value filter to adjust the lighting focus angle. These screenshots show the 3D video polygon lit from several different angles, from 225 to 45 degrees.

As you can see, the lighting gives a very realistic effect to the 3D cylinder. Of course, it would be even better if we could make the lighting less banded, but would put an even greater strain on the processor....

You can develop your own effects by modifying the easing values and changing different parameters (such as xangle, yangle, curvature, *and* lighting*) at the same time.*

Attaching the component dynamically

Finally, let's look at dynamically creating a component instance with the `attachMovie` method at runtime. With this, we don't even need to place an instance on the stage.

Let's look at a really cool multimedia experience, using an incredible panoramic video developed by a team of researchers from the University of Southern California: Thomas Pintaric, Ulrich Neumann, and Albert Rizzo. They produce high-resolution panoramic video by employing an array of five video cameras viewing the scene over a combined 360 degrees of horizontal arc. My thanks to these fine people! Please visit their web site at: http://graphics.usc.edu/~tpintari/panoramic_video/panoramic_video.htm

These panoramic videos are the best companion to my effect because they have a full 360 degrees field of view, so the cylinder is the perfect surface to show these kinds of images.

I'm going to attach the movie dynamically, so we don't need to drag and drop an instance of the component onto the stage. However, we still need to define all the parameters. We also need to place an instance of the video (`canyon.wmv`) inside an exportable movie clip – give it the Linkage ID canyon.

Now attach this code to the first frame of the main timeline:

```
properties = {};
properties.linkId = "canyon";
properties.slices = 8;
properties.curvature = 360;
properties.showgrid = false;
properties.animation = true;
properties.focusangle = 180;
properties.xangle = -30;
properties.yangle = 90;
properties.lighting = false;
properties.filllight = 100;
properties.raylight = 100;
```

The very first line creates an object and is simply a shorthand form of the new `Object()` constructor. We set properties on this object that correspond to the properties of our cylinder component – most should be fairly self-explanatory. Note that I'm using a polygon of just ten sides (a decagon) as the video file's quite large and I don't want to crash my CPU.

Now we call `attachMovie` to place an instance of the component on the stage:

```
this.attachMovie("FCylindricalVideoSymbol", "img",327, properties);
```

Note that we use the fourth parameter to specify our `properties` object. This is how we pass all the necessary property values to the new component instance.

Once attached, we can set the position and scale of our cylinder. Add the following to the first frame on the main timeline:

```
img._x = 200;
img._y = 200;
img._xscale = 100;
img._yscale = 100;
```

Now add the code we used in our first couple of examples (`tennis_panorama.fla` and `mimo_00.fla`), so that we can use the mouse to control the cylinder's rotation:

```
function yangleControl() {
  // performs y axis rotation
  var deltax= this._xmouse-img._x;
  speed += (.1*deltax-speed)/20;
  img._yangle += speed;
}

function xangleControl() {
  // performs x axis rotation
  var deltay= this._ymouse-img._y;
  img._xangle += (-.3*deltay-img._xangle)/10;
}
this.onEnterFrame = function() {
  this.yangleControl();
  this.xangleControl();
}
```

These screenshots show the 3D panorama viewed for various different values of `yangle`:

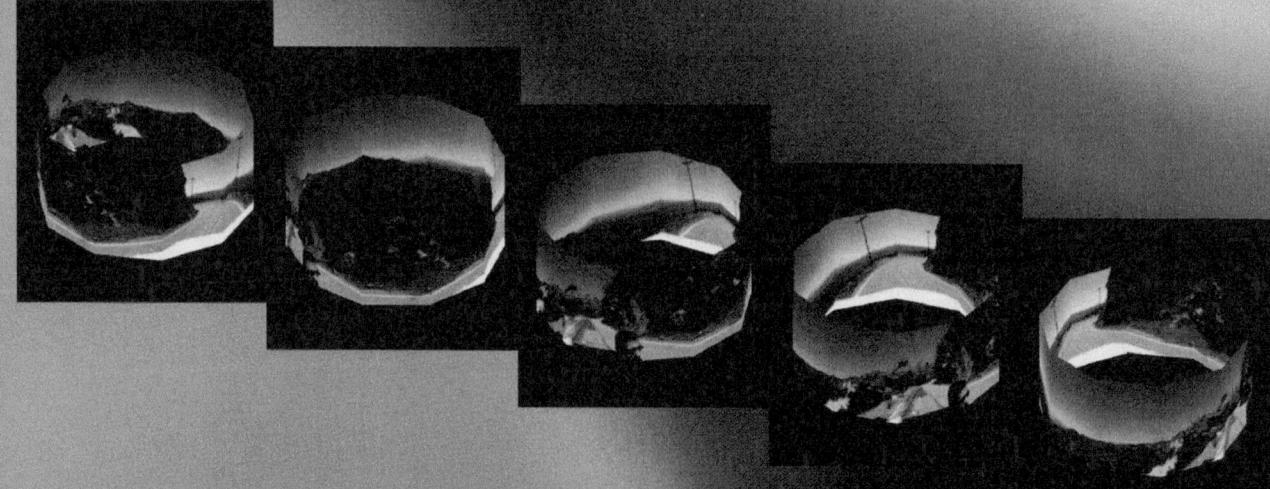

As you can see, this gives us a really cool effect: a 360° video that we can rotate with the mouse. On a slower computer though, it may be find this example just a bit too much... So, is there anything we can do to help?

Optimizing the effect for slower machines

Well, the first thing to try is reducing the number of slices, possibly down to six, or even five. This is the most critical performance factor, as it directly affects the amount of work you're asking the computer to do.

You should also try to avoid using videos with a lot of movement or image transitions. The "mimo" is a good example of video with a small amount of motion.

If you can afford to lose a little video quality, try using a higher compression ratio when you import the video. The image will become more pixelated, but the speed trade-off may just be worthwhile. Likewise, you can try scaling down when you import the video – again, this will be a matter of trial and error.

Conclusions

We've finished, and I'm sure this effect will be so useful. For instance it can be projected into a giant screen during a music concert. Of course, this is a very processor-intensive effect. If you want to run it at speed with high quality video footage, you'll need a computer with a powerful CPU (at least a Pentium 4).

If you are a hard coder, you can develop your own mutations of this effect by modifying the component code: for instance you could change the code in order to obtain two concentric video rings... another stunning effect for the next version of the component!

Anthony Onumonu works at Saffron
Interactive (www.saffroninteractive.com),
where he is a Senior Developer. Anthony's
first experience with web development goes
back to when Flash 3 was on the market and
has seen the Web through its ups and downs.
Anthony is a very active member of the web
community and is a moderator at Ultrashock
(www.ultrashock.com). He's also a news
editor for BD4D (www.bd4d.com),
MediumArt (www.mediumart.co.uk), and 3
Man Army (www.3manarmy.com).

Anthony thanks;

- His family for their continued support.

- Ketan Amin and family for their continued support.

- Bel Chand for his technical support.

- Nicky Sutton (www.nickysutton.com) for her graphical support.

- Ben and Pete (www.mediumart.com) for technical assistance.

- Ken (www.themenace.com) & Craig (www.broxi.com) for Red Back Support ;)

- friends of ED and Danny Franzreb for making this possible.

Video Half
Anthony Onumonu

Inspiration is around us all the time. The real challenge is finding it. I've often wondered if there are any differences in the type of inspiration that a graphic designer gets compared with a developer. What I've found is that inspiration is the same. The only difference is in the way we interpret it.

Yugop.com was one of the first sites that showed me the true power of ActionScript. The various studies on the site amazed me. A prime example is the industrial clock (www.yugop.com), where the concept of time is expanded and measured with animation. Just watch the way each figure for time is drawn. This study just whetted my appetite to learn ActionScript.

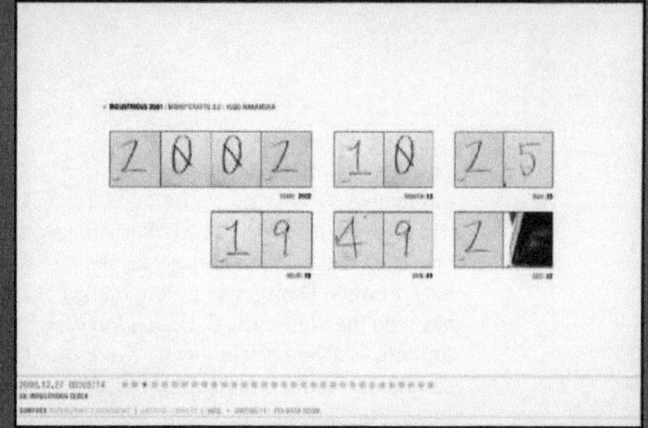

One of the latest additions to the Macromedia designer's toolbox is **Flash Communication Server MX**. This server solution makes it possible to deliver real-time audio and video straight to your browser. Slowly but surely, we are going to see an increase in the amount of video content online, and with broadband becoming readily available, more and more companies are seeing the potential of online video. One of the major benefits I see is the way that the video content can blend with your site. Gone will be the days of having to download additional plug-ins to view video content.

A site that's making great use of the Flash Communication Server is DateCam (www.datecam.com). What separates this site from the rest of the dating agencies out there is that their subscribers are able to use live video and chat.

Away from the Web, I think the one place where I've drawn the most inspiration is BD4D. By Designers 4 Designers (which has a website at www.bd4d.com) is an independent, non-profit, creative designer collective that encourages and inspires new media design around the world.

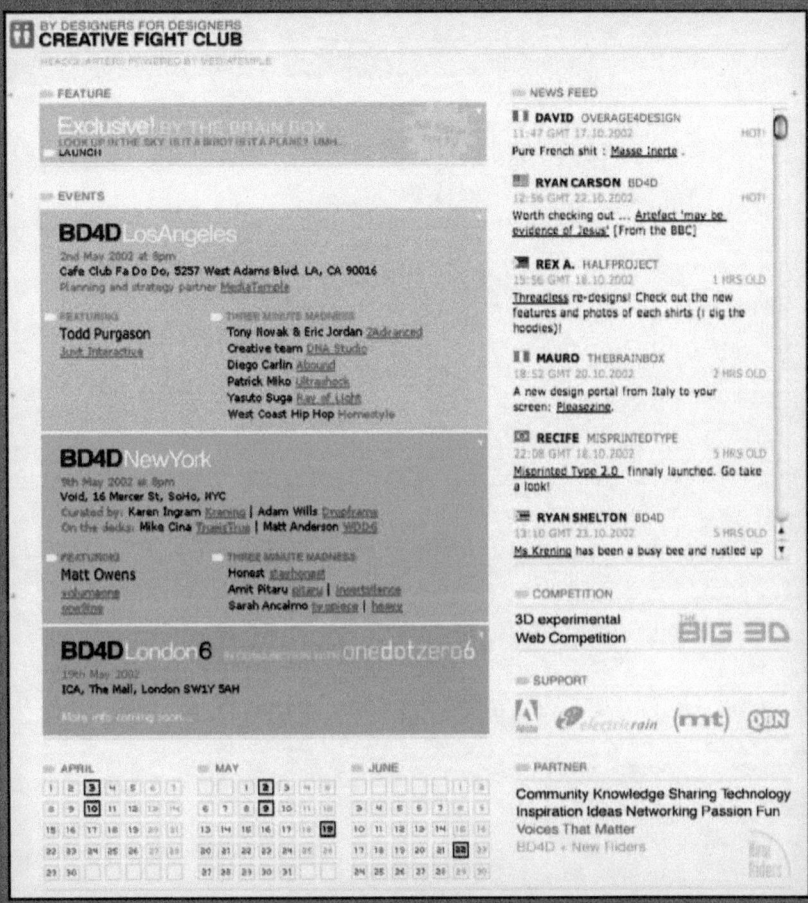

I was a bit intimidated the first night I attended one of their events. I guess I was worried that I wouldn't fit in or know anybody. My fears were proved unfounded though, because not only did I meet some very cool people, but I ended up bumping into some friends from secondary school – I guess we all know that small world feeling!

What I find so special and fascinating about BD4D is that it's a web community that is away from the computer. You get to distinguish people by their faces rather than their screen names. I guess this was one of the aims of the founders, Ryan Carson and Ryan Shelton.

A normal night consists of three or four sessions of three-minute madness, during which people from the community show their work and talk about it. The main section of the night is a talk from a guest speaker – to name just a few examples Brendan Dawes, Pete Barr Watson, Andy Beaumont, Hillman Curtis, Hoss Gifford and Jemma Guru, all inspirational designers.

Now, even though the name of the community is By Designers 4 Designers, this is far from the truth. You get a diverse crowd of people from the new media industry. If you ever do go to one of the events, take the time out to look around the room at your peers. What you will find if you look carefully is pure creative energy. Imagine if all these people came together on one project. There would probably be a lot of arguments, but you can bet the results would be worth it.

Life on a video wall

Now on to my inspiration for this project. One thing that has always fascinated me since childhood is the technology that goes into creating video walls. I'm talking about the type that you see at concerts that at a touch of a button can split into two, then four, then up to thirty screens. For this project I wanted to build my own video wall, playing a live stream from my webcam.

Later I'll extend the video wall concept by applying various effects like audio and motion detection, but let's start with streaming the video into Flash.

Live stream into Flash

I began by bringing a live stream into Flash, with a feed from my webcam. This is actually very simple.

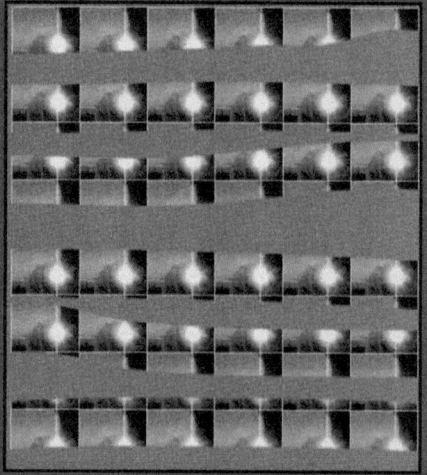

Start with a new movie, and open the Library. Using the Options menu in the right-hand corner of the Library, select New Video. An Embedded Video object will now appear in your Library.

Drag it from the Library on to the main stage.

Head into the Properties inspector and give the Embedded Video object an instance name; I called it live.

We now need to create our camera object, and we do so by attaching the following code to the first frame:

```
// Create cam object.
cam = Camera.get();
```

We now attach our live stream to our camera object by adding:

```
live.attachVideo(cam);
```

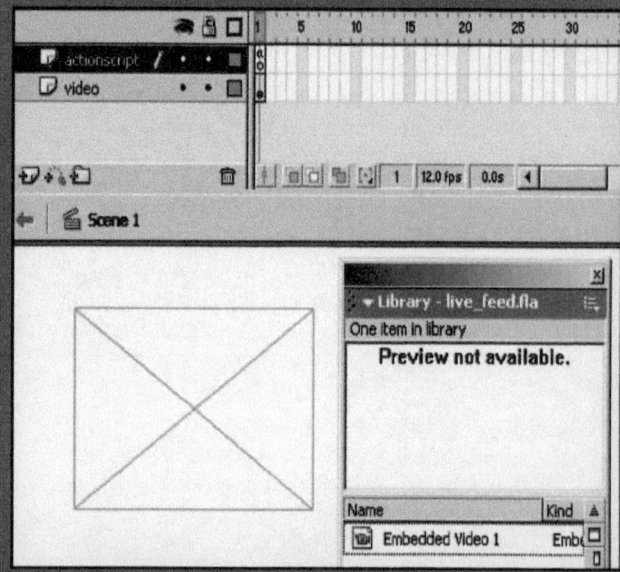

Now export and test your movie. When you run your movie the Privacy dialog will greet you with a message requesting your permission to access the camera.

Select Allow so that Flash can access your camera. Once this is done, a live stream will appear in your Flash movie.

You can bring up the Settings dialog (which contains the Privacy tab) whenever you like, simply by calling `System.showSettings`. The file `settings_dialog.fla` on the CD demonstrates this by using a button to activate the Privacy dialog.

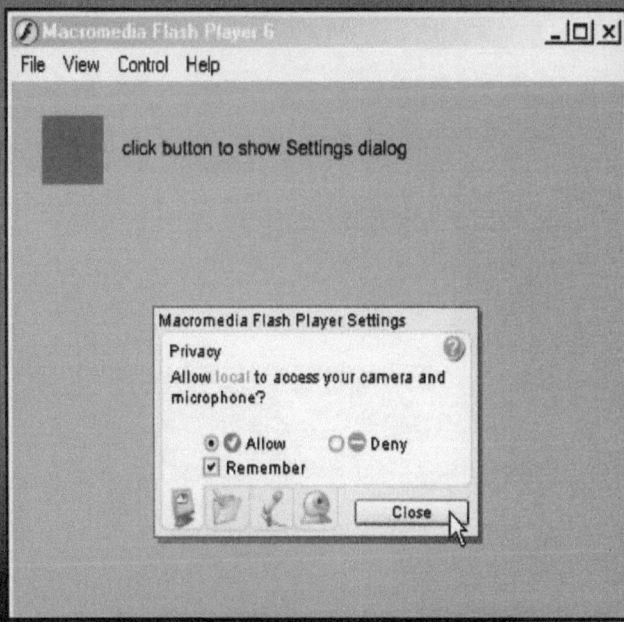

I saved this file as `live_feed.fla`, and you can find it on the CD.

Our next object is made up of movie clips forming a grid. Now there are two ways we can undertake this task. Method one is very painstaking and time-consuming, and involves you having to individually place each clip on the main stage. Now I'm pretty sure you don't fancy placing fifty-odd movie clips on the main stage and lining those movie clips up in a grid format (even if you do have the Align tool to help you).

The second method requires a little thought, along with some ActionScript, but it can be done in a fraction of the time.

Open a blank movie and create a blank movie clip – Insert > New Symbol...

Drag your blank movie clip from the library on to the main stage. Then use the Properties panel to give your blank movie clip an instance name. For our example we are going with clipholder.

Create another movie clip and call it square. But this time add a square to the movie clip using the Rectangle tool. Now select the square, and using the Info panel, set the width and the height of the square to 40 pixels. Then set the x and y positions of the square to 0.

We are now going to give our movie clip a bit more power and make it dynamic by giving it a Linkage identifier. Once our movie clip has this Linkage ID, we can use ActionScript to attach as many instances as we want to the stage. Each new instance has all the same characteristics as the original movie clip.

Open the Library, and right-click the movie clip square. If you move down the context menu, you will come to Linkage.... The Linkage Properties dialog appears.

Check the Export for ActionScript box. The Linkage identifier has been enabled and you can add your identifier. For our example we are going to call our identifier video_object. Click OK.

> You can also add a Linkage identifier when you are inserting a new symbol.

Now add the following code to the first frame of your movie:

```
var grid_row = 8;
var grid_col = 6;
video_wid = 40;
video_hei = 40;
for (var i = 0; i<grid_row; i++) {
  for (var j = 0; j<grid_col; j++) {
    clipholder.attachMovie("video_object", "v_"+i+"_"+j, zIndex);
    clipholder["v_"+i+"_"+j]._x = (j*video_wid);
    clipholder["v_"+i+"_"+j]._y = (i*video_hei);
    zIndex++;
  }
}
stop();
```

grid_row and grid_col are used to set the size of our grid. So if we wanted a grid that had four blocks we would set var grid_row = 2 and var grid_col = 2.

video_wid and video_hei are used as factors for positioning our movie clips in a grid format. Let's say we wanted each movie clip to be spaced out by 10 pixels. We would then set video_wid = 50 and video_hei = 50.

We now use a nested for loop to add our movie clips to the stage to form the grid. This sure beats adding each clip by hand!

So let's look at the outer loop first. In our example we have set the grid_row to 8. This loop will continue to execute while var i is less than the grid_row. This loop will be executed eight times. Each time the loop is executed, the second loop is executed and var i goes up by 1.

Then comes the second loop, nested inside the first. In our example we have set the grid_col as 6. This loop will continue to execute while var j is less than the grid_col. It will be executed six times, each time the external loop executes.

This loop is responsible for attaching our movie clip square to the movie clip on the main stage called clipholder.

video_object is the linkage name of our square movie clip. It is used to call the movie clip from the Library.

"v_"+i+"_"+j is the new instance name for a clip that has been dynamically added.
So the first clip will be called v_0_0.

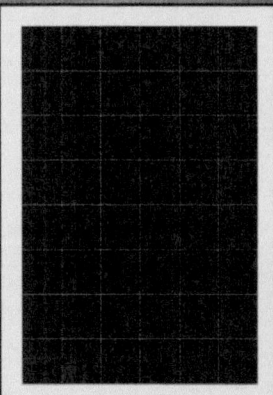

zIndex sets the depth of the dynamically attached movie clip. Each time the loop is executed the zIndex goes up by 1.

You can only have one movie clip per level attached to the main stage using the attachMovie method.

This second loop is also responsible for setting the position of each of the clips that have been attached to clipholder.

I saved this file as object2.fla. As you can see when you test, the code lays out an eight by six grid.

2 become 1

Now that we've built our objects, we're ready to join them up to make our video wall.

Still in your `object2.fla` file, edit the square movie clip – time to make our square into a rectangle!

You need to resize the rectangle graphic on the outline layer to 80 by 60. Once you have finished remove the fill so that you are just left with the outline.

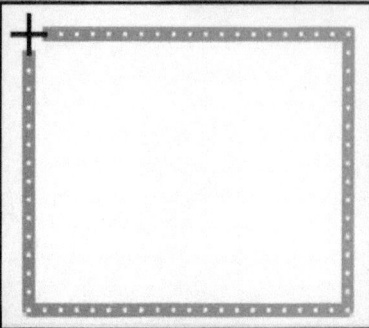

Next open `live_feed.fla` as a Library file – File > Open as Library...

From the Library, drag the Embedded Video object onto the stage of the square movie clip. Using the Info panel, set the width to 80 px and the height to 60 px. Then set the x and y positions of the Embedded Video object to zero.

Using the Property inspector, give the Embedded Video object an instance name of video.

Now go back to the main stage, and add the following line at the top of our frame 1 code listing:

```
cam = Camera.get();
```

This uses the Camera object to get us a reference to a physical camera, which we store as cam.

Next, change the `video_wid` and `video_hei` values to reflect our new rectangle size. The opening lines of code should now look like this:

```
cam = Camera.get();
var grid_row = 8;
var grid_col = 6;
video_wid = 80;
video_hei = 60;
```

We now attach the live video stream to each movie clip that makes up the grid. Inside the for loop, add in the line that's highlighted below:

```
for (var i = 0; i<grid_row; i++) {
    for (var j = 0; j<grid_col; j++) {
        clipholder.attachMovie("video_object", "v_"+i+"_"+j, zIndex);
        clipholder["v_"+i+"_"+j]._x = (j*video_wid);
        clipholder["v_"+i+"_"+j]._y = (i*video_hei);
        clipholder["v_"+i+"_"+j].video.attachVideo(cam);
        zIndex++;
    }
}
```

Now export and test your movie. When you run your movie the Privacy dialog may pop up, but this all depends on how you set up your privacy permission when you finished building the first object.

Our video wall is now complete. I saved mine as `wall.fla`. You could maybe try experimenting with a different size grid. You could also try rotating the movie clips or changing the alpha. It's really all up to you: the possibilities are endless!

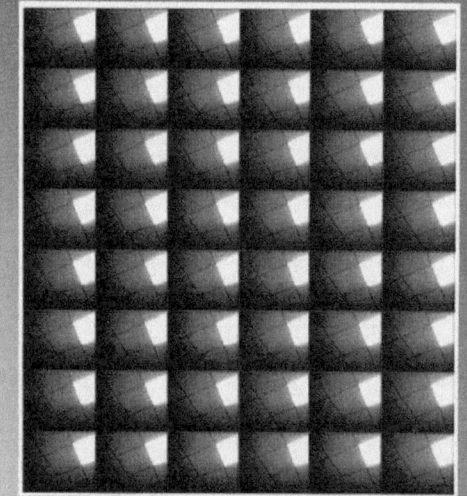

Let the remixing begin

For this serving, I've decided to apply a dynamic mask to the video wall. To reveal what is under the mask, you have to use your mouse and roll over the active area. Interesting patterns and shapes can be drawn. I also find that the live video stream gives a textured feel to the overall output.

185

Code analysis

The mask was applied to the movie clip (called `clipholder`) using the following code:

```
this.clipholder.setMask(line);
```

The code tell us is that we are setting `clipholder` with a mask, and that `clipholder` is being masked by a movie clip with the instance name of `line`. We use a dynamic mask instead of a layer mask so that our mask can change.

We are only going to be adding one movie clip and this clip is added to the main stage. The `attachMovie` method is used. Our new name instance is `video_object_new` and the movie clip will reside on depth 1.

```
this.attachMovie("video_object", "video_object_new", 1);
```

We then create a variable to hold the friction:

```
var fri = .2;
```

Then add an `onEnterFrame` handler to the main stage. The handler executes our code that is used to follow the cursor:

```
this.onEnterFrame = function() {
  xsquare = x;
  ysquare = y;
  xdiff = this._xmouse-xsquare;
  ydiff = this._ymouse-ysquare;
  xmove = xdiff* fri;
  ymove = ydiff* fri;
  x = (xsquare+xmove);
  y = (ysquare+ymove);
  this.video_object_new._x = x;
  this.video_object_new._y = y;
};
```

`xsquare` and `ysquare` are the last (x,y) position of the block movie clip:

```
xsquare = x;
ysquare = y;
```

`xdiff` and `ydiff` is the total distance the block movie clip needs to travel to get to the cursor:

```
xdiff = this._xmouse-xsquare;
ydiff = this._ymouse-ysquare;
```

`xmove` and `ymove` is the amount the block movie clip is going to move in the current cycle:

```
xmove = xdiff* fri;
ymove = ydiff* fri;
```

x and y is the block movie clip's new position:

```
x = (xsquare+xmove);
y = (ysquare+ymove);
```

`this.video_object_new._x` and `this.video_object_new._y` set the new position of the block movie clip:

```
this.video_object_new._x = x;
this.video_object_new._y = y;
```

Drawing a line

Now that we know how to make a movie clip follow a cursor, we need to find out how to draw the line that reveals all the content under our mask.

In `object4_drawsquareline.fla` you'll find an example of drawing a line:

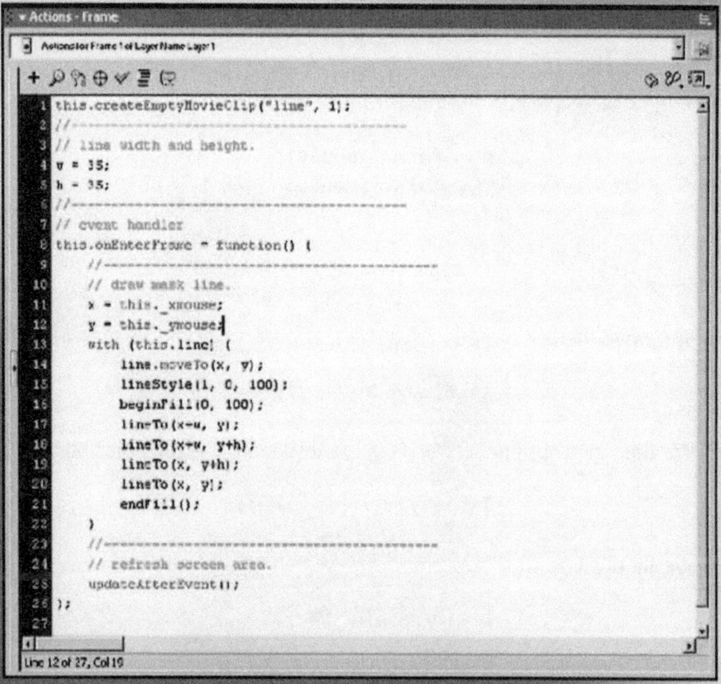

Code analysis

Before we can start, we are going to need to create an empty movie clip to attach our drawing to. Instead of creating an empty movie clip as in previous objects, we are going to create our new movie clip dynamically.

```
this.createEmptyMovieClip("line", 1);
```

The new movie clip is attached to the main stage and has an instance name of line. The new clip has a depth of 1.

w and h are the width and height of the square that makes up our line:

```
w = 35;
h = 35;
```

Again we use an onEnterFrame handler to execute the code:

```
this.onEnterFrame = function() {
    x = this._xmouse;
    y = this._ymouse;
    with (this.line) {
        line.moveTo(x, y);
        lineStyle(1, 0, 100);
        beginFill(0, 100);
        lineTo(x+w, y);
```

```
            lineTo(x+w, y+h);
            lineTo(x, y+h);
            lineTo(x, y);
            endFill();
        }
        updateAfterEvent();
    };
```

x and y store the cursor's current position:

```
        x = this._xmouse;
        y = this._ymouse;
```

We then use a with statement to draw our line. By using the with statement, we save ourselves from having to add this.line to each following statement.

We move the line to its starting point. The starting point is defined by x and y:

```
        line.moveTo(x, y);
```

We then give our line a style. (1 = the thickness, 0 = the color black, 100 = the alpha):

```
        lineStyle(1, 0, 100);
```

We fill our line. (0 = the color, 100 = the alpha):

```
        beginFill(0, 100);
```

We now draw our line. All the points join to form a square:

```
        lineTo(x+w, y);
        lineTo(x+w, y+h);
        lineTo(x, y+h);
        lineTo(x, y);
```

Once our square has been completed we end the fill:

```
        endFill();
```

We then refresh our screen using updateAfterEvent();

We now need to join the two objects and encase them in one event handler.

If you open object5_followanddraw.fla, this will show you how it's done:

```
 2  // attach emptymovieclip to the main stage.
 3  _root.createEmptyMovieClip("line", 1);
 4  //------------------------------------------
 5  // set the friction.
 6  var fri = .2;
 7  //------------------------------------------
 8  // line width and height of squares line.
 9  w = 35;
10  h = 35;
11  //------------------------------------------
12  // event handler
13  this.onEnterFrame = function() {
14      xsquare = x;
15      ysquare = y;
16      xdiff = _root._xmouse-xsquare;
17      ydiff = _root._ymouse-ysquare;
18      xmove = xdiff*fri;
19      ymove = ydiff*fri;
20      x = (xsquare+xmove);
21      y = (ysquare+ymove);
22      with (_root.line) {
23          line.moveTo(x, y);
24          lineStyle(1, 0, 100);
25          beginFill(0, 100);
26          lineTo(x+w, y);
27          lineTo(x+w, y+h);
28          lineTo(x, y+h);
29          lineTo(x, y);
30          endFill();
31      }
32      //--------------------------------------
33      // refresh screen area.
34      updateAfterEvent();
35  };
```

When joining the event handlers into one, you need to do a bit of rearranging.

You need to remove the attachMovie code that adds our video_object to the main stage (object3_followthecursor.fla). You won't need this, because you add an empty movie clip to the stage:

```
            this.attachMovie("video_object", "video_object_new", 1);
```

You also need to remove the setting of the _x and _y properties:

```
            this.video_object_new._x = x;
            this.video_object_new._y = y;
```

This is no longer required because we use line.moveTo(x, y);

You could experiment by changing the width and height of the square. Maybe try negative numbers. You never know, it might produce an interesting effect.

After playing with the file I thought it was best if I let somebody else use the video wall and take it in another direction. Danny Franzreb of www.taobot.com fame is here to remix the file and talk a bit about what Flash and video means to him.

Perspective (taobot)

In my opinion, one of the truly fascinating things about Flash MX video is perspective. Video shown in other players like QuickTime is normally represented by a flat rectangle, which often fits to your design, but sometimes it just doesn't feel right. In Flash, I can distort, mask and script video however I want, within an environment I am used to. Not only that, but you'll also use the same plug-in for video that you are already using all over your project, which means no additional download. These two factors were also two key arguments, along with multi-user games with the Flash Communication Server and others, that convinced one of our clients to use Flash MX on their new website.

When we developed www.smirnoff-ice.de, our client already had a very successful TV spot running, which they wanted to include in a unique and fresh way on their website. So we choose to distort the spot a little and put it on a video wall that fit perfectly into the site's design.

We distorted the video clips in After Effects, optimized them with the help of Squeeze and masked them in Flash. In that case, this made perfect sense, because we had to distribute the files for slower connections and machines in high quality. However, if you have a little more processing power you can do even more and distort movies in real time.

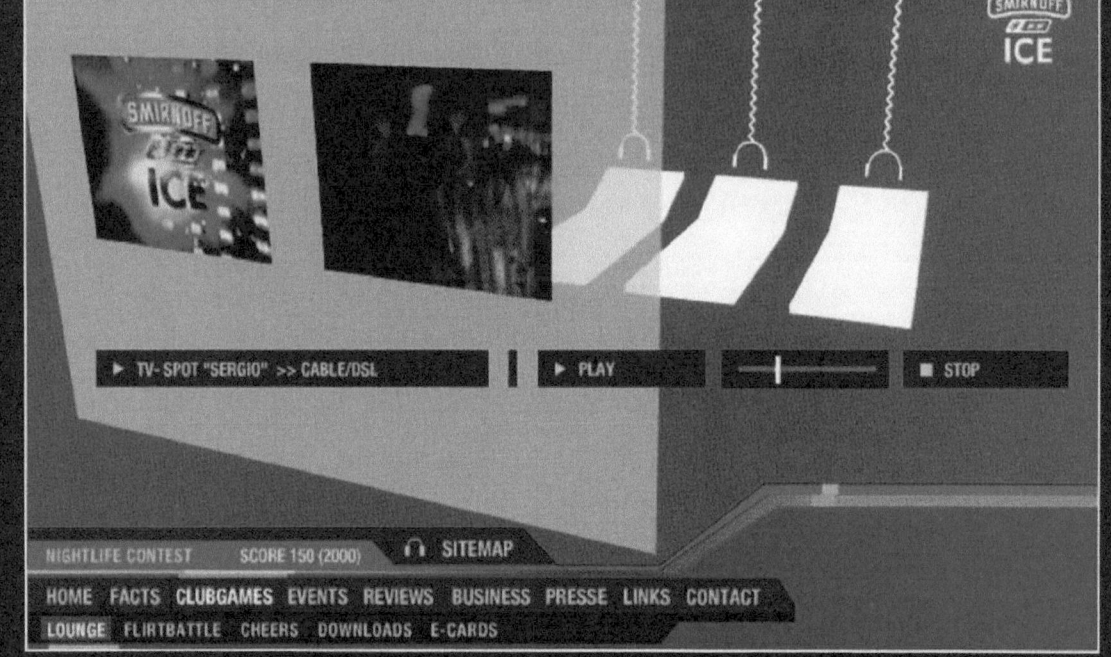

The idea for my remix came along when Ryan Shelton and Anthony stayed a few days at my house here in Germany for a BD4D I was curating. I showed Anthony a SWF file which used bitmap textures together with some ActionScript to create a real-time rotating 3D book within Flash. That example can be found on my personal website www.franzreb.com. Anthony was pretty fascinated by it, so I thought I should use a basic example for the remix of his chapter, to give you an idea of how 3D could work within Flash. Due to the fact that real-time Flash 3D includes a lot of advanced math calculations, I'll only do a simple version to get you thinking and inspire you.

The effect I created is based on scaling and rotating movie clips. First, a movie clip is created in a specified location. Second, we create another movie clip inside that clip, and that's basically it. The scaling is applied to the outer movie clip and rotation to the inner one, which creates the effect of distortion, or in other words fake 3D.

Now you can load pretty much every movie into that inner clip and distort it. I also added some sliders to the file in order to let you control distortion. Feel free to experiment with every variable to get a better impression on how it works. There are also some commented-out lines in the FLA, that you can use to alter the effect. Please note again that this technique is only the foundation of bitmap 3D in Flash.

Next I modified the background of Anthony's file; I included a little Vector-Builder. This Vector-Builder creates complex new vector shapes out of only a single symbol on the background.

I used that technique before to draw complex vector shapes on the fly for a few projects, which for me was pretty fascinating, because it took me about 30 seconds to create the original vector shape within Freehand and another 5 minutes to add the scripting within Flash.

Out of that I got thousands of different shapes, which would have taken me hours to create by hand. The technique is very simple; I just duplicate a shape, rotate it, change its position and sometimes give it the color of the background to imply a huge variation of shapes.

That's all from me – I tried to comment my remixed FLA file very well so you'll be able to understand what's going on. I hope you'll gain lots of inspiration from all these files; enjoy Cisnky's section and the rest of this wonderful book.

All the best,
Danny Franzreb

www.taobot.com

Recording wall

For this next section, you're going to need the Flash Communication Server installed. Why? Because we want to record a stream.

You can download a demo of Flash Communication Server MX from the Macromedia website at www.macromedia.com.

Once you have installed the server, you're ready to begin.

Now, recreating a video wall with 48 pre-recorded streams is pretty intensive stuff for your processor. How do I know? Well, my computer has crashed many times doing so. So we are going to create a video wall that plays back a number of single snapshot streams, which, when you mouse over them, scroll up or down, depending on where you have the mouse positioned. As the scrolling speed picks up, the illusion of playback will be created.

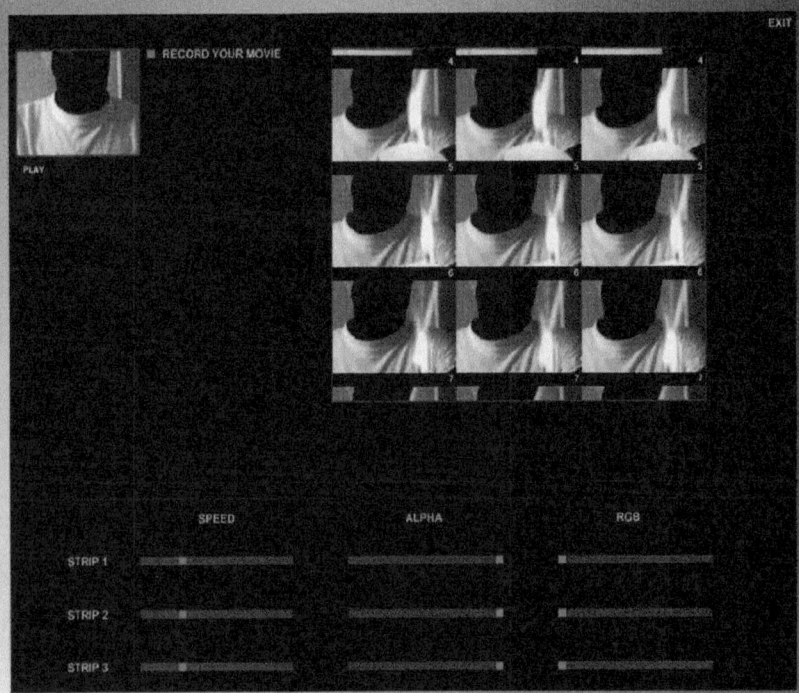

This video wall consists of three movie clips. Within each movie clip are twenty-three video objects, each like the one we created earlier. The only difference is that we attach the following code to each object, and give each one a unique instance name. So, the first object has an instance name of clip1, and the last clip23. The code is there so that the video object knows which single stream to load:

```
onClipEvent (load) {
    id = this._name.substring(4);
    video_play.attachVideo(eval("_root.replay"+id));
    eval("_root.replay"+id).play("file"+id);
}
```

The only painstaking bit of work is laying out the twenty-three video objects in a vertical strip. But this shouldn't take more than ten minutes (or you could just use the FLA provided, called vid_exp.fla on the CD).

We now need to duplicate our movie clip twice; this is done via the Library. Once this is done, we need to give our movie clips Linkage IDs: strip1, strip2, and strip3 respectively.

Let's record

```
// set up live stream.
client_cam = Camera.get();
Live_video.attachVideo(client_cam);
// initiate variables.
var i = 1;
var process = 0;
//
_root.play_button.enabled = false;
// connect to flash communication server.
connection = new NetConnection();
connection.connect("rtmp:/cisnky/001");
// create stream to flash communication server.
srcStream = new NetStream(connection);
replay = new NetStream(connection);
// record stream to flash communication server.
function record() {
  if (no_frames == 24) {
    //
    clearInterval(interval_id);
    _root.record_indicator.gotoAndStop(1);
    // reset bar indicator
    no_frames = null;
    _root.record_msg = " PLAY";
    play_button.enabled = true;
  } else {
    // If you're not recording, begin to record
    if (process == 0) {
```

```
                        // Take a snapshot
                        srcStream.attachVideo(client_cam, 0);
                        srcStream.publish("file"+i, "record");
                        // update the recording state
                        process = 1;
                        // If you're recording, stop
                } else {
                        // stop publishing recorded stream
                        srcStream.publish(false);
                        // close the stream so that we can use the same to publish again
                        srcStream.close();
                        // update the recording state
                        process = 0;
                        no_frames += 1;
                        i += 1;
                    }
                }
        }
        function startint() {
            _root.record_msg = " NOW RECORDING...........";
            interval_id = setInterval(record, 200);
        }
        function playback() {
            video_play.attachVideo(replay);
            replay.play("file"+i);
            result = "activated playback";
        }
        // stops at current frame.
        stop();
```

Code analysis

For the recording phase, we have attached an Embedded Video object to the stage so that we can view what we are recording (similar to the live stream into Flash).

Before anything can be recorded, we need to set up a connection with the server, and this is done using `NetConnection();` While we set up the net connection, we set up a directory to store our recorded streams (`connection.connect("rtmp:/cisnky/001");`).

The recording process involves twenty-three snaps being taken at a set interval. Each time we take a snapshot, we then publish it in the directory for recorded streams. Each stream is called `file(i)` with i being the stream number:

```
srcStream.attachVideo(client_cam, 0);
srcStream.publish("file"+i, "record");
```

Once we have finished recording we then close our stream:

```
srcStream.close();
```

Playback

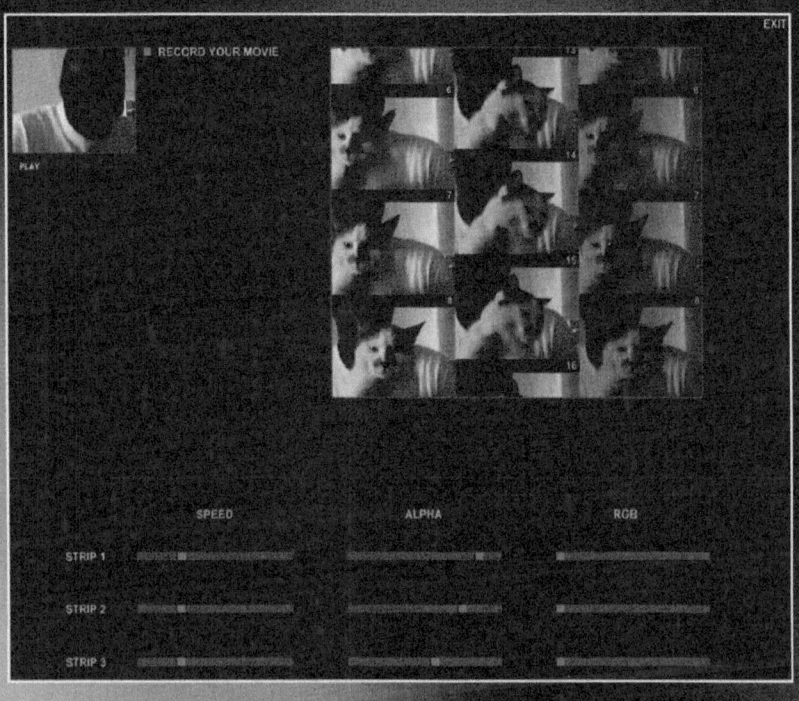

```
// create stream to flash communication server.
var start = 1;
var end = 24;
for (var i = start; i<end; i++) {
  this["replay"+i] = new NetStream(connection);
}
// create strip.
function createSlider(symbolID, name, depth, x, y,
                      w, h, cellHeight, maxSpeed) {
  // fail safe if width, height and max speed are not set.
  if (!w) {
    w = 160;
  }
  if (!h) {
    h = 400;
  }
  if (!maxSpeed) {
    maxSpeed = 50;
  }
  this.createEmptyMovieClip(name, depth);
  var me = this[name];
  me.maxSpeed = cellHeight*maxSpeed;
  me._x = x;
  me._y = y;
  // create mask for strip.
  me.createEmptyMovieClip("mask", 1);
  var mask = me.mask;
```

```
                    mask.moveTo(0, 0);
                    mask.beginFill(0, 0);
                    mask.lineTo(w, 0);
                    mask.lineTo(w, h);
                    mask.lineTo(0, h);
                    mask.lineTo(0, 0);
                    mask.endFill();
                    me.setMask(mask);
                    me.attachMovie(symbolID, "strip1", 3);
                    me.attachMovie(symbolID, "strip2", 4);
                    me.strip2._y = me.strip2._height;
                    me.tick = function() {
                        if (this.ticking) {
                            var mh = this.mask._height;
                            var sh = this.strip1._height;
                            var st1 = this.strip1;
                            var st2 = this.strip2;
                            var dy = -(this._parent._ymouse-mh/2);
                            var yv = this.maxSpeed*dy/(mh/2);
                            st1._y = Math.round(st1._y+yv);
                            st2._y = Math.round(st2._y+yv);
                            if (st1._y>mh) {
                                    st1._y = st2._y-sh;
                            }
                            if (st1._y<-sh) {
                                    st1._y = st2._y+sh;
                            }
                            if (st2._y>mh) {
                                    st2._y = st1._y-sh;
                            }
                            if (st2._y<-sh) {
                                    st2._y = st1._y+sh;
                            }
                        }
                    };
                    me.onEnterFrame = me.tick;
                    // start strip scrolling.
                    me.onRollOver = function() {
                        t1.ticking = true;
                        t2.ticking = true;
                        t3.ticking = true;
                    };
                    // stop strip scrolling.
                    me.onRollOut = function() {
                        t1.ticking = false;
                        t2.ticking = false;
                        t3.ticking = false;
                    };
                    return me;
                }
// activate and attach strip to the stage.
stripobject1 = createSlider("strip1", "t1", 1, 420, 40, 160, 400, 120, 3);
stripobject2 = createSlider("strip2", "t2", 2, 580, 40, 160, 400, 120, 3);
```

```
stripobject3 = createSlider("strip3", "t3", 3, 740, 40, 160, 400, 120, 3);
// attach playback window outline to main stage.
_root.attachMovie("playback_outline", "playback_outline", 1000);
_root.playback_outline._x = 420;
_root.playback_outline._y = 40;
// create colour object.
col_strip1 = new Color("t1");
col_strip2 = new Color("t2");
col_strip3 = new Color("t3");
set_strip = new Object();
set_strip.ra = 0;
set_strip.ga = 0;
set_strip.ba = 0;
col_strip1.setTransform(set_strip);
col_strip2.setTransform(set_strip);
col_strip3.setTransform(set_strip);
//
this.onEnterFrame = function() {
  // set speed.
  stripobject1.maxSpeed = slider1s.percentage;
  stripobject2.maxSpeed = slider2s.percentage;
  stripobject3.maxSpeed = slider3s.percentage;
  // set alpha.
  t1._alpha = slider1a.percentage;
  t2._alpha = slider2a.percentage;
  t3._alpha = slider3a.percentage;
  // set rgb value.
  set_strip.rb = slider1sc.percentage;
  set_strip.gb = slider2sc.percentage;
  set_strip.bb = slider3sc.percentage;
  // set colour alpha value.
  set_strip.ra = slider1sc.percentage2;
  set_strip.ga = slider2sc.percentage2;
  set_strip.ba = slider3sc.percentage2;
  // set rgb and alpha colour.
  col_strip1.setTransform(set_strip);
  col_strip2.setTransform(set_strip);
  col_strip3.setTransform(set_strip);
};
//stops at current frame.
stop();
```

Code analysis

First, we create twenty-three streams for playback, using a loop and the `netStream` function.

Next is a function that creates our strip. Various parameters are set; for example, where the strip should be positioned. The width and height of each strip and the speed that the strip should move.

The clip scrolling is activated using the `onrollover` and `onrollout`.

We then activate the function as an object so that we can access the various parameters mentioned before.

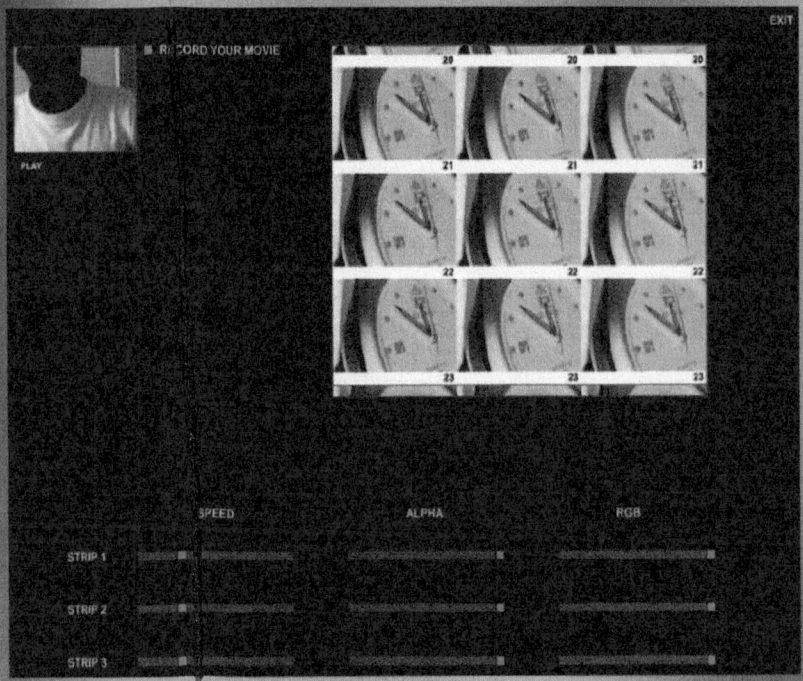

Variation

Using the scrollbars you can apply variation to your playback. You can adjust the speed of each strip, alpha a strip or change its RGB value. I found that if you move the RGB values to the far right, your image playback becomes negative.

The speed is adjusted by changing the `maxSpeed` via the object `stripobject1` which we created when adding the strip to the stage initially:

```
stripobject1.maxSpeed = slider1s.percentage;
```

The alpha is adjusted by changing the `_alpha` property of the new instance name created when adding the strip to the stage:

```
t1._alpha = slider1a.percentage;
```

The RGB is adjusted by changing the color of the video object using the `setTransform` method:

```
col_strip1.setTransform(set_strip);
```

Reactivity

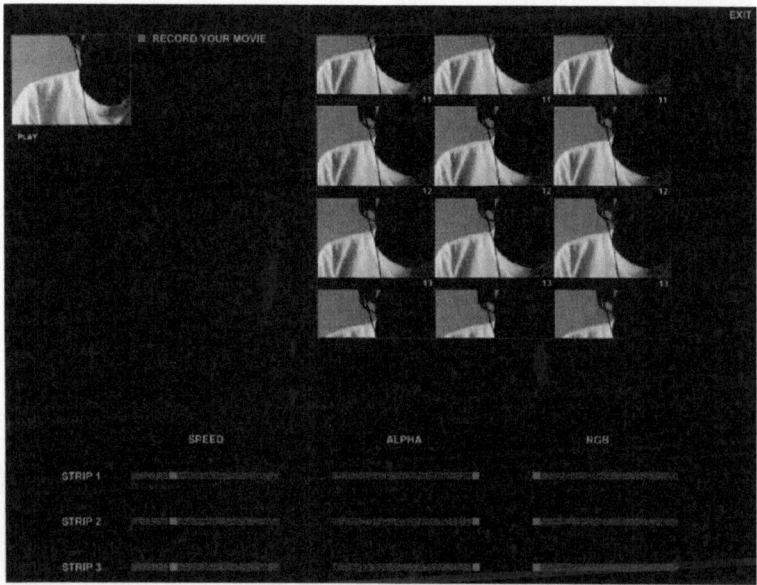

Mouse interaction is not the only method we can use to get the strips scrolling. It's also possible to use audio and motion detection.

Audio reactivity

To capture audio, we need to add a `mic` object, and this is done using `attachAudio`:

```
client_mic = Microphone.get();
_root.attachAudio(client_mic);
```

We monitor sound level by evaluating the microphone's activity level. The level varies from 0 to 100:

```
// set microphone sound activity.
_root.soundact = client_mic.activityLevel;
```

This is then picked up by the `var` `dy` causing the strips to scroll during high microphone activity and slow down during low microphone activity.

We also need to remove the `onRollover` and the `onRollOut` functionality and set the strips to true, so that they are listening to microphone activity:

```
t1.ticking = true;
t2.ticking = true;
t3.ticking = true;
```

Motion reactivity

Motion detection is captured in a similar way to audio. The main difference is that with motion we need to set our motion detection levels:

```
client_cam.setMotionLevel(30, 10);
```

30 indicates the amount of detection that is required to set off motion detection.

10 indicates the amount of time it waits before it sets the motion level back to no detection.

We also have a function that is used to clear the motion detection activity level once the motion has stopped:

```
client_cam.onActivity = function(mode) {
  if (mode == true) {
    _root.motion = client_cam.activityLevel;
  } else if (mode == false) {
    _root.motion = "";
  }
};
```

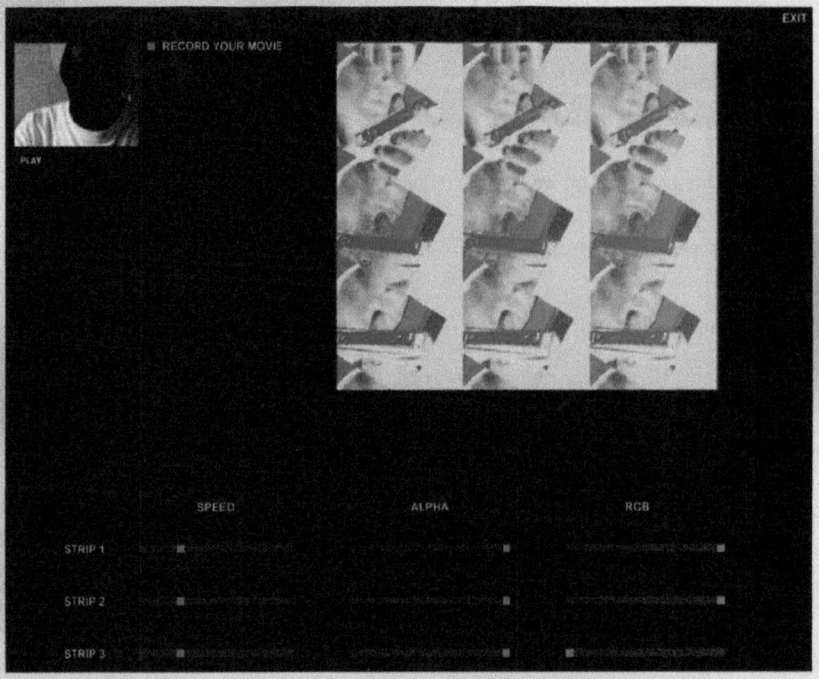

I hope your mind is now working overtime, and that you're ready to go and explore and experiment with the live streaming abilities of Flash. I think the future looks bright, and we can expect more high quality seamless web video experiences.

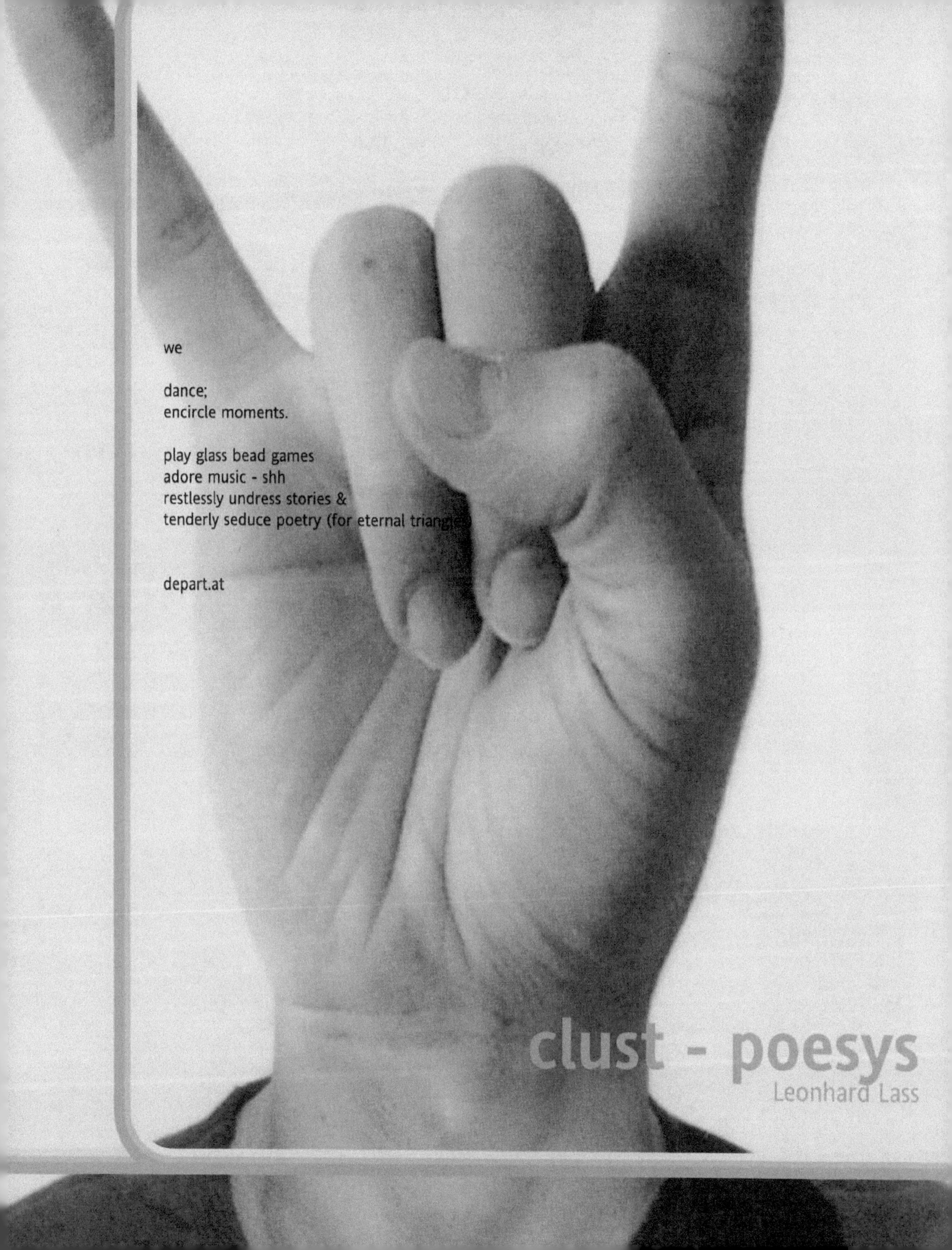

we

dance;
encircle moments.

play glass bead games
adore music - shh
restlessly undress stories &
tenderly seduce poetry (for eternal triangles)

depart.at

clust - poesys
Leonhard Lass

We're all interested in what possibilities the future holds for video. Linearity may still be the best solution for a lot of projects, but the analog videotape is all but dead. Now that Flash MX lets us put video into our movies, there's no reason to force all our ideas into a linear structure. Nor do we need to be so rigid in combining visual and audio elements. In Flash, the individual media elements are all just entities in the system, so they can be treated equally and independently.

In my opinion, the greatest thing about working with video in Flash MX is the possibility it offers to dynamically combine these different media types, and to trigger them with flexible and non-linear scores – scores in the musical sense, meaning the arrangement of elements in time.

The project

For this project, I wanted to develop a system that offers an alternative to the common arrangement of linear video editing, aiming for a more open and organic approach, which supports non-narrative editing. I often work with partly algorithm-based clips, which don't always have a fixed duration, and can therefore be hard to squeeze into a rigid linear timeline.

My 'timeline' is a rectangular space in which you can place your media assets. These can be text, sound, video, or images (or any combination thereof), and each one is represented on the screen as a filled circle.

You can then drop a playhead onto any part of the timeline space, and it will produce a ripple growing outwards in a circle. Whenever the edge of this expanding circle touches a media element, it will cause that element to start playing.

The concept's very like throwing a stone into water and watching how the ripples affect the other things in the water. This gives a more content-related approach, allowing you to cluster related media together quite intuitively.

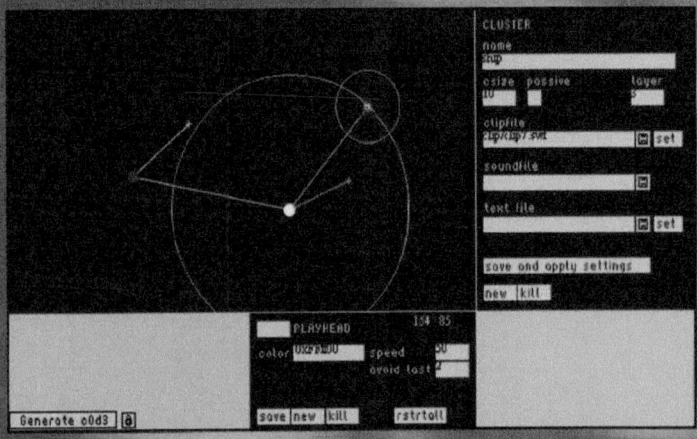

To be a truly flexible non-linear system, it needs to be able to support more than one playhead running at the same time – even with different behaviors – and also to adjust the media cluster parameters (for example, adding a masking clip from an external source) in real time.

Allowing more playheads radically increases the possibilities available, but also raises the system's complexity. Of course, you can still create linear scores by restricting yourself to one playhead and by lining up your media nodes. In addition though, you can throw all thoughts of linear editing overboard and experiment with whole new score structures: multiple playheads spreading simultaneously to trigger a whole collection of media clips. I also felt it was important to give users the chance to save their arrangements, and some way to present the outcome to an audience. We'll achieve this by building a playback-only mode for the application.

I view the pieces created with this application as 'poetic arrangements', allowing a great deal of potential for expression, and quite different to the limited, linear editing process. What's more, the idea of revealing underlying structure in the work interests me a lot. We should be able to get an almost musical appreciation of where individual playhead paths entangle and disentangle.

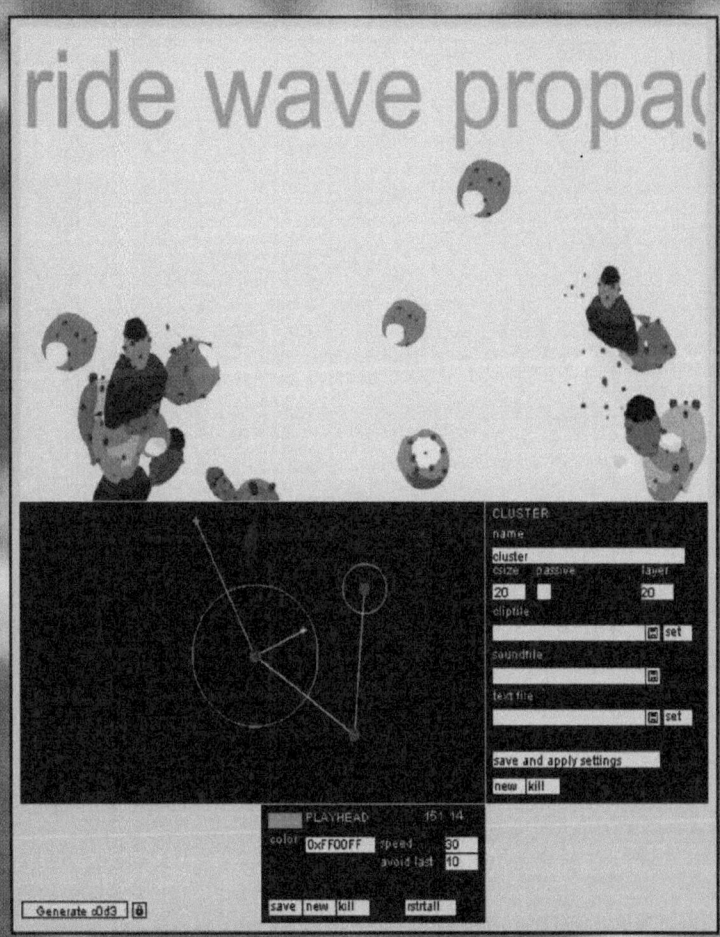

A complex system like this opens a broad space for subtle metaphors, from concrete (like physical space mapping) to abstract. You might think of arrangements that start out really synchronized and linear but evolve into a chaotic finale, or the other way round. You might as well consider the playheads as autonomous characters in the overall composition.

Let's take a look at how the finished application works.

Finding your way around

The interface may initially look a bit tricky, and you'll definitely need to read on to get a strong sense of what's going on. However, as you get deeper into the concept, you'll discover that it's really quite easy to use. You can load it up for yourself from a file (just 29KB!) on the CD called `clust.swf`.

When you first run the movie, a finished application comes up. As you'll see, the clips I've chosen for this sample arrangement aren't pure video media, as I wanted to carry the whole idea to its limit and incorporate non-linear clips. However, there's nothing to stop you using pure video clips as source material.

If you'd rather have it start out blank, simply rename the configuration file `init.dat`, which you'll find in the same folder as the SWF. Later on, we'll take a proper look at what this file does and how it works.

First though, let's define some terms that we'll use to describe the different parts of the interface.

- The **screen** is the large area at the top where the clips play.

- The **timeline** is the area below the screen where you place clusters and playheads to compose your arrangement.

- The **cluster panel** lets you create, edit, and destroy **clusters**, which are our basic media elements, represented as small filled circles within the timeline.

- The **playhead panel** lets you create, edit, and destroy **playheads**, which control when the different media elements are triggered, and are represented as growing circles within the timeline.

- The **c0d3 panel** lets you generate code describing your composition, so that you can save the fruits of your labor.

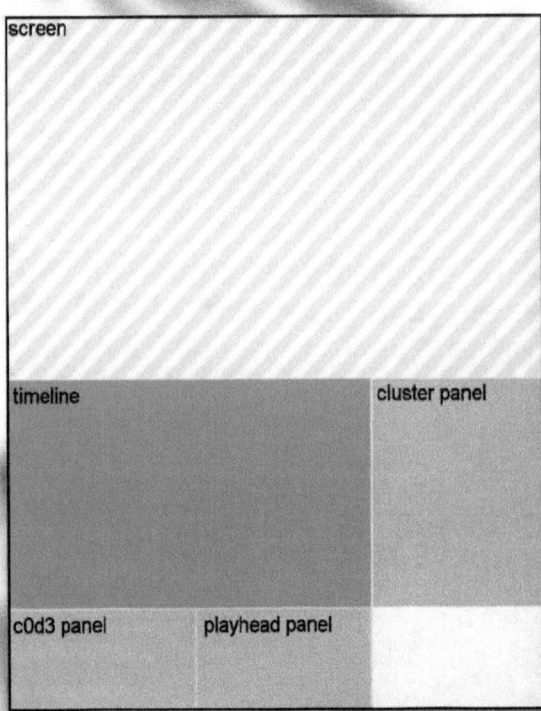

The details shown in the different panels will change according to which cluster is selected. To change a cluster's parameters, simply click on the cluster in the timeline; likewise, to change a playhead's settings, click on the little cross that marks its origin.

If you start the application without an init.dat file in the same folder, the timeline will start out blank. In this case, you can create new clusters and playheads by pressing the new button in the respective panels.

Let's take a closer look at the specific parameters we can modify for each cluster and playhead.

The cluster panel parameters

Click on one of the clusters shown in the timeline to select it – we can now take a look at the various parameters that define what it does. You can also change those parameters, though these changes will only take effect if you then click on the button marked save and apply settings.

The first input field lets us type in a name for the cluster. This is simply to help us identify clusters, and can really be anything you like.

csize determines the diameter of a cluster's circle in the timeline. Note, that this also has an effect on the fading in and out of the media. Bigger diameters result in longer fades.

Normally, when a playhead hits a cluster, that cluster will re-emit the playhead, making it an active participant in the composition. We may not always want this though, so there's an option here to set clusters to be passive, and not re-emit playheads.

The layer setting controls which clips will appear over which others.

clipfile specifies a clip file (SWF or JPEG) that will be attached to the cluster.

soundfile specifies an attached sound file (MP3).

textfile specifies an attached (URL-encoded) text file.

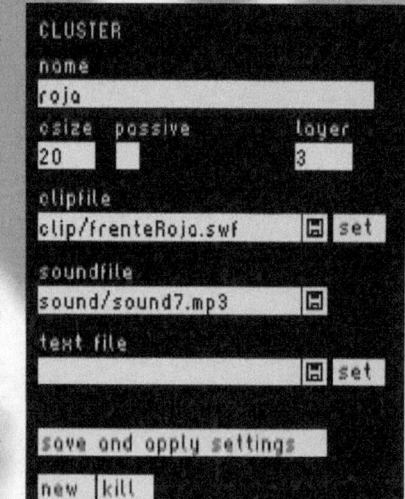

Just to the right of each of the media file input fields, you'll see a button marked with a disk icon . This is just a shortcut to load example files, making it easier to instantly play around with the system.

Next to the clipfile and textfile fields you'll see buttons labeled set. Assuming you have relevant media attached to the cluster, this will call up a settings subpanel in the bottom right corner, giving you access to further parameters relevant to the media in question.

I've already mentioned the save and apply settings button - but it's worth another mention, since it's very important! Any changes you make in the panel (or in the settings subpanel) will only take effect and get stored when you press this button.

Finally, at the bottom of the cluster panel, we have two buttons that we can use to create a new cluster (at the center of the timeline, and using the current parameter settings), or kill the currently selected one, removing it from the timeline.

The playhead panel parameters

Now click on one of the playhead crosses, and we'll turn our attention to the parameters shown in the playhead panel.

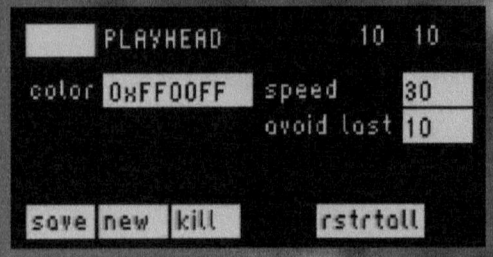

The rectangle just to the left of the word PLAYHEAD represents the currently selected playhead's color. The two numbers after it are the starting coordinates of a playhead cue (the position of the little cross in the timeline area).

color lets you adjust the color of the playhead, though note that you won't see the result until you click rstrtall to restart the sequence. The color has to be entered in hexadecimal code in the following format: 0xRRGGBB.

speed sets the speed at which the playhead circles grow. I suggest keeping it below 100.

avoid last prevents looping by telling the playhead to ignore clusters that it's recently encountered. For example, if you set a value of 2, the playhead won't have any effect on the last two clusters it's interacted with.

> 0x is the Flash color identifier, which makes Flash recognize the following hexadecimal value. The first two numbers behind the x are the red amount, the second two are the green amount and the last two make up the blue amount. For example, pure red would be 0xFF0000 and white would be 0xFFFFFF.

As with the cluster panel, you need to click save to apply your changes, while new creates a new playhead. After you have pressed this button, move your mouse over the timeline area. There you get a crosshair, which allows you to define the initial coordinates by clicking. Kill removes a playhead (and its current path), and rstrtall restarts all playheads at their original position. It's important to re-sync all your playheads while you're working on an arrangement.

Using Clust

Before we go any further, let's create a simple arrangement, to get a better idea of how the application works. First, rename the init.dat file from the Clust folder and start up the application. It should come up with a blank timeline and a blank screen.

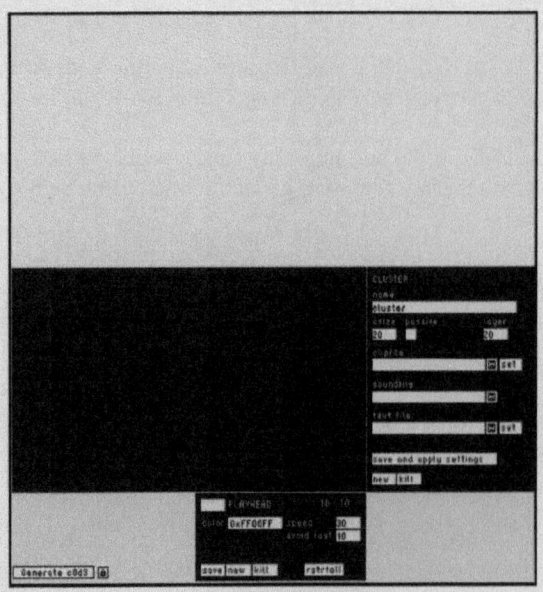

Making a new cluster

First of all, let's use the cluster panel to plant a few clusters on the timeline. In the name field, enter a descriptive title like testCluster_1. Let's make the cluster 40 pixels in diameter - so, enter 40 into the csize field.

We want this cluster to be active, so that it can emit a playhead once it gets hit – we therefore leave the passive checkbox untouched. Likewise, we can leave the layer setting alone for now.

Click on the disk icon next to the clipfile field, and select option number 1. Note that you can also enter the filename of a SWF or JPEG directly. Select a sound file in the same way; again, I've used option number 1.

Finally, click the new button to bring the new cluster into existence; there we are, our new cluster is born!

We can now drag the new cluster around in the timeline and place it wherever we want.

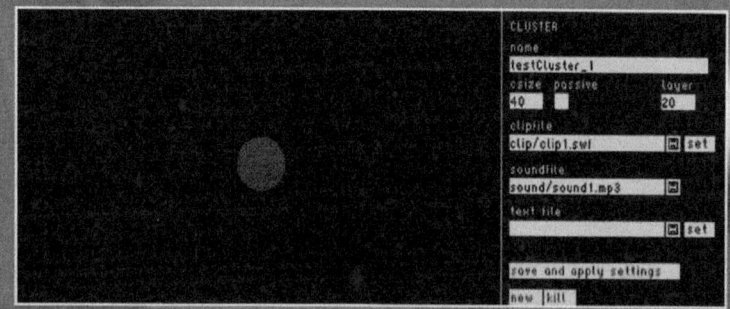

Making a text cluster

Our next step is to create a second cluster – this one will be passive, and only use text. Once again, we need to use the cluster panel.

Enter a new name (I suggest testCluster_2_text) in the name field. Change the csize to 20, making it less dominant in the timeline, and check the passive checkbox. If you're still not really sure of what passive means, wait just a bit longer... everything will become clear after you drop the first playhead.

We now need to empty the clipfile and soundfile fields, because we don't want these media in our current cluster. Add a text file from our samples by clicking on the disk icon and selecting text file 1.

Next to the text file disk icon is a set button. Press it and the TEXT.SETTINGS subpanel appears right below the cluster panel. Here, we can specify how the text is to be displayed.

Set the fontsize to 15, and enter 2 into the mode field – this will select the second text mode. There are several different text animation modes, which I'll talk about later.

Leave the other settings as they are, and press the new button to create the cluster. Again, the new cluster appears at the center of the timeline, and we can then drag it to the desired position. Note that if you haven't moved the first cluster from its initial position, you won't be able to see the new one, as both will appear in exactly the same place. When you click on it, it will become active and turn white.

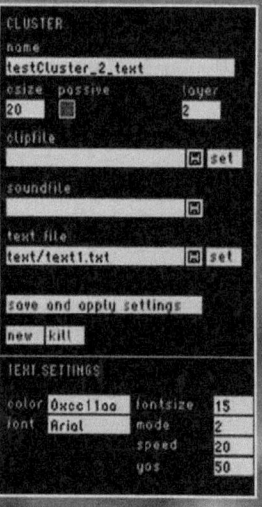

Making a playhead

Now, to get things moving we need to add a playhead, and that means using the playhead panel, just below the timeline. Leave all the settings as they are for now and just press the new button.

Now move your mouse over the timeline. You'll see a crosshair follow your mouse around the screen – this allows you to place the playhead exactly. To drop a playhead, click on the desired position.

When you click, the playhead starts to grow immediately.

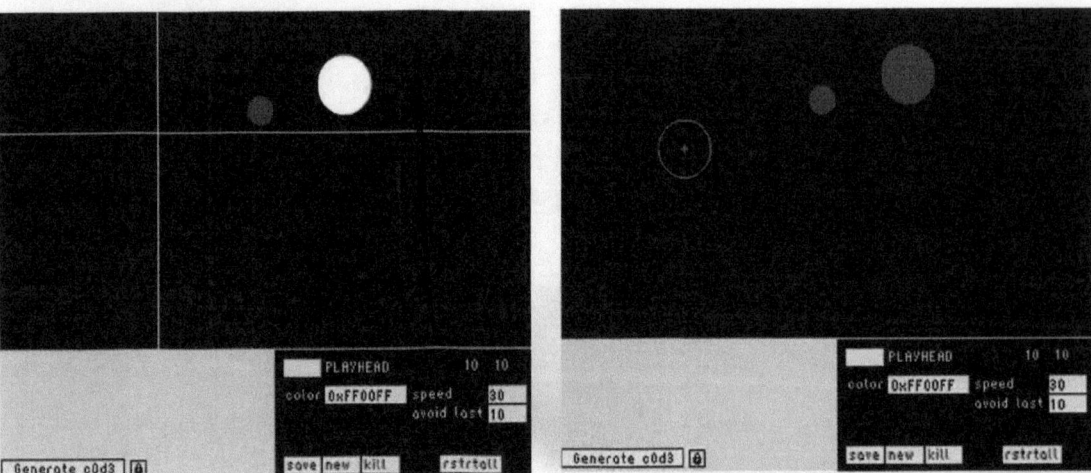

Now, as you'll remember, we set one of the clusters to **passive** and one to **active**. Watch closely what difference it makes as the playhead reaches the clusters:

■   When it touches the active cluster, the cluster starts to play and the playhead path is altered, so that the circular path comes from the center of the cluster.

■   When it reaches the passive cluster, the cluster starts to play, but the path continues in the same direction, with the circle continuing to grow from the active cluster.

Changing a cluster's parameters

Click on the cluster you want to change in the timeline area. It will turn white, showing that it's active, and the cluster panel will update to show its current values.

Inside the cluster panel, alter the field parameters as you wish, and click on save and apply settings. Now click on rstrtall (in the playhead panel) to view your changes.

Changing a playhead's parameters

Click on the origin of the playhead you want to change, represented in the timeline area by a little cross that marks the start of its path. The playhead panel will update to show the relevant parameters. Adjust the parameters as required and click on save. Finally, click on rstrtall to reboot the timeline.

Removing a cluster or a playhead

Click on either the origin of the playhead or the cluster to select the element you want to remove. In the related panel, click the kill button to remove the cluster or playhead from the timeline area.

How to save an arrangement

If you want to preserve your work, you can save a configuration file. When you save, you have the option of saving it with the possibility of opening it up in editable form, or opening the application in playback-only mode to play it.

On the bottom left of your interface you will find the generate c0d3 button, and next to it a little lock icon. Click on the icon to change its state. The closed lock means that the code you are going to generate will call the application in playback-only mode. The open lock means the application will open and play your saved arrangement, but you will still be able to edit it. Once you've decided whether to lock or unlock the arrangement, click on the generate c0d3 button.

Now a window appears, containing the code for your arrangement saved in text file format. Click into this window and select all the text (*CTRL+A* or *APPLE+A*). Then copy and paste it into a blank text file. This text file needs to be saved to the same folder and called init.dat.

Now if you exit the application, and then restart it with the file in the right place, your saved setting will be loaded.

Further population

To get a bit more used to how the system works, I'd suggest that you create some more clusters or another playhead and alter the parameters. Watch the different playhead paths and play around with the avoid last counter in the playhead panel. Using the application will give you a good grasp of how it works, so looking at the code won't be so difficult.

Defining the System

The way I work is to begin by assembling a comprehensive picture of my system, its parts, inhabitants, and rules. The nature of a system requires individual functional parts, which are able to communicate efficiently. This will result in synergies, what means that we will get something that is more than the sum of its parts. We can classify this system as cybernetic (self-steering) but not auto-poetic (self-producing).

I start by making an exact list of parts and responsibilities, as a first step to get my idea beyond the abstract. Step by step, I then move closer to an ActionScript syntax that will make the system a reality.

The parts – division of labor

The most interesting and also the most complex part of the system is the timeline area, which basically represents the whole triggering system. The other parts are simply the result of what's in the timeline area (screen) or controlling devices to design and control the inhabitants of the timeline and their behaviors. So for defining the system and its rules, we need to focus on the timeline.

The inhabitants and their environment

Actors in a system are elements with their own behaviors and abilities, and the ability to interact and communicate with either the system itself or the other actors (or both). We've already determined the two main actors in our environment; the cluster (represented by a filled circle) and the playhead (represented by an extending circle outline). As we'll see later on, we're going to need a few side actors as well, but let's cross that bridge when we come to it. For now, let's take a closer look at our stars.

The basic aim of the cluster is to represent media. It actually has nothing more to do than to store data, stay in a given place on the timeline, and wait to be touched by a playhead.

It acts as a representative of the media files and contains a link to their real entities (which will appear in the screen area). So whenever a new cluster is generated, a corresponding container for the media is created in the screen. Already we can see that only sound and movie clips could be played without further definition, while text will need some more parameters and even algorithms for a satisfying display. But let's delegate this task to the media container in the screen. The cluster only contains the links to the media files and their parameters and doesn't care about how they are played. It should only send them the command to start and stop.

For more flexibility we also need a way to weight the individual clusters, which we can easily achieve by allowing different diameters.

So we define its abilities, which we need to build into the code, as:

- is able to be positioned on the timeline
- is able to store data (sound, text, clips links)
- knows which playheads are currently on it
- may have different diameters
- can die (be removed from the timeline area)

The playhead

While the cluster is pretty much passive in its behavior, the playhead has its own life. By our definition, it is started at a user-defined position inside the timeline, from where it spreads in a circle. Whenever it touches a cluster, it starts to play the attached media and fades it in. Furthermore, if it touches an active cluster's center (core) it will start a new playhead emanating from the cluster's core while the current playhead dies.

As the playhead has an implicit movement, we want to be able to adjust its speed. The color should also be flexible for a better overview when more than one head is playing.

So, the abilities we need to build into the playhead are:

- checks for cluster collisions, and discriminates between collisions and core collisions
- fades in the media attached to clusters
- expands with a given speed
- remembers its starting position
- dies (removed from the timeline area)
- may have an individual color and speed
- remembers its path

We'll add some more things to our list later on, but when I was first thinking about the design, this was what I came up with.

The environment

Our composition environment (the timeline) is aware of what's going on within it, and has the ability to create and destroy inhabitants. Most of the time, when the inhabitants are functioning, it's in a more passive 'surveillance' mode, but the main abilities it needs are:

- creates a new playhead
- deletes an existing playhead
- restarts all playheads
- creates a new cluster
- deletes an existing cluster
- selects and deselects clusters

The system's outcome – the screen

We have already mentioned that the cluster is simply an abstract representation of a media-bundle that will be played in the screen area. So, as mentioned earlier, for every cluster we need a container in the screen, holding the real media. The container with its files is hidden until its representative cluster is touched by a playhead in the timeline area.

Therefore we note the following abilities:

- creates a container for every cluster in the timeline, which is able to hold the attached media files
- destroys this container when the related cluster in the timeline is deleted

A container needs to be able to handle the three media accordingly. This is easy for sound and movie clips, because they are already prepared for direct display. It gets trickier for text, where we need to set up a flexible (and therefore generic) text animation, which uses a text file as its data source. Another thing this container must handle is the external masking file for a media clip.

So, for our container's list of necessary abilities we have:

- handler for the masking file
- generic text animator that can display the text from the file

System weaknesses, exceptions and special cases

Now that we have the core of our system worked out, we can start to think through different scenarios to hopefully get some awareness of its weaknesses. I find this part of the process useful, as it enables me to think ahead and anticipate some of the pitfalls that lie ahead.

Infinite loops (a weakness)

The first thing that came to my attention when thinking about how this system would function is that it would have a tendency to get lost in infinite loops. This would happen if the distance to the next cluster is larger than the distance to the previous cluster.

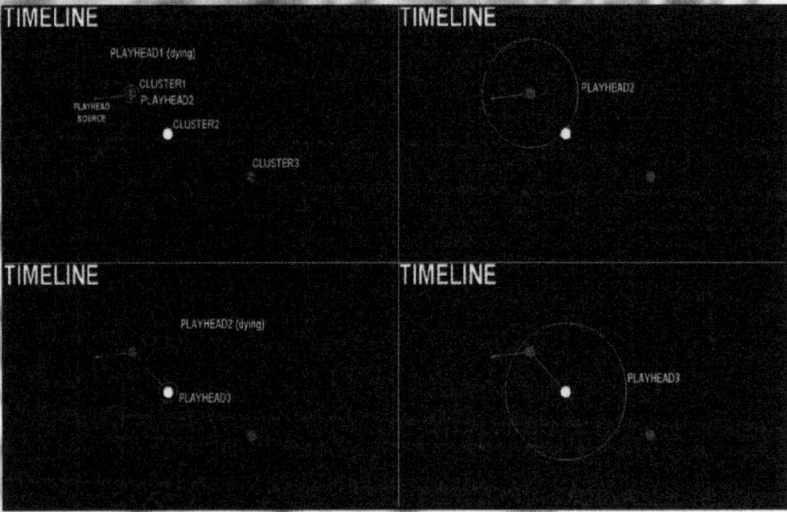

While this might be an interesting stylistic element, it could be pretty annoying if it couldn't be controlled. I want the system to be flexible, but if you had to put all the clusters in ever-nearer proximity to each other this would be very limiting.

So, we need some way to get rid of this, or, even better, a way to control it.

An easy way to completely erase the problem would be to only allow the playhead to play a cluster once, so that all former clusters in the playhead's path are avoided. However, this would be a quite radical restriction, which also limits our non-linear goal dramatically.

A better solution is to introduce the **avoid counter**, which lets us specify how many prior clusters should be avoided. With this concept in place, we'll be free to choose whether we want to allow endless loops (by setting the avoid counter to zero), totally prevent them (by setting the counter according to the maximum amount of clusters), or restrict the loop to a group of clusters.

So, to our list of the playhead's desirable abilities, we add:

- knows the path's previously-played clusters, and is able to avoid some, all, or none of them

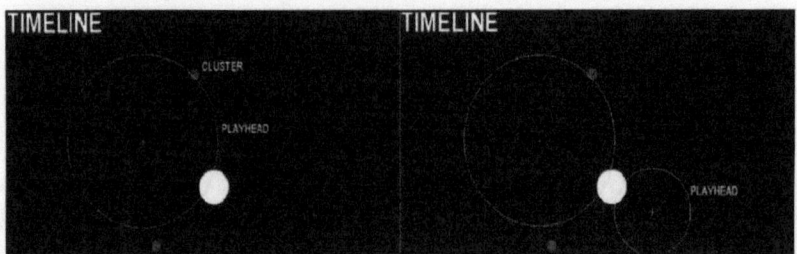

More than one playhead on a cluster at one time

Since I decided to allow more than one playhead in the timeline, it was vital to think about how they should be handled. What happens if two playheads are inside a cluster? One idea would be to generate an instance of the media cluster for every playhead, so that the cluster's media in fact appear twice on the screen.

Logically though, it feels more intuitive to have each cluster only represent one output on the screen, and therefore I think it's best if the cluster is shared between the playheads. In this case the cluster has to be aware of how many playheads are currently on it, and only stop playing the media files attached to it if all the playheads have left it again. Let's keep that in mind for later.

The code – to the keyboards!

First of all, some general notes about the code. What I'm using here for clarity's sake is 'fake' object-oriented programming. That means that I don't really instantiate and write classes, but nevertheless keep up an object-based structure.

I've tried to make all the panels and components as individual and portable as possible. Because of this, all code is kept on the individual component itself, rather than on the main timeline.

I've also included extensive comments within the ActionScript in the FLAs, which should further help you to understand the code.

Exploring the library

Before you start looking at the code in detail, it's worth taking a look at the Library panel and familiarizing yourself with the organization of symbols I've used. Most of the movie clips, buttons, and bitmaps I've used are stored away in folders, according to their usage in the movie – in fact, only the screen and timeline movie clips are located in the library root, as you can see just below:

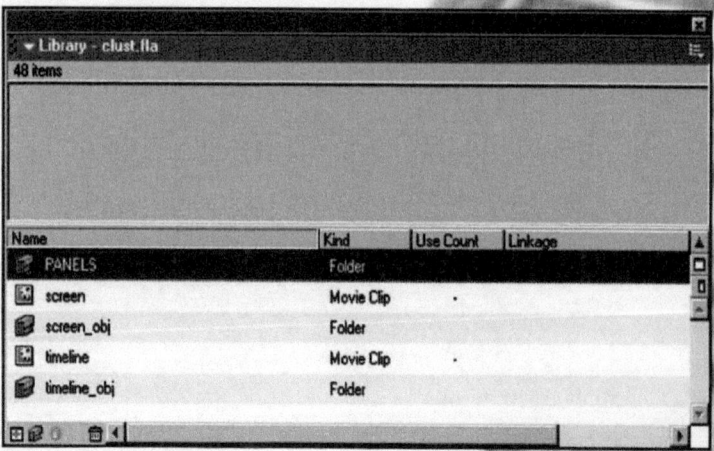

The three folders you see contain all the symbols we need to populate the screen and timeline, along with all the panels (and their own resources). Look inside, and you'll find all the bits and pieces that make up the application.

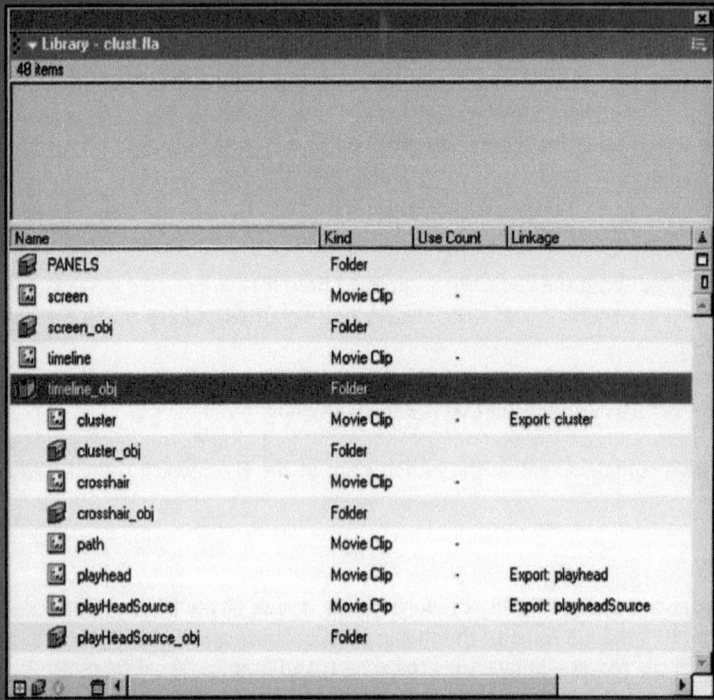

As you'd expect, we find our main actors (which belong exclusively in the timeline) defined inside the timeline_obj folder. Let's take a look at how they all fit together.

We'll start with the cluster and playhead movie clips. Both of these clips are applied dynamically, so you'll only be able to find them as symbols in the Library panel. They're both stored in the timeline_obj folder.

Defining the cluster

There isn't really much to see inside cluster symbol – there's a single instance of the circle movie clip (called circle), which contains a button whose instance name is circle_but. Double-click on it to take a quick peek inside.

circle

Even the code inside circle is nice and simple:

```
circle_but.onPress = function() {
  _parent.startDrag(false);
  _root.timeline.selectCluster(_parent);
  _root.panel.update(_parent);
  _root.textSettings.update(_parent.container.txt);
  _root.clipSettings.update(_parent.container);
};
circle_but.onRelease = function() {
  stopDrag();
};
```

It basically allows the cluster to be draggable, but only within the timeline area. It also ensures that when we click on a cluster, that cluster becomes active, and the relevant panels are updated with all relevant information.

cluster

The real action takes place in the first frame of cluster itself, in the actions layer.

The first couple of lines ensure that the cluster is visible (by maxing its _alpha property), and that it has the ability to change color when clicked upon:

```
this._alpha = 100;
circle.col = new Color(this);
```

We then go on to set up the functions and variables that will support the abilities we want all our clusters to have.

setData

First, we have a function to set and update the basic information of a cluster:

```
function setdata(name, clipfile, soundfile, textfile, csize, passive, layer){
   this.csize = csize;
   this.name = name;
   this.clipfile = clipfile;
   this.soundfile = soundfile;
   curContainer = _root.screen["container"+absId];
   if (soundfile="") {
      curContainer.sound = null;
   }
   this.textfile = textfile;
   this.passive = passive;
   if (passive) {
      _alpha = 50;
   } else {
      _alpha = 100;
   }
   circle._width = csize;
   circle._height = csize;
   this.swapDepths(Math.round(layer));
}
```

I'm sure you recognize all the parameters from looking at the application earlier. This function picks up all the variables it needs as input parameters, and makes local copies – for example:

```
this.csize=csize
```

If it didn't do this, the parameters would only be available inside the function, and not all over the clip instance (as required).

The variable curContainer stores the path to the relevant screen container, which holds the media (again, remember we talked about this earlier). So, if there is no sound file included in the cluster, the following line:

```
curContainer.sound = null;
```

...makes sure that the sound is unset.

Remember that clusters can be active (changing the playhead path) or passive. The `if...else` loop ensures that users can see if the cluster is passive, by setting its `_alpha` property to 50%.

The last line makes sure that the cluster is placed at the right depth (rounded to the nearest integer, just in case the user doesn't enter a whole number).

We also noted earlier that it's important to track how many playheads are inside a clip at any given moment. We therefore create a new array...

```
headsOnMe = new Array();
```

...and set up a few functions to manipulate it.

addHead

This lets us push a playhead object onto the end of the headsOnMe array:

```
function addHead(headObj) {
  headsOnMe.push(headObj);
}
```

removeHead

Now, a function to remove the playhead from the array when it's no longer over the cluster:

```
function removeHead(headObj) {
  i = -1;
  do {
    i++;
  } while (headsOnMe[i] != headObj && i<(headsOnMe.length));
  if (i<headsOnMe.length) {
    if (i<(headsOnMe.length-1)) {
      headsOnMe[i] = headsOnMe.pop();
    } else {
      headsOnMe.pop();
    }
  }
}
```

This removes the playhead from the array and fills the hole with the current last element in the array.

Let's look at the code for this in a bit more detail, because it's used several times for all kinds of arrays.

We start with:

```
i = -1;
```

because there is an `i++` counter in the `do...while` loop, and we want to make sure we count through the array elements from the very bottom.

Then we have:

```
do {
  i++;
} while (headsOnMe[i] != headObj && i<(headsOnMe.length));
```

This finds the place of our element in the array. Basically, while the `headObj` isn't the array element we've reached using the i++ counter, and we haven't gone all the way through the array yet as i is still less than the length of the array, we carry on counting up by incrementing i each time the loop runs. It will stop when it has found the placement of the `headObj` in the array.

If i has got past the length of the array, then our object was not found in the array, but if i is less than the length of the array, we want to go ahead and remove the element:

```
if (i<headsOnMe.length) {
```

If the object was found in the array, we then check that it's not the last element:

```
if (i<(headsOnMe.length-1)) {
```

This is important, because if it already is the last element we can simply remove it, without getting a hole in the list.

Remember that an array index always starts with 0. For that reason an array with three elements has a maximal index of 2 (0,1,2). This is why we compare with `length-1`.

So if it's *not* the last element in the array, we remove it and fill the gap:

```
headsOnMe[i] = headsOnMe.pop();
```

We overwrite the element we want to delete with the currently last element of the array, using `array.pop`. This returns the last element of an array and then removes it from the array.

If it's the last element of the list, we simply remove it:

```
} else {
    headsOnMe.pop();
```

isHeadOn

The function isHeadOn checks if headObj is in our array, and sets a flag to tell the cluster that the playhead is on it:

```
function isHeadOn(headObj) {
  isOn = false;
  for (i=0; i<headsOnMe.length; i++) {
    if (headsOnMe[i] == headObj) {
      isOn = true;
    }
  }
  return isOn;
}
```

It counts through the length of the array and sets isOn to `true` if the playhead is found.

howManyHeadsOn

Then we have the function howManyHeadsOn:

```
function howManyHeadsOn() {
  return headsOnMe.length;
}
```

This returns the number of playheads currently inside the cluster.

Together, these functions handle pretty much everything our cluster needs to know, setting up all the capabilities that we talked about earlier.

The only other action is a simple

```
stop();
```

With that, we're done looking at the cluster. Now let's move on to the playhead symbol – again, you'll need to open it up from the timeline_obj folder in the Library panel, as there aren't any instances on the stage.

Defining the playhead

If you take a look at the playhead symbol in the Library panel, it really doesn't look like much: just a red circle with a few sets of actions attached to the timeline. Well I'm sorry to break the news, but the ActionScript for the playhead is probably the trickiest piece of coding in the whole application.

It needs to detect collisions and decide on whether a cluster is started, stopped or left in peace. What's more, the playhead itself has behaviors. First of all, it grows until it hits the core of a cluster. Assuming the cluster is neither in passive mode, nor on its list of clusters to be avoided, the playhead dies and recreates itself at the center of the cluster. So, instead of talking about a single playhead, it's better to think of it as a **playhead path**.

Every playhead path has a source, represented by a little cross, where it starts (and restarts) and through which it is defined. This playheadSource is another movie clip, which is called whenever the user starts a new playhead. It contains all the information that needs to remain constant throughout the playhead path: things like speed, color, starting coordinates, and the avoid count.

playheadSource

We delegate jobs like removing and restarting a playhead to the playheadSource clip; a reasonable move, since they're closely related to the source data.

The movie clip itself contains a button, an instance of headBut, which means that we can do things like select it and drag it about the timeline. Once the clip is selectable, we can write code allowing its modification or removal.

The button code is very simple:

```
on (press) {
  this.startDrag(false);
  _root.playheadPanel.update(this);
}
on (release, releaseOutside) {
  stopDrag();
  _root.playheadPanel.update(this);
}
```

This makes it draggable, and ensures that when a playhead is clicked upon, the playhead panel updates to reflect its particular parameters. Likewise, when the user stops dragging it, the change in its position will be reflected in the panel.

Now onto the code on frame 1 of playheadSource. First, we need to track the container that's currently being played by the playhead:

```
activeContainer=null
```

Then we need to make some values available:

```
function setdata(col, speed, avoidCnt) {
  this.col = col;
  this.speed = speed;
  this.avoidCnt = avoidCnt;
}
```

You'll recognize these parameters from the list of capabilities we looked at earlier: variables for the playhead's color, speed, and avoid count are defined.

The next function codes what happens when we want to remove a playhead from the timeline:

```
function remove() {
  activePlayhead.removeMovieClip();
  myGraphicPath = _root.timeline.graphicPath["path"+id];
  myGraphicPath.removeMovieClip();
  i = 0;
  while (_root.timeline.activePath[i] != this
➡        && i<_root.timeline.activePath.length) {
    i++;
  }
  if (_root.timeline.activePath.length>1
➡        && i != (_root.timeline.activePath.length-1)) {
    _root.timeline.activePath[i] = _root.timeline.activePath.pop();
  } else {
    _root.timeline.activePath.pop();
  }
  this.removeMovieClip();
}
```

Let's look at this in a bit more detail. First we have:

```
activePlayhead.removeMovieClip();
```

activePlayhead contains a reference to the currently playing playhead. This variable is set by the playhead movie clip, after a collision has been detected between the playhead and a cluster's core. Here, we use the reference to remove the currently active playhead.

Then we need to remove the current graphic path that has been drawn between the visited clusters as the playhead path has developed:

```
myGraphicPath = _root.timeline.graphicPath["path"+id];
myGraphicPath.removeMovieClip();
```

We work out the path to it, and then remove it:

```
i = 0;
while (_root.timeline.activePath[i] != this
        && i<_root.timeline.activePath.length) {
  i++;
}
if (_root.timeline.activePath.length>1 && i !=
            (_root.timeline.activePath.length-1)) {
  _root.timeline.activePath[i] = _root.timeline.activePath.pop();
} else {
  _root.timeline.activePath.pop();
}
```

We're keeping track of all currently active playhead paths in an array called timeline.activePath[]. So, when we remove the playhead, we also need to remove the playhead path from the array. We use the method we saw before: cycle through the array to find the particular playhead's place in it, and remove it, replacing it (if necessary) with the last playhead in the array so that we don't leave a gap.

When we've done all this, finally we remove the playheadSource movie clip from the timeline:

```
  }
  this.removeMovieClip();
}
```

restart

The next function deals with what happens when we restart all the playheads. It needs to restart all set playheads at their original position. So the already-drawn path needs to be erased, the currently playing head must be removed, and all active playheads must be sent back to their original coordinates and told to play again:

```
function restart() {
  this.path = new Array();
  activePlayhead.restart();
  myGraphicPath = _root.timeline.graphicPath["path"+id];
  myGraphicPath.clear();
}
```

First, we reinitialize the path array. Initially, this contains all the clusters on the playhead path that have already been played. By reinitializing it, we erase all that data. We then call the currently active playheads to start playing again from their original positions. Finally, we get rid of the graphic path that's been drawn on the stage. We do this by working out its path, and using the clear method to erase all formerly drawn graphics.

isInPath

The last function in playheadSource simplifies the task of finding out if a cluster has to be avoided by the current playhead:

```
function isInPath(obj, avoidCnt) {
  i = path.length-2;
  while (path[i] != obj && i>((path.length-2)-avoidCnt)) {
    i--;
  }
  return (i>((path.length-2)-avoidCnt));
}
```

To accomplish this task, we search through the playhead `path` array, starting at the end of the queue, counting down by the number of elements specified in the `avoidCnt` counter.

As I'm sure you already know, the index number of the last element in an array is `array.length-1`, because the first element is `array[0]`. What's more, the last element in the array will be the currently playing cluster, which we're not interested in. This means the last queued cluster is stored in `path[i]` where i is `path.length-2`.

Then we have the loop that actually goes through the `path` array. This is a `do...while` loop that cycles through the array elements until we either find an element matching the one we want to probe, or the counter goes out of the range specified by `avoidCnt`. So the loop itself has no direct work to do: what's important is the value of the counter when it stops.

Once the loop has stopped, we know that one or other of the exit conditions must have been met. We check the second condition again: if it's true, we know the first must have been false – and vice versa.

> We wanted to find out is if there's an element in the array that we need to look at. The simple true or false value returned by this piece of code is enough to tell us this.

Once again, the only other action in the playheadSource code is a

```
stop();
```

playhead

Now let's move on to the actual playhead movie clip. It's a multi-frame movie clip, containing a loop, which we'll look at in a minute. The most important playhead functions are contained within the first frame, so let's take a look at the code here first.

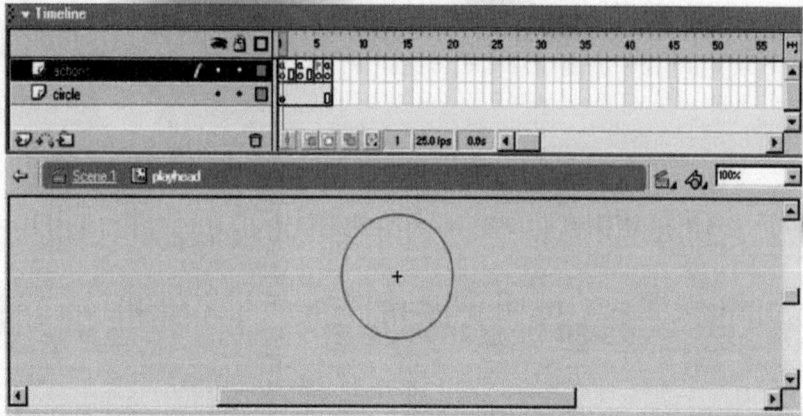

Before creating any functions, we set the clip's dimensions and initialize the `fadeStarted` variable:

```
_width = 3;
_height = 3;
fadeStarted = false;
```

fadeStarted is used to determine if a cluster fade has been started – remember we want the media to fade in and out.

checkCollision

Next comes a function to check if the playhead has collided with a cluster. Unfortunately, we can't use the `hitTest` function provided by Flash for our collision detection, as we're using circular objects (rather than rectangular) and we need it to be accurate. Don't panic, but can you remember learning Pythagoras in math?

OK, so we begin with these lines:

```
function checkCollision() {
    collided = false;
    collisions = new Array();
    i = 0;
```

This sets a flag variable with an initial Boolean value of `false`, initializes an array to hold our collisions, and begins a counter.

Then we start a `do...while` loop, which will do our math. First we need to exclude the current cluster that is emitting the playhead from the loop:

```
do {
    curObj = _parent.activeCluster[i];
    if (emitter != curObj) {
```

Now, in order to detect the collision, we need to calculate the distance between two objects (from center to center) and then subtract the combined value of their radii:

```
dx = _x-curObj._x;
dy = _y-curObj._y;
d = Math.sqrt(dx*dx+dy*dy);
```

`dx` is the horizontal difference between the playhead and the cluster. `dy` is the vertical distance. `d` is therefore the direct distance between the playhead and the cluster. Trust me, it may be evil math but it works! The following diagram shows what these variables actually represent in terms of a typical cluster and playhead:

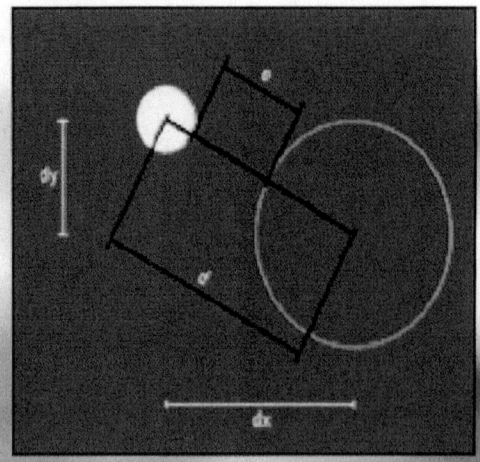

We use these values to determine whether the playhead is inside the cluster's circle:

```
if ((d<(_width/2+curObj._width/2)
➥ && (d>(_width/2-curObj._width/2))){
```

Let's break this down a little:

- `curObj` is the current cluster
- `_width/2` is the playhead's current radius
- `curObj._width/2` is the cluster's radius.

So, as long as the sum of the radii is greater than d, and the difference is less than d, we know that the playhead is inside the cluster. We therefore push the cluster object onto the end of the collisions array – otherwise, we do nothing.

We then carry on looping through all of the other clusters:

```
        if ((d<(_width/2+curObj._width/2)) && (d>(_width/2-curObj._width/2))) {
          collisions.push(curObj);
        }
      }
      i++;
    } while (i<_parent.activeCluster.length);
```

The counter i increases incrementally, and while it's less than the length of the activeCluster array, the code continues to loop. Once the whole array has been cycled through, we take a look at the length of the collisions array. If that's greater than 0, we return the whole collisions array; if not, it's because we've not detected any collisions, so the code returns false.

```
    if (collisions.length>0) {
      return collisions;
    } else {
      return false;
    }
  }
```

In fact, we're not just interested in playhead collisions with the edge of the cluster: it's collisions with the cluster's *center* that we want to use to change the playhead path's direction. The current playhead will then die and be replaced by one emanating from the center of the cluster with which it collided.

checkCoreCollision

The difference between this and the last function is that in checkCoreCollision we're ignoring the actual size of the cluster, and looking out for the playhead's collision with a *fictional* circle (with a diameter of two pixels) placed at the center of the cluster.

As well as the actual collision detection, this code needs to detect whether the cluster is active or passive, and ignore the collision if the cluster is in passive mode.

```
        function checkCoreCollision() {
          collided = new Array();
          curCollided = false;
          i = 0;
          do {
            curObj = _parent.activeCluster[i];
            if (emitter != curObj) {
              dx = _x-curObj._x;
              dy = _y-curObj._y;
              d = Math.sqrt(dx*dx+dy*dy);
              if ((d<(_width/2+1)) && (d>(_width/2-1)) && (!curObj.passive)) {
                collided.push(curObj);
              }
            }
            i++;
          } while (i<_parent.activeCluster.length);
          if (collided.length>0) {
            return (collided);
          } else {
            return false;
```

Most of this code is just the same as that in checkCollision. The only notable changes can be found in the first if condition:

```
if ((d<(_width/2+1)) && (d>(_width/2-1)) && (!curObj.passive)) {
```

We effectively change the target radius (previously curObj._width/2) to 1, and add an extra condition to ensure that passive clusters are ignored:

restart

This function sets all playhead variables and clusters back to their initial values:

```
function restart() {
    startedClusters = new Array();
    emitter = null;
    _x = source._x;
    _y = source._y;
    collision = false;
    coreCollision = false;
    source.activePlayhead = this;
    gotoAndPlay(1);
}
```

We reinitialize the startedClusters array, set the emitter to null (so that if a cluster was emitting a playhead, it's now stopped), set the _x and _y playhead values back to those of the source, set the collision and coreCollision variables back to false, send the playheads back to their source, and restart the playhead movie clip back on frame 1.

die

This is the last function defined on frame 1 of the playhead, and is responsible for making the playhead vanish in an aesthetically pleasing manner when it dies:

```
function die() {
    steps = 20;
    gotoAndPlay("die");
}
```

We want the dying playhead to fade out rather than vanish instantaneously, so we set up a frame loop, steadily decreasing its alpha value until the circle disappears. We've defined all that functionality on frame 6 (just after the frame labeled die) so this function simply tells Flash how many steps are required and sends us on to the relevant frame.
So, we have the following code on frame 6:

```
if (_alpha>3) {
    _alpha -= 100/steps;
    gotoAndPlay(_currentframe-1);
} else {
    this.removeMovieClip();
}
```

We simply step down the value of _alpha, once each time the frame is played, and keep looping back to the previous frame (which leads straight into this one) until _alpha is less than 3. Once that happens, we remove the clip completely.

Controlling the playhead

Under normal circumstances, the movie clip will loop continuously between frames 1 and 3, and the code in these frames can be seen as the functional heart of the system, where all the real decision-making occurs.

So, let's take a look at the code in frame 3. We begin with a couple of calls to our collision detection functions:

```
coreCollision = checkCoreCollision();
collision = checkCollision();
```

Remember that both functions return an array of clusters where collisions have been detected (or false if nothing was detected).

We now move on to processing the collision. If variable collision doesn't have a value of false, we know that some collision has been detected, so we cycle through all of the array elements it contains:

```
if (collision != false) {
    for (i=0; i<collision.length; i++) {
```

For each one, we check if it involves a cluster that needs to be avoided on account of being in avoidCnt:

```
if (!source.isInPath(collision[i], source.avoidCnt)) {
```

If not, we create a new reference to the container related to the cluster with which the playhead collided:

```
newContainer = _root.screen["container"+collision[i].absId];
```

We then calculate the number of steps required for the fadeIn, according to the cluster's radius:

```
steps = (collision[i]._width/2)/(source.speed/50);
```

We check that the container isn't already playing (so as to avoid multiple fadeIns). If so, we fade it in:

```
if (!newContainer.playing) {
    newContainer.fadeIn(steps);
}
```

We finish off the loop body with the following code:

```
        if (!collision[i].isHeadOn(source)) {
          collision[i].addHead(source);
          startedClusters.push(collision[i]);
        }
      }
    }
  }
```

This helps us keeps track of how many playheads there are inside a given cluster. First, it checks if this playhead has already been recorded. If not, it's added to the queue, and the collision is added to the `startedClusters` array – `startedClusters` lists all the clusters started by this particular playhead. There may be more than one, and we need to keep track of them all, because we need to fade them out again, if a `coreCollision` occurs.

Interesting core collisions

Next, we have the code that deals with each `coreCollision`. We have to deal with the fact that there may have been more than one `coreCollision`, but that some may have been on clusters that should be avoided; ultimately, only one `coreCollision` can trigger the next playhead.

First of all, we set up some variables:

```
      interestingCoreCollision = false;
      found = false;
```

Then we start an `if` block – the following code will only run if we've detected a core collision:

```
      if (coreCollision != false) {
        i = 0;
```

Now we have a do...while loop that checks all currently detected core collisions to see if they should be avoided or not:

```
        do {
          found = !source.isInPath(coreCollision[i], source.avoidCnt);
          i++;
        } while (i<coreCollision.length && !found);
```

The `isInPath` function of a `playheadSource` returns `true` or `false`. So, if a collision is *not* in the avoidance path, `found` will be set to `true` and the loop will stop.

We decrement the counter i (since it'll be one too high by the time the loop stops) and use `interestingCoreCollision` to store the specific `coreCollision` we're interested in:

```
        i--;
        if (found) {
          interestingCoreCollision = coreCollision[i];
        } else {
          interestingCoreCollision = false;
        }
      }
```

If we don't find one, interestingCoreCollision is set to false – this being the case, we run the following code:

```
if (interestingCoreCollision == false) {
  _width += source.speed/50;
  _height += source.speed/50;
  if (_height>350) {
    _root.timeline.restartAllHeads();
  } else {
    gotoAndPlay(_currentframe-1);
  }
```

This code continues to expand the playhead and loop through frames 2 and 3, until the playhead's height is greater than 350, at which point all the playheads are restarted.

On the other hand, if an interesting core collision *has* been found, we first need to create a new (descendant) playhead at the relevant cluster's center, and then remove the existing playhead:

```
} else {
  _root.timeline.createPlayhead(interestingCoreCollision, source);
  source.activeContainer =
➥        _root.screen["container"+interestingCoreCollision.absId];
```

We must then stop all the clusters that were started by the playhead collision. Remember that there may also be other playheads on those clusters. We therefore need to look at each of the clusters in turn, and check if the playhead we just removed was the *only* one on them, before deciding whether or not to fade them out:

```
for (i=0; i<startedClusters.length; i++) {
  if (startedClusters[i].howManyHeadsOn()>1 &&
➥      startedClusters[i].container != source.activeContainer) {
    startedClusters[i].removeHead(source);
  } else {
    if (startedClusters[i].container != source.activeContainer) {
      startedClusters[i].container.fadeOut(startedClusters[i]._width);
      startedClusters[i].removeHead(source);
    }
  }
}
```

Finally, we remove the playhead:

```
  this.die();
}
```

Well, that was quite a bit of work! Now that we have our main actors assembled though, we can start to look at building up the environment, and adding user interactivity and functionality. We'll start by taking a look at the timeline movie clip.

The timeline

The timeline is where our actors live, and as such, it's responsible for passing on the user-specified parameters and behaviors. Double-click on the timeline symbol to see what it contains.

It's basically a two-frame movie clip – the two frames corresponding to editable and non-editable modes – containing several masked layers and a bunch of function definitions. The whole of the timeline area is masked so that when, for example, the playheads grow larger than the timeline, they won't intrude into other areas of the application.

In the top left corner of the stage (on the path layer) is an instance of the path movie clip called graphicPath. This is actually an empty movie clip: we'll use it to dynamically draw the graphic path, our visual representation of our playheads' journeys.

In the center of the stage (on the crosshair layer) is the crosshair movie clip. This helps users to place new playheads within the timeline – let's take a closer look.

Inside the crosshair

Double-click on the crosshair symbol, and you'll see that it's a simple three-frame movie clip with three layers: actions, button, and crosshairs. In the first frame, the stage is empty, and the actions layer simply contains a stop action.

If you move to frame 2, the stage now has some content. The button layer contains a button the same size as the timeline, with an instance name of coordbut. Lock off the button layer, and you can click on the horizontal and vertical lines – they are in fact just movie clips, called horHair and vertHair respectively.

Now look at the actions on frame 2 of crosshair, which is labeled as active. First, you have two lines controlling horHair and vertHair:

```
horHair._y = _ymouse;
vertHair._x = _xmouse;
```

These set the x and y coordinates of the movie clips' registration points to the mouse position, so that a crosshair will follow the user's mouse. Remember the crosshairs that appeared when you went to place a new playhead on the timeline? Yes, these are they.

The next lines control the actual placement of the new playhead:

```
coordbut.onRelease = function() {
  _parent.createPlayheadAt(_parent._xmouse, _parent._ymouse,
                           col, speed, avoidCnt, endMode);
  gotoAndStop(1);
};
```

The function createPlayheadAt (which we'll study in a moment) takes the parameters passed in from the panel and places a new playhead accordingly, before taking the crosshair movie clip back to the first frame, where the stage is empty once more.

Now let's get back to the timeline movie clip itself. As I mentioned earlier, it contains two frames, for editable and non-editable states of the application. The ActionScript attached to frame 1 of its actions layer defines seven functions, which contain all the functionality we need to have clusters and playheads appear in the timeline.

Before we start defining any functions though, we need to initialize all the variables and arrays we'll need for the timeline:

```
activeCluster = new Array();
selectedCluster = null;
absCnt = 0;
absPlayheadCnt = 0;
absPathCnt = 0;
activePath = new Array();
```

We're going to use `absplayheadCnt` to keep track of the number of playheads created in the current session. Likewise, `absCnt` will store the number of clusters, and `absPathCnt` the number of timeline paths. The arrays will store information about the active cluster/path and `selectedCluster` (not so surprisingly) will tell us which cluster is currently selected.

Now let's investigate those functions.

Timeline functions related to playheads

The first three timeline functions all deal with different aspects of creating playheads in the timeline. There are two different ways for a playhead to be born:

- When the user activates the crosshair (via the New button in the playhead panel) and clicks on the timeline while it's active.

- When an existing playhead hits the center of an existing cluster (defined as a `coreCollision`) and that cluster emits a new playhead.

We therefore define our playhead-related functions as follows. For the first scenario:

- `startPlayhead` initializes the crosshair movie clip.
- `createPlayheadAt` creates a new playhead at specified coordinates, and at the *start* of a new playhead path.

And for the second:

- `createPlayhead` creates a new playhead at the *end* of an existing playhead path.

Let's take a closer look.

startPlayhead

This is the function that's called whenever the user clicks on the playhead panel's New button – here's what it looks like:

```
function startPlayhead(col, speed, avoidCnt, endMode) {
    crosshair.col = col;
    crosshair.speed = speed;
    crosshair.avoidCnt = avoidCnt;
    crosshair.endMode = endMode;
    crosshair.gotoAndPlay("active");
}
```

There's not a great deal to this function: it simply assigns certain necessary variables to the crosshair movie clip (so that it's ready to perform its function) and jumps to the crosshair frame labeled active.

From there, the crosshair itself takes over for a while, until the user clicks and releases the mouse button. At that point (as you may recall) it calls the `createplayheadAt` function – and that's our very next step.

createPlayheadAt

This is evidently the more important function of the two. It's responsible for creating a brand new playhead path and placing a playhead instance at the start of it. So, we begin by attaching a new playhead movie clip to the timeline movie clip:

```
function createPlayheadAt(startx, starty, col, speed, avoidCnt, endMode) {

    curPlayhead = this.attachMovie("playhead", "playhead"+absPlayheadCnt,
                                        absCnt+absPlayheadCnt+100);
```

If you take a look back at the Library panel, you'll see that I gave the playhead symbol a Linkage Identifier (also playhead) so that we could dynamically import it into the movie.

Each new instance of playhead is given its own name, and placed at a different depth, so as to avoid overwriting existing instances. Remember that absplayheadCnt tells us how many playheads there are in the current session. Since this number will change with each new playhead, we use it to make each instance name and depth unique.

We then use curPlayhead to store the newly created movie clip, and set lots of fairly self-explanatory parameters:

```
    curPlayhead._x = startx;
    curPlayhead._y = starty;
    curPlayhead.emitter = null;
    curPlayhead.startedClusters = new Array();
```

Likewise, absCnt will store the number of clusters, and absPathCnt the number of timeline paths. The arrays will store information about the active cluster/path and selectedCluster (not so surprisingly) will tell us which cluster is currently selected.

We now prepare to draw the path – in other words, the line connecting all the clusters that have been triggered by a particular playhead:

```
    curGraphicPath = graphicPath.createEmptyMovieClip("path"+absPathCnt,
                                                absPathCnt);
```

We use the new (and very handy) Flash MX function createEmptyMovieClip to create an empty movie clip within the graphicPath clip (which we saw on the stage earlier). We give it a unique instance name (based on absPathCnt, the current path count) and store it in curGraphicPath.

Next, we move the graphic cursor to the starting position and update the playhead count:

```
    curGraphicPath.moveTo(startx, starty);
    absPlayheadCnt = (absPlayheadCnt+1)%99;
```

Bear in mind that we don't want more than a hundred playheads on the timeline simultaneously, so we use %99 to loop the count back round to zero should it ever get too high.

We now go through essentially the same routine once again for the playheadSource movie clip:

```
    curSource = this.attachMovie("playheadSource",
                            "playheadSource"+absPathCnt, absPathCnt+500);

    activePath.push(curSource);

    curSource._x = startx;
    curSource._y = starty;
    curSource.id = absPathCnt;
    curSource.crossCol = new Color(curSource);
    curSource.crossCol.setRGB(col);
    curSource.speed = speed;
    curSource.col = col;
    curSource.avoidCnt = avoidCnt;
    curSource.endMode = endMode;
    curSource.path = new Array();

    absPathCnt = (absPathCnt+1)%99;

    curPlayhead.source = curSource;
    curPlayhead.circleColor = new Color(curPlayhead);
    curPlayhead.circleColor.setRGB(col);
```

We attach a movie clip, push it onto the activePath array, and set a bunch of properties. This time, as well as setting the position and updating the count (this time the path count, though once again limited to a maximum of 100), we're assigning path-wide properties such as color, speed, and path source.

Finally, we update the playhead panel, so that it shows information that's relevant to the new playhead:

```
    _root.playheadPanel.update(curSource);
    curSource.activePlayhead = curPlayhead;
}
```

createPlayhead

This function is called whenever we detect an interesting core collision. We know that the original playhead needs to die, while the cluster it collided with should emit a new playhead with the same properties as its late progenitor.

The cluster code we looked at earlier takes care of most of this, but when it comes to creating a brand new playhead, we still have a little work to do. That's what the function createPlayhead is for, and we need to feed it with two parameters:

- emitter specifies the cluster instance that must emit the new playhead.

- source specifies the source of the current playhead path (as submitted by the dying playhead).

First we attach the new movie clip in the location of the emitter cluster:

```
function createPlayhead(emitter, source) {
    curPlayhead = this.attachMovie("playhead", "playhead"+absPlayheadCnt,
                                         absCnt+absPlayheadCnt+100);
    curPlayhead._x = emitter._x;
    curPlayhead._y = emitter._y;
    curPlayhead._width = emitter._width+2;
    curPlayhead._height = emitter._height+2;
    curPlayhead.emitter = emitter;
```

We now pass source on to the new playhead (so that it knows which playhead source it came from) and push emitter onto the source.path array.

```
    curPlayhead.source = source;
    source.path.push(emitter);
```

This means that the array property path of the playhead instance specified by source builds up a list of all the clusters our path has visited.

We create another new array for keeping track of the currently playing clusters, and push a reference to our emitter onto the end:

```
    curPlayhead.startedClusters = new Array();
    curPlayhead.startedClusters.push(emitter);
```

We set the color of the new playhead, based on the color of the source:

```
    curPlayhead.circleColor = new Color(curPlayhead);
    curPlayhead.circleColor.setRGB(source.col);
```

...and use the source.id property to specify a particular path within the graphicPath movie clip – we store this as curPath:

```
    curPath = graphicPath["path"+source.id];
```

Next comes the drawing of the playhead path. In order to make the playhead path visible we want to draw lines, connecting the triggered clusters. Remember that we've stored all played clusters in the path array (in the playheadSource movie clip):

```
    if (source.path.length>1) {
        curPath.moveTo(source.path[source.path.length-2]._x,
                          source.path[source.path.length-2]._y);
        curPath.lineStyle(0.01, source.col, 100);
        curPath.lineTo(emitter._x, emitter._y);
    } else {
        curPath.moveTo(source._x, source._y);
        curPath.lineStyle(0.01, source.col, 100);
        curPath.lineTo(emitter._x, emitter._y);
    }
```

The if statement checks to see if there are two or more clusters on the path. If so, we draw a line from the previous emitter to the current emitter. If not, it's because only one cluster has been triggered, so we draw a line from the source position to the first emitter cluster.

> curPath is a movie clip (we created it using createEmptyMovieclip), so we're able to apply methods of the drawing API. moveTo sets the graphic cursor to a defined coordinate (relative to the curPath movie clip), while lineTo plots a line from the graphic cursor's current position to the coordinates specified. The lineStyle method defines the line appearance, with parameters specifying line thickness, color (as a hexadecimal value), and alpha transparency respectively.

Finally, we update the total number of playheads (once again, limited to one hundred), and update the source clip's activePlayhead property so that it refers to the new playhead:

```
absPlayheadCnt = (absPlayheadCnt+1)%100;
source.activePlayhead = curPlayhead;
}
```

restartAllHeads

There's actually one more playhead-related function to look at, which restarts all currently active playhead paths:

```
function restartAllHeads() {
    for (i=0; i<_root.timeline.activePath.length; i++){
        _root.timeline.activePath[i].restart();
        _root.screen.turnAllOff();
    }
    for (i=0; i<_root.timeline.activeCluster.length; i++){
        _root.timeline.activeCluster[i].headsOnMe = new Array();
    }
}
```

You may recall that the createPlayheadAt function keeps a list of all active playhead paths in the activePath array (stored as a property of timeline). This makes it quite simple to restart all our playheads: we just loop through this array and call a restart method for each referenced instance of playheadSource.

This function also stops and hides all media playing in the screen. This abrupt ending of the playheads alone doesn't tell the clusters anything, so we need to manually reset their headsOnMe array, which tracks the playheads currently running inside them.

Timeline functions related to clusters

Now for the rest of the timeline functions, the ones that tell it how to handle clusters. There are four altogether:

- createCluster
- deleteCluster
- deselectAllClusters
- selectCluster

I'd say it's fairly obvious what each one does, but it's still important to see *how* – let's investigate.

createCluster

This function begins by attaching a new instance of cluster to the timeline. Specifying parameters set (by the user) in the cluster panel, it's very similar to how we created a new playhead:

```
function createCluster(name, clipfile, soundfile, textfile, csize, passive) {
    absCnt++;
    newCluster = this.attachMovie("cluster", "cluster"+absCnt, absCnt+1);
    activeCluster.push(newCluster);
    newCluster._x = _width/2;
    newCluster._y = _height/2;
    newCluster.absId = absCnt;
    newCluster.id = activeCluster.length-1;
    newCluster.name = name;
    newCluster.clipfile = clipfile;
    newCluster.soundfile = soundfile;
    newCluster.textfile = textfile;
    newCluster.csize = csize;
    newCluster.circle._width = csize;
    newCluster.circle._height = csize;
    newCluster.passive = passive;
```

We assign appropriate values to each of the cluster's properties, and push a reference to the new cluster onto the `activeCluster` array, which holds a list of all our active clusters.

Now, assuming the cluster parameters contain references to a clip, sound, or text file, we create a related container in the screen movie clip – this is where all the media will be played:

```
    if (clipfile != "" || soundfile != "" || textfile != "") {
        newCluster.container = _root.screen.createNewContainer(absCnt,
                                       clipfile, soundfile, textfile);
    }
}
```

The `createNewContainer` function (which we'll investigate when we look at the screen movie clip) is designed to return the object that it's just created. That means we create a new container *and* get a direct reference to it (in our new cluster) at the same time.

deleteCluster

This function removes a cluster from the timeline, as well as dealing with the repercussions. We begin by identifying the screen container housing the cluster's content:

```
function deleteCluster(which) {
```

```
    container = _root.screen["container"+which.absId];
    _root.screen.deleteContainer(container);
```

Assuming which has been specified, we extract the id property that tells us where to find this cluster in the activeCluster array.

```
    if (which != null) {
        dyingid = which.id;
```

We remove the current Container from the activeCluster array and fill the hole with the current last element.

We now need to remove the deleted cluster from the activeCluster array. We do this by popping an element lastElement off the end of the array. Then, assuming lastElement isn't the one we want rid of, we assign it to activeCluster[dyingid], writing over the unwanted element value. We then update the surviving element's id property, according to its new position in the array:

```
    lastElement = activeCluster.pop();
    if (dyingid<=(activeCluster.length-1)) {
        activeCluster[dyingid] = lastElement;
        lastElement.id = dyingid;
    }
```

Finally, we remove the specified cluster movie clip instance, and make sure it's no longer selected.

```
    which.removeMovieClip();
    }
    selectedCluster = null;
}
```

That's most of the heavy work here done. Just a couple of functions left.

deselectAllClusters

This function simply loops through each of the active cluster clips, using setRGB to change them back to their original (unselected) color of dark gray:

```
    function deselectAllClusters() {
        for (i=0; i<activeCluster.length; i++) {
            activeCluster[i].circle.col.setRGB(0x4F6171);
        }
    }
```

selectCluster

This function uses the previous one to deselect all the clusters before changing one to bright white, marking it out a currently selected. It also stores a reference to the specified cluster in selectedCluster:

```
function selectCluster(which) {
    _root.timeline.deselectAllClusters();
    which.circle.col.setRGB(0xFFFFFF);
    selectedCluster = which;
    }
}
```

Apart from a closing stop action, that's it for the timeline code. Quite a lot to get through for sure, but hopefully it's a making some kind of sense to you.

Now that we've seen how the timeline looks after itself and its inhabitants, we're ready to move on to the other mai players in our application: the screen (for viewing the content of our media clusters) and the panels (which we use t manipulate them). We'll start with the screen.

The screen

The screen movie clip is where we play all the media clips represented by clusters on the timeline. It's a simple, single frame movie clip, and all the actions are attached to that frame. This is where we need to make the container that hold the individual media clips. So, first of all we initialize a containerList array, which will help us to keep track of a currently existing containers in the screen:

```
containerList = new Array();
```

After this, we define the functions to create, destroy and reset containers.

createNewContainer

This will create a new container within our screen movie clip. Depending on which media are attached, the container w ensure that they load and play correctly when needed:

```
function createNewContainer(cnt, clipfile, soundfile, textfile, layer) {
```

cnt represents the unique ID of a container through which it's connected to a cluster in the timeline. The other parameter are the filenames of the media files, and the layer – this governs the depth at which the movie clip is played, and s determines whether it will appear in front of (or behind) the others.

Next, we attach a new container movie clip, initialize its variables and add it to our global list containerList of all activ containers:

```
newContainer = this.attachMovie("container", "container"+cnt, cnt+1);
newContainer.clipfile = clipfile;
newContainer.soundfile = soundfile;
newContainer.textfile = textfile;
newContainer._visible = false;
newContainer.playing = false;
containerList.push(newContainer);
newContainer.id = containerList.length-1;
```

Now we have to prepare all the media files that need to be attached to a container/cluster. These steps should all be fair self-explanatory:

```
            if (clipfile != "") {
              newContainer.createEmptyMovieClip("clip", 1);
              newContainer.clip.loadMovie(clipfile);
              newContainer._x = 0;
              newContainer._y = 0;
              if (_root.clipSettings.maskfile != "") {
                newContainer.createEmptyMovieClip("mask", 999);
                newContainer.mask.loadMovie(_root.clipSettings.maskfile);
                newContainer.maskfile = _root.clipSettings.maskfile;
                newContainer.maskLoader.loading = true;
              }
            }
            if (soundfile != "") {
              newContainer.snd = new Sound();
              newContainer.snd.loadSound(soundfile, false);
              newContainer.snd.stop();
            }
            if (textfile != "") {
              newContainer.attachMovie("txt", "txt", 3);
              newContainer.txt.loadVariables(textfile, newContainer.txt);
              ts = _root.textSettings;
              newContainer.txt.fontcolor = ts.col;
              newContainer.txt.fontname = ts.fontname;
              newContainer.txt.fontsize = ts.fontsize;
              newContainer.txt.mode = ts.mode;

              newContainer.txt.yos = ts.yos;
              newContainer.txt.speed = ts.speed;
            }
            return newContainer;
          }
```

The mask code is interesting because it takes advantage of the new Flash MX ability to apply a mask dynamically - I'll talk more about this in a minute.

Note that in the text files section, we have to assign all the values directly, because the setdata function of the new txt movie clip will only be available in the next frame.

239

deleteContainer

This function removes the container from the containerlist array and deletes it from the screen:

```
function deleteContainer(dyingContainer) {
  if (dyingContainer != null) {
    dyingid = dyingContainer.id;
    lastElement = containerList.pop();
    if (dyingid<=(containerList.length-1)) {
      containerList[dyingid] = lastElement;
      lastElement.id = dyingid;
    }
    dyingContainer.removeMovieClip();
  }
  selectedCluster = null;
}
```

Note that this is always connected to the death of a cluster in the timeline.

turnAllOff

Last up is the turnAllOff function, which allows us to stop all media files from playing:

```
function turnAllOff() {
  for (i=0; i<containerList.length; i++) {
    containerList[i].clip.stop();
    containerList[i].playing = false;
    containerList[i].sound.stop();
    stopAllSounds();
    containerList[i]._visible = false;
  }
}
```

This is called when the user restarts all the playheads.

The container

The container is attached dynamically (inside the screen movie clip) and can be found in the Library, within the screen_obj folder. It has a Linkage identifier of container.

The container represents the media display of one cluster. Each cluster has exactly one related container. A container may contain sound, video or animation or image, and text. So there needs to be a central fading in and out function that takes care of all media. This is controlled by the setup of the container movie clip to run a frame loop, as we saw before in the playhead movie clip. Besides that, we also implement an update function (similar to the setdata function of the cluster).

fadeIn

The first function on the first frame of the container movie clip is the fadeIn function:

```
function fadeIn(steps) {
   _visible = true;
   clip.play();
   txt.startText();
   //starts the text-engine in the selected mode
   if (this.snd) {
      snd.start(0, 666);
   }
   this.steps = steps;
   playing = true;
   value = 0;
   fadingIn = true;
   gotoAndPlay("fadeInLoop");
}
```

The single parameter steps determines how many frames the fading operation should last for. The concept's quite simple: the container is stopped at the first frame. When it gets a call for fadeIn(steps), it makes itself visible and starts playing the clips, text and sound. It does this by first making the steps value available throughout the clip (as this.steps), indicating that this container is playing (playing=true), and jumping right into a frame loop.

As you can see, the function tells the movie clip to go to the frame labeled fadeinLoop. This takes us to frame 2, which contains the following code:

```
value += 100/steps;
_alpha = value;
if (this.snd) {
   this.snd.setVolume(value);
}
```

The value we want to reach after steps frames is 100 (100% alpha and 100% volume), so we add 100/steps once each frame to get the required amount. Then we can directly assign it to our alpha and volume settings.

The movie will then continue to frame 3, where some code sees if the fade-in is complete; if not, it sends the movie clip back to frame 2 to loop again:

```
if (value<100) {
   gotoAndPlay(_currentframe-1);
} else {
   stop();
}
```

If the fade-in is complete, we stop the container timeline – though note that this doesn't stop the timeline of whatever's playing inside it.

fadeOut

The fade-out works in just the same way. We begin with the fadeOut function, defined on the first frame:

```
function fadeOut(steps) {
   this.steps = steps;
   value = 100;
   gotoAndPlay("fadeOutLoop");
}
```

Then in the frame labeled fadeOutLoop, there's code to control the fade:

```
playing = false;
value -= 100/steps;
this._alpha = value;
snd.setVolume(value);
gotoAndPlay(_currentframe+1);
```

This pushes the movie clip onto the final frame, which houses the code required to actually fade the container:

```
if (value>0) {
  gotoAndPlay(_currentframe-2);
} else {
  clip.stop();
  snd.stop();
  _visible = false;
}
```

update

Now let's get back to frame 1, and move on to the update function. This is responsible for setting the container's data, loading and unloading the different media, and making them available to the rest of the code.

```
function update(clipfile, soundfile, textfile,
                       layer, textSettings, clipSettings) {
  this.swapDepths(int(layer));
  this.maskfile = clipSettings["maskfile"];
```

The input parameters indicate the media files and settings to be used. The settings are packed into arrays, and we use the variable names to identify elements – for example clipSetting["maskfile"] contains the maskfile string.

Next, we initiate the playing of the sound file:

```
if (this.soundfile != soundfile && soundfile != "") {
  this.snd = new Sound();
  this.snd.loadSound(soundfile, false);
  this.snd.stop();
}
if (soundfile == "") {
  this.snd = null;
}
```

We check if the new soundfile string is different from the current soundfile (and not empty). If that's the case we create a new Sound object called snd – if a soundfile was already attached there, this simply replaces it.

We now use our new snd object to call the loadSound function. The first parameter specifies the filename/path, while the second tells Flash if the sound is streaming or not. If there's no soundfile string attached, we remove the currently loaded sound by setting our snd object to null.

Next comes the part of the function to update and initiate the clip file:

```
if (this.clipfile != clipfile && clipfile != "") {
    if (!this.clip) {
        this.createEmptyMovieClip("clip", 1);
    }
    this.clip.loadMovie(clipfile);
```

Again, we check if the `clipfile` string has changed and make sure there's a value in `clipfile`. We then figure out whether there's already an object called `clip` – if not, we create an empty movie clip (called `clip`) to serve as the container for the `clipfile`.

The next part of the function deals with applying a mask for the clip – we use an external file, which can be any suitable SWF:

```
if (this.maskfile != "") {
    maskLoader.createClipMask(this.maskfile);
```

To apply a mask dynamically, we use the Flash MX function `setMask`. First though, we need to make sure that our mask file has been completely loaded, otherwise the masking has no effect.

We don't know how this loading may take, and since we have other things to be getting on with, we delegate the loading to the `maskLoader` movie clip and to its `createClipMask` function – we'll look at that in a minute.

If we don't have a masking file, we need to turn the masking off and remove the current masking clip (assuming there's one there). To remove a dynamically applied mask you can simply set it to `null`.

```
} else {
    clip.setMask(null);
    mask.removeMovieClip();
}
}
```

We now have a bit of code that deals with what happens if there's no clip file attached:

```
if (clipfile == "") {
    this.clip.removeMovieClip();
    mask.removeMovieClip();
    maskfile = "";
}
this.clipfile = clipfile;
this.textfile = textfile;
```

The current clip and its mask are removed, and the variables are reset.

Following this, we've some code to update and initiate the text file. To display the text of a text file (in an animated way) we need some extra work. For that reason we will create a movie clip that accomplishes this task (more on that right after the initialization). But first of all we continue to update the data:

```
if (textfile != "") {
  if (!this.txt) {
    this.attachMovie("txt", "txt", 3);
    txt.speed = textSettings["speed"];
    txt.fontname = textSettings["fontname"];
    txt.fontsize = textSettings["fontsize"];
    txt.fontcolor = textSettings["fontcolor"];
    txt.yos = textSettings["yos"];
    txt.mode = textSettings["mode"];
  } else {
    this.txt.setdata(textSettings);
  }
  this.txt.loadVariables(textfile);
```

If a `textfile` name is entered, we create a new movie clip (called `txt`) by attaching an instance of txt to the stage. Its variables are set according to the parameters set in the panel. We also need to load the text contained in the text file as variables into `txt`. Besides that we pass all the `textSettings` to it as well.

If `textfile` has no value, the `txt` movie clip is removed:

```
  } else {
    this.txt.removeMovieClip();
  }
}
```

Once again, the last action in the frame is:

```
stop();
```

The text engine: system and framework

The `txt` movie clip (which you'll find inside the screen_obj folder) is responsible for handling text content on the screen. It's attached to the stage dynamically, inside a container.

Open it up from the Library panel, and you'll see that it's a multi-frame clip, containing an initialization section (frame 1), and two modes (frames 5-9 and frames 10-12), identified by frame labels mode1 and mode2, which we can move between.

We want to be able to handle text as a dynamic element. Due to that, we have to provide a versatile system that is able to animate the text from a file, based on various parameters. We also want it to have the flexibility of extensibility, so that we can add further animation algorithms when we feel like it.

One way to accomplish this is to collect a number of useful but abstract parameters that all these algorithms could use: `speed`, `textsize`, `font`, `color`, `yoffset`, and so on would meet this aim.

So, we create a function that makes these values available for all text modes. In our case, the `textSettings` (which we enter through the text settings panel) are again packed into an array.

We introduce the mode variable to allow for using more than one animating algorithm. Each animation algorithm is placed on a distinct frame on the timeline and carries a frame label like mode1 or mode2. Depending on the mode value the gotoAndPlay command calls the appropriate mode by going to the relevant frame.

init

First we have the function that initializes the text file and loads in the variables:

```
function init(file) {
  this.file = file;
  loadVariables(file, this);
}
```

startText

The next function sends the movie clip to the appropriate frame for the required mode:

```
function startText() {
  gotoAndPlay("mode"+mode);
}
```

setData

Then we have the function that applies the settings:

```
function setdata(textSettings) {
  this.fontcolor = textSettings["fontcolor"];
  this.fontsize = textSettings["fontsize"];
  this.fontname = textSettings["fontname"];
  this.mode = textSettings["mode"];
  this.speed = textSettings["speed"];
  this.yos = textSettings["yos"];
  if (_parent.playing) {
    gotoAndPlay("mode"+mode);
  }
}
```

Now I want to talk about the two (very simple) text modes. The following code is a bit of an extra, as it is not really video-essential, but it helps a lot if you like using text overlays on video material, for instance. So for those of you who are still with me...

text mode 1 (frames 5-7)

We want the variables from the text field to be displayed one after the other, with a flexible speed, textsize, and font. Further to this, we want to fade out the text, before we continue with the next variable.

Notice that in this mode we put one dynamic text field directly on the stage. This text field has the instance name centertxt. In Flash MX there are two ways to put text into a text field dynamically:

- The first is to give the field a variable name. In this case the text field acts like any other variable, with the only difference being that it also displays its content.

In Flash MX, we can also use the fact that the text field on the stage corresponds to an ActionScript `TextField` object, with its own methods and properties. One of these properties is `text`, which can be used to control the field's text. So, we just need to give the text field an instance name, and we can control the text dynamically like this:

```
centertxt.text="shwurbel"
```

What's great about this new `textField` object is that you have full control over the text appearance as well, by applying a `textFormat` object. So, in the first frame of mode1, (which is frame 5 of the txt movie clip) we find:

```
i = 1;
value = 0;
curFormat = new TextFormat();
curFormat.color = fontcolor;
curFormat.font = fontname;
curFormat.size = fontsize;
curFormat.align = "center";
```

First, we instantiate a new `textFormat` object (called `curFormat`) and set the properties we want to control. Notice that this has no effect at the moment, because it isn't applied to any text field yet. `i` is our counter, with which we step through all variables of our text file.

Next we assign the text variables from the text file to the text field, and set some more properties:

```
centertxt.text = eval("txt"+i);
centertxt.selectable = false;
```

Then we apply the `textFormat` we prepared earlier:

```
centertxt.setTextFormat(curFormat);
centertxt.embedFonts = true;
```

In the second frame of mode1 we find:

```
value += speed/10;
centertxt._alpha = 100-value;
centertxt._y = yos;
```

Here we take care of the fading out, and ensure that the vertical offset is applied.

In the third frame, we begin with:

```
if (value<100) {
  gotoAndPlay(_currentframe-1);
```

If `value` is still smaller than 100 (indicating that the current text has not finished fading out), we continue our loop, going back to the second frame until `value` is 100 and the text is invisible.

Otherwise, we need to proceed to the next variable of our text field until all variables have been processed:

```
} else {
  i++;
  if (i>txtcnt) {
    i = 1;
  }
  value = 0;
  centertxt.text = eval("txt"+i);
  curFormat = new TextFormat();
  curFormat.align = "center";
  curFormat.color = fontcolor;
  curFormat.font = fontname;
  curFormat.size = fontsize;
  centertxt.setTextFormat(curFormat);
  gotoAndPlay(_currentframe-1);
}
```

When all the values have been processed (i>txtcnt) we start from the beginning again, reassigning the textFormat, since the user may have changed it in the meantime.

The second text mode works in just the same way, but uses its parameters in a slightly different way. I won't go into it in detail here, but you may want to take a look for yourself. To add another mode of your own design, simply add a new frame label mode3 and place your code in a loop starting there.

The panels

Now that we have prepared all these parametric functions, we need an interface to call them up and set their values. This is what the panels are here for:

- the playhead panel
- the cluster panel
- the text settings panel
- the clip settings panel

Every panel has an update(object) function that changes the parameters in the panel fields to reflect the currently selected object.

The cluster panel

The update(object) function for clusterPanel is triggered whenever the user clicks on a cluster – it's defined as follows:

```
function update(cluster) {
  name = cluster.name;
  clipfile = cluster.clipfile;
  soundfile = cluster.soundfile;
  textfile = cluster.textfile;
  csize = cluster.circle._width;
  passive = cluster.passive;
  layer = cluster.getDepth();
  if (passive) {
    check.gotoAndStop(2);
  } else {
    check.gotoAndStop(1);
  }
}
```

Each of these variables (except for passive) is represented in the panel by an input text field, whose Var setting wires the field directly up to the variable's current value. All we therefore need to do is set our local variable values with the corresponding variables in the passed movie clip instance. All other panel update functions work similarly.

check

The passive variable is controlled by a movie clip called check. This is a one-frame clip, containing a button called check_butt (instance name checkbut) and a movie clip called fill (instance name fill). It also contains the following code:

```
function passiveon() {
    fill._visible = true;
    _parent.passive = true;
}
function passiveoff() {
    fill._visible = false;
    _parent.passive = false;
}
```

These functions help us turn the Boolean variable _parent.passive on or off, making the fill visible or invisible as appropriate.

We then wire up the onPress event of check_btn to alternate between passive and non-passive states:

```
check_btn.onPress = function() {
    if (fill._visible) {
        passiveoff();
    } else {
        passiveon();
    }
};
```

Finally, we set the (default) non-passive state, and stop the timeline:

```
passiveoff();
stop();
```

fileshortcut

The next interesting feature of the cluster panel is the file shortcut control, which you'll see in several places on the panel in the form of a little disk icon. Each of these is actually an instance of a two-frame movie clip called fileshortcut. The first frame simply contains a button, along with some code:

```
quadbut.onRelease = function() {
    gotoAndStop(2);
};
stop();
```

This ensures that when the button is pressed, the movie clip goes to frame 2. That frame contains numbered buttons representing each of the clips that can be loaded via this shortcut device, and contains this code:

```
quadbut.onRelease = function() {
  setFile("x");
  gotoAndStop(1);
};
quadbut1.onRelease = function() {
  setFile(1);
  gotoAndStop(1);
};
quadbut2.onRelease = function() {
  setFile(2);
  gotoAndStop(1);
};
quadbut3.onRelease = function() {
  setFile(3);
  gotoAndStop(1);
};
quadbut4.onRelease = function() {
  setFile(4);
  gotoAndStop(1);
};
```

```
stop();
```

If the user presses the disk button again (without selecting a clip file) the movie clip goes straight back to the first frame. If one of the numbered buttons is clicked though, we call setFile to set the relevant file in the text field, and only then is the movie sent back to the first frame.

The setFile function is actually defined out in the clusterPanel clip, and defined slightly differently for each of the three instances. For example, we have:

```
clipfileshortcut.setFile = function(val) {
  path = "clip/clip";
  if (val != "x") {
    clipfile = path+val+".swf";
  }
};
```

When the top instance of fileshortcut (instance name clipfileshortcut) calls its setFile function, the parameter val is used to generate a clipfile name of the form:

```
clip/clip1
```

Likewise, the following code enables each of the other two instances:

```
soundfileshortcut.setFile = function(val) {
  path = "sound/sound";
  if (val != "x") {
    soundfile = path+val+".swf";
  }
};
```

```
textfileshortcut.setFile = function(val) {
  path = "text/text";
  if (val != "x") {
    textfile = path+val+".swf";
  }
};
```

In each case, the appropriate text field variable (soundfile or textfile) is updated with the relevant text – for example:

sound/sound2
text/text4

All the rest of the button functionality is defined exclusively on the first frame of the clusterPanel movie clip. We have handler functions for changing the panel display:

```
clip_set.onRelease = function() {
  _root.textSettings._visible = false;
  _root.soundSettings._visible = false;
  _root.clipSettings._visible = true;
};

text_set.onRelease = function() {
  if (textfile != "") {
    _root.textSettings._visible = true;
    _root.soundSettings._visible = false;
    _root.clipSettings._visible = false;
  }
};
```

These buttons control the appearance of any extra panels to deal with parameters for masking, text and so on, the data being set to the cluster and the container, and the creation and deletion of clusters.

Another one for applying the new settings:

```
cluster_apply.onRelease = function() {
  obj = _root.timeline.selectedCluster;
  if (obj != null) {
    obj.setdata(name, clipfile, soundfile, textfile,
                              csize, passive, layer);
    obj.swapDepths(int(layer));
    ts = _root.textSettings.packSettings();
    cs = _root.clipSettings.packSettings();
    obj.container.update(clipfile, soundfile,
                         textfile, layer, ts, cs);
  }
};
```

Due to the fact that cluster data isn't just needed by the cluster itself, but also in its related container, we need to pass the data to both. We also need to pass the data of the subordinate panels (text and clip settings). As we'll see in a moment, these panels provide a packSettings function that returns all the variables packed together in one array.

Finally, a pair of functions for creating and destroying clusters:

```
new_but.onRelease = function() {
    _root.timeline.createCluster(name, clipfile, soundfile,
                                    textfile, csize, passive);
};

kill_but.onRelease = function() {
    _root.timeline.deleteCluster(_root.timeline.selectedCluster);
};
```

textSettings

Open up the textSettings movie clip (which houses the text settings panel) and you'll find the following code:

```
_visible=false
function packSettings() {
    settings = new Array();
    settings["fontcolor"] = col;
    settings["fontsize"] = fontsize;
    settings["fontname"] = fontname;
    settings["speed"] = speed;
    settings["mode"] = mode;
    settings["yos"] = yos;
    return settings;
}
```

We also define an update function for this panel, to apply any text settings set there:

```
function update(txtobj) {
    if (!txtobj) {
        _visible = false;
    } else {
        col = txtobj.fontcolor;
        fontsize = txtobj.fontsize;
        speed = txtobj.speed;
        mode = txtobj.mode;
        yos = txtobj.yos;
        fontname = txtobj.fontname;
    }
}
```

clipSettings

This movie clip defines the clip settings panel, which is located just below the text settings panel in the interface. It works in exactly the same way as that panel, with functions as follows:

```
_visible = false;
function packSettings() {
    settings = new Array();
    settings["maskfile"] = maskfile;
    return settings;
}
function update(clipobj) {
```

```
            if (!clipobj) {
                visible = false;
            } else {
                maskfile = clipobj.maskfile;
            }
        }
```

The playhead panel

The playhead panel is updated whenever a playheadSource instance is selected. All the code is attached to frame 1 – the update function is as follows:

```
source = null;
function update(source) {
    this.source = source;
    col = source.col;
    speed = source.speed;
    avoidCnt = source.avoidCnt;
    colDisplay.setRGB(source.col);
    startx = Math.round(source._x);
    starty = Math.round(source._y);
}
```

This works in exactly the same way as the cluster's update function: the playhead color is set according to the color value entered into the text field whose variable name is col.

The next function deals with setting the color of the box to reflect the color of the currently selected playhead:

```
this.onEnterFrame = function() {
    colDisplay = new Color(colPad);
};
```

colPad is the instance name of the movie clip placed there whose color is changed to provide this visual reference within the panel.

The rest of the code deals with button functionality:

```
playhead_save.onRelease = function() {
    if (source != null) {
        source.setdata(col, speed, avoidCnt);
    }
};
playhead_new.onRelease = function() {
    _root.timeline.startPlayhead(col, speed, avoidCnt, endMode);
};
playhead_kill.onRelease = function() {
    source.remove();
};
playhead_rstrtall.onRelease = function() {
    _root.timeline.restartAllHeads();
};
```

Once again, this should all be self-explanatory. These are all functions we already applied with their full absolute path. In this case source is the passed playheadSource.

Saving settings

Now that we have almost finished setting up a complex editing system, we also want a way to keep our arrangements and to present them. Unfortunately Flash MX still doesn't offer a decent way to save and retrieve data from a file. Although the Shared Object concept may come to mind, which is a cookie-like function that actually allows us to store variables locally, there are some reasons why this won't suit in our case. With shared objects, we have very limited control over where the file is stored. Due to its cookie-like nature, it is always stored on the local computer, so if we are thinking about adapting it for online viewing, we won't be able to supply the initialization file. So it would be also hard to transport an arrangement to another computer.

For all these reasons I decided to implement a copy and paste solution.

The c0d3 panel

This is now the only panel we haven't looked at – it's where we access the functionality of generating code.

The c0d3Panel movie clip consists of a labeled button (codegen_but), a lockCheck movie clip instance, and a single handler function.

The lockcheck movie clip works as a toggle button, in a similar way to the passive check button in the cluster panel. This time, we have two frames, with each frame representing a state: either locked or unlocked. Here's the code (attached to both frames) that makes it work:

```
function seton() {
  gotoAndStop(1);
  _root.setlock = true;
}
function setoff() {
  gotoAndStop(2);
  _root.setlock = false;
}
check_butt.onPress = function() {
  if (_root.setlock) {
    setoff();
  } else {
    seton();
  }
};
seton();
stop();
```

If it's locked, a press of the button unlocks it; if it's not locked, another click locks it up. In either case, we set a variable setlock in the root timeline to reflect the state of the button.

Back in the c0d3Panel movie clip,
we wire up the button that will generate our code:

```
codegen_but.onRelease = function() {
_root.c0d3.generateInitCode();
};
```

This calls the function generateInitCode, which we will look at in the next section.

c0d3

If you look at the top left-hand corner of our timeline interface, you'll find an instance of this clip. It's normally quite invisible when the movie's running, but in development you'll see it as a white circle. If not, you can always open it up from the Library panel.

If you look inside, you'll see it's a two-frame movie clip, with nothing but actions on the first frame, and a large dynamic text field (with the Var name code) on the second, along with a button for returning the movie clip to the first frame.

The main functionality is attached to frame 1. We start by hiding the clip, loading setup variables from the file init.dat, and setting up the variable eof (which we'll use shortly to detect the end of that file):

```
_visible = false;
eof = "";
this.loadVariables("init.dat");
```

Next we have the function that's responsible for generating those variables in the first place.

generateInitCode

This function collects together all the data that describes our current arrangement and arranges it in the form of pathless (that is, all within the same hierarchy) variables. In fact we have to create a single string that contains the Flash-syntax code of all the variables, using the & symbol to separate values. Further we can use \r to add a carriage return, to make the resulting string more readable.

```
function generateInitCode() {
_visible = true;
code = "&clusterCnt="+_root.timeline.activeCluster.length+"&\r";
```

We start a string variable that contains a variable name clusterCnt= plus the total number of clusters in the timeline. If there were four clusters in the timeline when we generated the code, it would look like this:

```
&clusterCnt=4&
```

At the end of an expression we add the line break and continue to add the next variable:

```
code += "&lock="+_root.setlock+"&\r";
for (i=0; i<_root.timeline.activeCluster.length; i++) {
  ac = _root.timeline.activeCluster[i];
  code += "&name"+i+"="+ac.name+"&\r";
  code += "&csize"+i+"="+ac.csize+"&\r";
  code += "&passive"+i+"="+ac.passive+"&\r";
  code += "&layer"+i+"="+ac.getDepth()+"&\r";
  code += "&clipfile"+i+"="+ac.clipfile+"&\r";
  code += "&soundfile"+i+"="+ac.soundfile+"&\r";
  code += "&textfile"+i+"="+ac.textfile+"&\r";
  code += "&posx"+i+"="+ac._x+"&\r";
  code += "&posy"+i+"="+ac._y+"&\r";

  curContainer = _root.screen["container"+ac.absId];
  ct = curContainer.txt;
  if (ct) {
    code += "&fontcolor"+i+"="+ct.fontcolor+"&\r";
    code += "&fontname"+i+"="+ct.fontname+"&\r";
    code += "&fontsize"+i+"="+ct.fontsize+"&\r";
    code += "&textspeed"+i+"="+ct.speed+"&\r";
    code += "&textmode"+i+"="+ct.mode+"&\r";
    code += "&textyos"+i+"="+ct.yos+"&\r";
  }
  if (curContainer.clip) {
    code += "&maskfile"+i+"="+curContainer.maskfile+"&\r";
  }
}
```

This block of code basically just cycles through all the clusters in our arrangement, and generates a variable for each one. We now do likewise for each of the playheads:

```
code += "\r";
code += "&playheadCnt="+_root.timeline.activePath.length+"&\r";

for (i=0; i<_root.timeline.activePath.length; i++) {
  ac = _root.timeline.activePath[i];
  code += "&playhead_startx"+i+"="+ap._x+"&\r";
  code += "&playhead_starty"+i+"="+ap._y+"&\r";
  code += "&playhead_col"+i+"="+ap.col+"&\r";
  code += "&playhead_speed"+i+"="+ap.speed+"&\r";
  code += "&playhead_avoidCnt"+i+"="+ap.avoidCnt+"&\r";
}
```

We finish off defining the code string, by adding eof, which signifies the end of the file. This will come in very handy when we want the application to load this data back in:

```
code += "&eof=true";
gotoAndStop(2);
}
```

Since code is specified in the Var setting for our (selectable) dynamic text field, the user can now read it and copy it into a text file. Once it's copied, it must be saved in the same folder as the SWF under the filename init.dat, and the application will load it back in the next time it's run.

parseInitCode

This serves as a counterpart to the last function: this time we reverse the concept, taking variables from init.dat and using them to set up all our elements in the timeline.

We begin by checking that eof has been processed – this ensures that we have all the data we need to begin processing:

```
function parseInitCode() {
    eof = "processed";
```

We stored the total number of clusters in a variable called clusterCnt, so we can directly start the loop that will generate all our clusters:

```
for (i=0; i<int(clusterCnt); i++) {
    curCluster = _root.timeline.attachMovie("cluster","cluster"+i, i+1);
```

We attach a new cluster movie clip and then assign the variables directly. Unfortunately we can't use its setdata function for this, as we can't rely on it being available so soon after instantiation.

We now go on to recreate all the elements from the text variables:

```
        curCluster._x = eval("posx"+i);
        curCluster._y = eval("posy"+i);
        curCluster.circle._width = eval("csize"+i);
        curCluster.circle._height = eval("csize"+i);
        curCluster.name = eval("name"+i);
        curCluster.passive = eval("passive"+i);
        curCluster.clipfile = eval("clipfile"+i);
        curCluster.soundfile = eval("soundfile"+i);
        curCluster.textfile = eval("textfile"+i);
        curCluster.absId = i;
        curCluster.id = i;
        _root.clipSettings.maskfile = eval("maskfile"+i);
        curCluster.container = _root.screen.createNewContainer(i,
            curCluster.clipfile, curCluster.soundfile, curCluster.textfile);
        if (curCluster.textfile != "") {
          curContainer = eval("_root.screen.container"+i);
          curContainer.txt.fontcolor = eval("fontcolor"+i);
          curContainer.txt.fontsize = eval("fontsize"+i);
          curContainer.txt.fontname = eval("fontname"+i);
          curContainer.txt.speed = eval("textspeed"+i);
          curContainer.txt.mode = eval("textmode"+i);
          curContainer.txt.yos = eval("textyos"+i);
        }
        _root.timeline.activeCluster.push(curCluster);
    }
    for (i=0; i<int(clusterCnt); i++) {
        l = eval("layer"+i);
        curCluster.swapDepths = int(l);
        curCluster.container.swapDepths = int(l);
```

```
    }
    _root.timeline.absCnt = clusterCnt;
    for (i=0; i<int(playheadCnt); i++) {
      _root.timeline.attachMovie("playhead",
              "playhead"+i, _root.timeline.absCnt+i+100);
      curPlayhead = eval("_root.timeline.playhead"+i);
      curPlayhead._x = eval("playhead_startx"+i);
      curPlayhead._y = eval("playhead_starty"+i);
      curPlayhead.emitter = null;
      curPlayhead.startedClusters = new Array();
      curGraphicPath = _root.timeline.graphicPath
                              .createEmptyMovieClip("path"+i, i);
      curGraphicPath.moveTo(eval("playhead_startx"+i),
                              eval("playhead_starty"+i));

      curSource = _root.timeline.attachMovie("playheadSource",
                              "playheadSource"+i, i+500);
      _root.timeline.activePath.push(curSource);
      curSource._x = eval("playhead_startx"+i);
      curSource._y = eval("playhead_starty"+i);
      curSource.id = i;
      curSource.crossCol = new Color(curSource);
      curSource.crossCol.setRGB(eval("playhead_col"+i));
      curSource.speed = eval("playhead_speed"+i);
      curSource.col = eval("playhead_col"+i);
      curSource.avoidCnt = eval("playhead_avoidCnt"+i);
      curSource.endMode = eval("playhead_endMode"+i);
      curSource.path = new Array();
      curPlayhead.source = curSource;
      curPlayhead.circleColor = new Color(curPlayhead);
      curPlayhead.circleColor.setRGB(eval("playhead_col"+i));
      curSource.activePlayhead = curPlayhead;
    }
    _root.timeline.absPlayheadCnt = playheadCnt;
    _root.timeline.absPathCnt = playheadCnt;
  }
}
```

These functions are both quite interesting, as they clearly illustrate where all the variables lie and how the actors are generated.

We now have an onEnterFrame handler function, which calls the parsing function.

```
onEnterFrame = function() {
    if (eof == "true") {
        parseInitCode();
        if (lock == "true") {
            _root.panel._visible = false;
            _root.textSettings._visible = false;
            _root.soundSettings._visible = false;
            _root.timeline.gotoAndStop(2);
            _root.playheadPanel._visible = false;
            _root.c0d3Panel._visible = false;
        }
    }
};
```

The first line checks to see that the init.dat file is fully loaded: eof=true should always be the last line in our init.dat. Once we know that all the variables from the file are available locally, we call the parseInitCode function.

If the code was saved in locked mode, we make sure that when the application is opened, the editing panels are not visible. We also jump ahead to frame 2, where the text can be seen and copied.

We finish off (as usual) with a stop action:

```
stop();
```

Over on frame 2, there's just a single 'close' button to wire up, so that users can get back to frame 1, hiding the code panel so they can access the main application:

```
close_btn.onRelease = function() {
    gotoAndStop(1);
}
```

So that's it. We now have a complete non-linear video editing system. As the complexity of our system is pretty dense, the performance isn't exactly amazing, but it is acceptable. The application itself only weighs in at less than 30K, and so it could easily be adapted for online use.

My example arrangement, init.dat on the CD, uses lots of masking and PNGs with alpha channels, as well as many generated movie clip instances. It's designed to test an extreme performance case.

Conclusions

I don't particularly want to talk about any specific usage of the system – after all, our goal was to create as versatile a concept as possible. However, I *strongly* encourage you to experiment, maybe adapt the interface (or even the whole system) to your own ideas. You could for example think about applying movement to the clusters as well, or have different types of playheads (like a line, a circle, an irregular shape). If you're adding something, or if you develop it further, I'd be pleased if you'd let me know. Thanks!

sample sounds are by zanshin (gregor ladenhauf) – go to www.depart.at *to get more of his music.*

thanks a lot to silvia (for love), zanshin, michael brandstetter, area3 and barcelona for sun and sea.

Digital evolution – small steps and giant leaps

Experience tells us that the world of tomorrow will be a digital one. From the home to the office, we see this happening in every aspect of our lives. The last twenty years have seen a technological revolution that's had a seismic effect on the world of creative media. From the advent of desktop publishing, to virtual recording studios, and onwards to digital film, the changes it's made to the theories, practices, and methods of modern design and creativity are countless.

We're going to round off this book with a look at how some of the most recent technologies are now affecting visual art forms, such as design and film.

Digital lifestyle, digital creativity

The scope of creative possibilities has never been more broad, thanks to the ever-evolving technology that allows artists and designers to take their abilities and extend them, while engaging in the new kinds of thinking and executions that can change an industry.

Technology shouldn't be seen as a free ride to excellence. It's not going to show up and hand you a degree, a career and a shelf full of awards. It's a shame that it can't, but technology is only a conduit to bigger and better things. It is, however, a road that will lead designers to new areas of creation.

Digital design

Design is the meeting of art and business. Design creates a balance of these two sides, ensuring that one area never outshines the other. Where the two sides meet in the middle, we can create, execute and sell.

The digital revolution has empowered people who aren't artists in a traditional sense to do the things they've always wanted to do, in a way they never thought would be possible. Just like the world of music, the world of design has evolved at the hands of the digital revolution. Twenty years ago, something as simple as cropping a photo would have been nearly impossible for the everyday computer user to pull off without the help of a pair of scissors. But now it's an everyday reality. With the modern tools of creation at our disposal, the world of design suddenly opens itself to everyone.

Once upon a time, we lived in a world where art was almost invariably created by hand. Then in 1984, Apple introduced a little box of tricks called the Macintosh, and almost overnight, everything changed in the publishing and design industry. The new technologies produced life-changing software that allowed the user to create and manipulate images without the burden of rulers, knives and sore wrists.

For a long time though, traditional design advocates (teachers and ink-stained typographers) fought the united embrace the world was giving computers. Sure, computers could make people lazy and possibly threaten certain jobs, but what these supposedly evil little machines were actually doing was making jobs easier. It wasn't long before the anti-computer people changed the way they looked at technology.
Your whole world can now be localized on one desktop. The tech industry has been busy focusing a lot of its energy on creating the image of a "desktop lifestyle". By making film, photography, and music fit in your pocket and in your laptop, a new type of necessity has been created. The accessories of a "desktop lifestyle" don't appear anywhere on Maslow's Hierarchy of Needs, but their ease of use and high quality certainly make consumers believe they need to get their hands on them in order to secure their place in the digital revolution.

By putting things like tiny cameras or iPods into the hands of the average consumer, computer companies are empowering people to be creative – to find new and great uses for these things they might have paid way too much for.

Digital music

Technological necessity can change the way an industry operates. Some of the greatest innovations come about because of the need for an easier or a better way of doing things. If we look to the past we can see how changing technology will have an effect on the future. In the 1940s, the creation of music changed forever when Les Paul developed multitrack recording, a method of production that allowed the recording of different parts of a song at different times, giving the ability to piece the parts together later. Instead of recording a song in one shot and hoping it came out well, a producer could now record music piece by piece and assemble it later to produce the best possible combination.

In the past, the only practical way for someone to play as a one-man band was to attach several instruments to their body and play for money on the street. Thanks to major revolutions in technology, creating and recording new material is a lot easier on aspiring musicians than ever before.

With the digital revolution, the creation of quality music went from an art form that only professionals in expensive studios could perfect, to a skill that any 16-year old kid can master in his bedroom. And when you add the texture supplied by audio production software, that 16-year old kid is suddenly an unstoppable one-man show. He now has complete control over his creation.

The digital revolution has brought a large amount of self-reliance to both amateur and professional musicians. There used to be a loss of control when a musician would have to hand his creation over to someone else to add finesse or finish off the piece. But now the creator can retain control. In addition, the financial burdens have been massively reduced. Decades ago, production would cost a musician thousands of dollars to get the job done right, but now with the help of a PC and some software, the same job can be done for next to nothing.

The tools of creation have become the instruments, producers, and studios for many new musicians. Thanks to the explosion of the Internet, distribution channels are nothing like they once were. A musician can use a grass roots effort to distribute music via the Web, rather than go through the perils of a soul-sucking record company. Granted, the results aren't quite the same, but it's just more proof that the digital revolution has changed the music industry in a major way. The technology is empowering people to make music and therefore changing the economics of the industry.

One Art Director I know talks about how composers/musicians offer him high quality music for free (or next to free) for use at his agency. This is a no-lose situation for him because he's willing to take a shot with the music on a project, and he's not going to see half of his budget eaten by recording, publishing and studio costs. If he has the finished piece in front of him, he can save time and money.

Digital video

As more digital products seep into the consumer market, greater numbers of men, women and children are arming themselves with digital video cameras. This could lead to a day when thousands of armchair directors will emerge from their living rooms with plans for the next great movie epic. In some cases, the future is already here – 90% of all cameras in Japan are digital. Today Japan, tomorrow the world!

Making a home movie of Junior's first birthday is one thing, but learning the fundamentals of editing and changing it into a slick piece of cinema verité is quite another. Feeling the need to take something mundane and make it into something you can be proud of is nothing new, but in this ultra-digital age the filmmaking process can be as easy as a paint-by-numbers kit when you're armed with some of the amazing editing and effects software available at consumer level. Dad can go from a guy who shoots a birthday video to a guy who now has the opportunity to shoot, transfer, edit and embellish his video into a short film.

Digital editing software like Avid and Final Cut help distill the filmmaking process down to its essence – shoot, capture, and cut. With basic three-point editing, the artist can build a whole movie from scratch. Just like Les Paul's multitrack recording method, digital editing gives the artist more control. Instead of the film school exercise of the in-camera edit which forces the filmmaker to shoot in linear and sequential order, he can go above and beyond normal story telling with the help of some simple editing.

If we go one step beyond creative control, we find the artist now has more freedom to create by adding digital effects and music to the production. Of course adding texture to a production is not just for the filmmaker. Designers in broadcast production find huge advantages in the latest software developments that allow them to easily composite, add effects, create motion graphics and titles. Editing, layering effects, adding music, and creating graphics all add to the depth of a piece. It's like creating a fresco – every layer of plaster, paint or varnish can make the finished product much richer.

Through these new technologies, designers and filmmakers are not only getting the job done faster, but they are creating wholly original pieces of art. New technologies are opening up new doors for artists and enabling them to work with fewer restraints. There exists a symbiotic relationship between the artist and technology. Technology allows the artist to work in previously unexplored ways, and the artist pushes existing technology towards industry-changing improvements. By providing new ways of doing things, technology is also shaping thought processes as well. This is not to say an artist should only rely on technology – that's wrong. Technology should not be used as a creative crutch – it should be seen more as a way to fulfill your creative intentions.

Digital film-making

Traditionally, movies are shot on film made from cellulose acetate (or something similar), which is costly – especially when you're shooting miles of it – and can't even be reused. Add in development and correcting costs to the process and you're looking at a pretty pricey art form if you want to do it right!

For some time, a majority of filmmakers objected to the substitution of digital video for film – after all, they're filmmakers, not digitalvideomakers. But as the century turned, so did the popular opinion of filmmakers. They saw that you could make a movie entirely on digital video and actually retain creative credibility, and even make some money on the side.

So will digital cameras take over the world of film? Digital has becom more of a style choice than anything else for modern filmmakers. It's a option for a filmmaker to express himself in a brand new way – a unexplored way. Sure, it's insanely cheaper than film, but the choice t use digital had more to do with aesthetics than price. Several majo directors have already made the choice to use digital in their wor Lynch, Soderbergh, Demme – they've all found a reason to use th cheaper medium. Danny Boyle talks about using DV to shoot his lates film, 28 Days Later, in an interview on www.28dayslaterthemovie.co.u He is just one of several directors who believe in the capability of digit video to democratize the creative process.

So some filmmakers are even abandoning film altogether in favor o digital video. The attraction to digital may have something to do with th fact that 24-frame video runs at the same speed as film. NTSC video run at a speed of 29.97-frames per second giving it a cold and realistic loo – almost too realistic. 24-frames per second strips away some of tha reality, and gives more grain and texture to the picture on the screen.

As of this writing, 24-frame video is slowly becoming a consumer realit When it finally saturates the consumer market, the entire film industr could experience massive change as more filmmakers start embracin the new technologies. Whether it's a good or a bad change remains t be seen.

Digital filmmaking has worked its way into projects of every scale.

Back in 2001, I was involved with a project called The Last Caravan O The Silk Road. It involved four explorers leading their camels along th ancient Silk Road over the course of eighteen months. Their story wa eventually told in various forms including photo exhibits, a coffee tabl book and an eight-episode documentary series. It was shot, edited, an distributed digitally. The use of film would have been far too costly an would have meant involving twice as many crewmembers and twice a many camels for the production.

On a much larger scale was the digital production of Star Wars: Episod II - Attack of the Clones. While George Lucas isn't destroying an conventions in terms of storytelling or directing, he's had majo involvement in the evolution of the digital medium. Shot and projecte digitally (in certain theaters), Episode II proved that even a majo blockbuster could be shot digitally and come out looking as good as traditional film production.

Thanks to pioneers like Lucas, digital filmmaking is now gainin credibility. From the largest film studios to smallest ad agencies, digital now being viewed as a serious option.

At the time of writing, many businesses are still behind in their adoptio of digital technology. A lot of businesses have old roots and are steepe in tradition, which makes the execution of major changes a rarity. Fror banking to insurance, change does not come easily. This is especially tru in the case of the advertising industry.

Agencies are reluctant to change because of the established ways tha they operate. This can severely hurt their abilities to compete fo business and stay afloat. A fear of going digital can kill an agency. Onc digital is embraced, it changes the way things work in the agency worl In an era when every business needs to find new ways to save and mak more money, agencies have started handling every aspect of productio within their own walls. Until recently, this was unheard of.

Not every agency is afraid of change. This is especially true of smaller and independent agencies. In a world where every company either gets eaten or destroyed by bigger companies, evolving with technology is one of the best ways to stay successful and alive. One agency in Boston, Massachusetts decided that becoming an early adopter of technology was the best plan of action for them in a rather stagnant economy. So far the decision has paid off.

State Street campaign

Allen and Gerritsen Advertising in Massachusetts is one of the largest independently owned agencies in New England, which is a rarity in an age of shops run by giant holding companies. As with all agencies, A&G knows there can be no resting on laurels or waiting for clients to come to them. They've always got to be working on new business. That's what they were doing when they tried to sell a full campaign to State Street Bank, a major financial services client. In the days of tight purse strings, it seemed like A&G had only a slight chance with the client.

The agency made a decision to bypass the usual ad agency process of meeting, planning, meeting again, budgeting, shooting, editing, and then meeting yet again. A&G instead created an unsolicited thirty-second spot for State Street. From start to finish, everything was created in-house. This was not a rough version of the spot – it was a finished piece.

State Street loved it. Virtually overnight, the project went through a major evolution in terms of its size and scope thanks to some simple editing and effects tools. From the original thirty-second spot, A&G went on to create a two-minute video.
State Street knew a good thing when they saw it and asked for the video to be expanded into a series of five TV spots for air in the US, Switzerland, Germany, Netherlands, China, Japan, and Hong Kong. They decided to expand the in-house video to four minutes and also requested that A&G take elements from the TV work and put them into a Flash-based CD-ROM.

All of this came from a simple thirty second speculative piece, created entirely inside the agency, and with no help from outside studios. If simple technology was responsible for changing an agency's method of doing business, the way its employees think and work, and the way clients look at them, think about what it can do when put to use in bigger and better ways.

Organizations like A&G can expect plenty more liberating experiences like this in the future, thanks to the fact that technology and innovation make the act of creation and execution easier than ever. Some agencies are even building in-house editing and effects capabilities to meet the changing needs of their clients.

It's a simple fact: the more people see something, the more they grow to expect it. As more agencies start taking these new, flexible approaches to their work, more clients will come to appreciate and even rely on it.

Portfolios

Another example of technology changing an industry is demonstrated by the way photographers put together their portfolios. There was a time when a photographer would have to create several different books with several prints in each. It could end up costing them a great deal of money just to get their work seen by an Art Director.

When photographers started coming into ad agencies with digital prints from simple inkjet printers, it seemed clear that technology had helped to change their game for the better. It not only saved them money – it saved them worrying about coffee getting spilled on their prints!

At this time, digital doesn't seem to be the perfect substitute for film. Digital lacks the tangible nature of film, the tactile experience, the smell, and the look of film. The bottom line for many is that digital is just not 'real'. But some photographers are willing to look past that and dedicate themselves to the digital form. With the quality of cameras going up and prices coming down, more and more photographers are embracing the technology with every passing day.

Creation by experimentation

Now we see that the sense of creation has changed. It's left the hands of the old school, educated purists who could only recognize one style of work: their own. It's now with the new designers, the ones who weren't satisfied with the purist mentality.

These new designers began experimenting as method of creation. Experimentation allows the realization of things that might have never been thought of through traditional means. Experimentation becomes second nature to us with technology.

Technology demystifies a whole industry for us. We used to just dream about doing things. But now we're doing them. Suddenly the dream is attainable. Technology allows anyone to do the things they want to.

More people can create.
More people are creating.

More people can make art.
More people are musicians, photographers, and filmmakers.

Of course, this realization means that an army of no-talents could saturate the market at any moment. But then this is the only way to discover the next Steven Spielberg, Brian Wilson or Tibor Kalman. The next new talent may well have gone undiscovered if it were not for the ability to obtain the technology that allows the creative instinct and talent to become a reality.

Today's artist is different from yesterday's in that he has access to some major technology that allows him to do his work in new and sometimes better ways. But the technology can be a blessing and a burden. Yesterday's artist would simply rely on their hands and their heads, whereas today's artists still need their hands and heads, but they also have to learn and keep up with new technologies to use them well. However, with proper application and study, these new ideas and technologies can allow for the possibility of meeting or exceeding one's potential. Forsaking the new ideas keeps you where you are – sluggish and redundant in your creativity. Learning the technology and how to best use it brings you a step closer to becoming great at what you do.

Executing your ideas

Just as there's no perfect way to embrace the new technology, there's never an ideal way to execute your ideas. One of the better ways to work on your creations is to scrap any linear thinking processes you may be saddled with and just dive into your work headfirst.

Working on the fly and eventually bringing everything together in the end may not seem like the most logical way to work, but you start doing things in ways you might not have considered before.

This method of work suggests that there will be some mistakes along the way. But mistakes get made. There's no need for perfection while working. You can always deal with your messes later. Why let perfection get in the way of creativity?

The best place to start is 'somewhere'. This just means you start wherever there's a good jumping off point and then go where the work takes you. This approach puts you in places and interesting dilemmas you might otherwise have ignored or avoided if you'd just started at the beginning and finished at the end.

Making, mixing and moving

When you're dealing with various media you should just keep moving. You should always be designing, editing, redesigning and re-editing simultaneously. Take your elements from your camera or your effects programs, or even your iPod, and just start mixing and refining and eliminating and reconstructing in your video editing software. You're surrounded by all of this great technology, but don't ever let it intimidate you. It's just a bunch of pricey stuff. Work with the elements you have and make them better with the technology you're blessed with.

So what about Flash? We've looked at how the digital revolution touched music, desktop publishing, movies and photography. Flash is very young by comparison with any of these, but that just means it has a long way to evolve. So where is Flash going?

In the old days, Flash was used as a vector-based animation tool. It's safe to say that it was pretty limited in its use. When designers got bored with its abilities they started trying to make it do different things. They began tricking the technology to get the results they desired. And while this seemed like enough for designers to creatively live off of for years, they were hungry.

They wanted more. More sound capabilities. More video capabilities. And most importantly, they wanted more emotional ways to tell their stories. This meant exploring how many different directions in which they could push the program. Once designers started importing media, they realized how much more this little animation tool could actually do. Technology paved the roads for designers to seek alternate routes to their destination of more effective communication.

As this process of experimentation continued, the digital revolution was still going on outside. The revolution gave designers access to the digital tools that they couldn't get their hands on before. Cameras, editing and effects software were now within financial reach. When you add FireWire technology and broadcast quality video to the mix, you get designers who can effortlessly cross the boundaries of TV and the Web.

Some of the most interesting new work in Flash has been done in video and ActionScripting. For example, a sequence of 6-15 frames per second can be exported from a QuickTime file and placed in a Flash movie to simulate realistic movie movement. With appropriate editing and looping, the results are impressive and much greater than what we're used to seeing on the Web. The introduction of Flash MX gives us better capabilities for video-to-Flash integration. With this major technological transition, Flash moves closer to becoming the content design and editing tool for the Web.

Major strides have also been made in the areas of streaming media in Flash. Everyone who's ever suffered through a slow connection knows the burdens of waiting for a download to finish. With streaming audio and video in Flash, there will be much less pulling of hair and gnashing of teeth. Flash can now broadcast the media to the user without the need to install 15 different pieces of proprietary software. With the development of Macromedia Flash Communication Server MX, a designer can easily broadcast video and music, have real-time messaging, or use it to creatively collaborate with a partner 1000 miles away.

While Flash is not (yet) perfect and Internet speeds are still slow, the program should evolve in such a way as to give users more control over how video is delivered and how it behaves and looks. Not so long ago, editing video and editing effects were two separate things that happened at different times. That has all changed and now many applications have built-in effects, color correction and titling tools. In the future, Flash could also have some of these capabilities. At the moment, Flash is still developing, but it could well become the next rich content editing tool for the Web.

Popular thinking suggests that we will live in a future where any and everything will be digital. The digital revolution has made its mark. The desktop revolution is complete. Music creation has reached a high level of maturity. Crisp digital prints of films can now be beamed from L.A. to Boston at the flip of a switch. Technology keeps advancing and so far there hasn't been a crazy movement to bring us back into the dark ages, so our iPods remain safe.

So now we're standing at the intersection of Technology and Creativity waiting for the next big thing to come along. Sure, life-changing pieces of technology will show up eventually, but right now we're better off waiting for the good things to get better. Since the result of your creativity is limited only by the technology that's available, we're going to have to keep pushing the technology further to make more groundbreaking work.

— Murat Bodur, 2003